Latinos in America

To the memory of Risieri Frondizi

Latinos in America

Philosophy and Social Identity

Jorge J. E. Gracia

Blackwell
Publishing

© 2008 by Jorge J. E. Gracia

BLACKWELL PUBLISHING
350 Main Street, Malden, MA 02148-5020, USA
9600 Garsington Road, Oxford OX4 2DQ, UK
550 Swanston Street, Carlton, Victoria 3053, Australia

The right of Jorge J. E. Gracia to be identified as the author of this work has been asserted in accordance with the UK Copyright, Designs, and Patents Act 1988.

First published 2008 by Blackwell Publishing Ltd

1   2008

Library of Congress Cataloging-in-Publication Data

Gracia, Jorge J. E.
    Latinos in America : philosophy and social identity / Jorge J.E. Gracia.
       p. cm.
    Includes bibliographical references and index.
    ISBN 978-1-4051-7658-3 (pbk. : alk. paper) – ISBN 978-1-4051-7659-0 (hardcover : alk. paper)   1. Hispanic Americans–Ethnic identity.   2. Hispanic Americans–Social conditions.
3. Hispanic Americans–Philosophy.   4. Ethnicity–United States–Philosophy.   5. Citizenship–United States–Philosophy.   6. United States–Ethnic relations–Philosophy.   I. Title.

    E184.S75G675 2008
    305.89´68073–dc22

                                                                                    2007046027

A catalogue record for this title is available from the British Library.

Set in 10 on 12.5 pt Minion
by SNP Best-set Typesetter Ltd., Hong Kong
Printed and bound in Singapore
by C.O.S. Printers Pte Ltd

The publisher's policy is to use permanent paper from mills that operate a sustainable forestry policy, and which has been manufactured from pulp processed using acid-free and elementary chlorine-free practices. Furthermore, the publisher ensures that the text paper and cover board used have met acceptable environmental accreditation standards.

For further information on
Blackwell Publishing, visit our website at
www.blackwellpublishing.com

Contents

Preface: The Latino Challenge

What is it to be Latino? What is the place of Latinos in America? And how do Latinos think about themselves and their identity? These questions require answers, for the extraordinary increase in the Latino population in the United States has generated fears and the perception of a threat to various aspects of the life of the nation. Thirty years ago, the number of Latinos was negligible, but particularly from 1990 to the present, this population grew substantially, so that now Latinos are the largest minority group in the United States.

The implications of this fact are staggering, and scientists and politicians are just beginning to realize it. Many see the increase of the Latino population with alarm, or even fear. In Samuel P. Huntington's controversial statement:

> The persistent inflow of Hispanic immigrants threatens to divide the United States into two peoples, two cultures, and two languages. Unlike past immigrant groups, Mexicans and other Latinos have not assimilated into mainstream US culture, forming instead their own political and linguistic enclaves – from Los Angeles to Miami – and rejecting the Anglo-Protestant values that built the American dream. The United States ignores this challenge at its peril.[1]

The attitude reflected by these words has resulted in much political action aimed at containing 'the Latino threat.' Consider the increasing attempts to pass laws banning the use of languages other than English and the initiatives to make English the official language of the United States. Some see the Latino threat as resulting from a conspiracy of Latinos who want to take over the

[1] Samuel P. Huntington, 'The Hispanic Challenge,' *Foreign Affairs* (March–April 2004): 30.

country and make it a Latino nation. But are we really trying to replace the hamburger with the taco? Facts tell another story, as the work of Alejandro Portes and others has demonstrated.[2] Still, facts have never bothered those who are afraid, because facts often stand in the way of feelings and it is much easier to feel than to think.

Whether we buy into the rhetoric of threat and fear or not, the ramifications of the growth of the Latino population are significant and justify that Americans begin thinking about who Latinos are and about their impact on the nation. Demographics is certainly one reason why we need to talk about Latino identity, the place of Latinos in American society, and the way Latinos think about themselves. Another reason has to do precisely with the fears and perceptions that the demographic phenomenon has helped produce.

The two groups of non-Latino Americans that feel more threatened by the growth of the Latino population are Anglo Americans and African Americans. Many Anglo Americans fear the impact of Latino customs, values, and language because they are different from those of the mainstream Anglo-American population. Changes in culture will mean a different country: out go hot dogs and the blues, and in come tamales and salsa. Of course, if it were just a matter of food and music, perhaps the threat posed by Latinos would not be perceived as so serious, but much more is taken to be at stake, such as American democracy and law. After all, so the argument goes, we need not look farther than to our neighbors to the South to anticipate what is in store for the United States.

African Americans feel threatened by Latinos because of our increasing visibility and political power. Until recently, African Americans had, to a large extent, monopolized the claims of justice made on American society as a result of both the egregious abuses that have been, and continue to be, committed against them and their substantial numbers in the population. But now Latinos are demanding, and getting, attention. Understandably, some African Americans feel that the more attention Latinos get, the less attention they get, for attention is a limited commodity. This issue has strong political dimensions, for it concerns the just and equitable distribution of resources, and the participation of various groups of Americans in government and society at large. The increase in Latino clout could diminish the clout of other minority groups.

It is not only Anglo Americans and African Americans who are apprehensive about the growth of the Latino population and its impact on American society. Latinos themselves have fears of their own. One originates in the

---

[2] Alejandro Portes and Rubén C. Rumbaud, *Immigrant America: A Portrait*, 2nd rev. ed. (Berkeley, CA: University of California Press, 1997).

general lumping of all Latinos into one group of people; another is the use of the labels 'Latino' and 'Hispanic' to refer to the group. Both are thought to be objectionable by many Latinos, because they neglect the differences among diverse groups. One problem with lumping all Latinos together is that it is often based on stereotypes. Stereotyping is a kind of generalization, and generalizations are of the essence of all knowledge. There is not one single, well-formed sentence in our discourse that does not contain a general term. We cannot think without them, so it makes no sense to ask us not to generalize. But stereotypes are not mere generalizations, they are *hasty* generalizations, and they are about people. Their danger lies in that they do not correspond to reality, but nonetheless can have momentous consequences. Federal funds are appropriated on the basis of bureaucratic classifications, and often these classifications are based on stereotypes about certain groups of people: African Americans, Latinos, Asian Americans, women, the elderly, gays, and so on.

Latinos suffer from stereotyping in a very bad way. Some Latinos have complained about this and have blamed the non-Latino American community for identifying us in ways that are inaccurate and we find unacceptable. But we share in the responsibility, because identities are the result of more than one party. The identity tango is danced by two. In some ways, you are as responsible for me as I am for myself, and you are as responsible for yourself as I am for you. The Latino stereotype has many dimensions, but two are particularly grating: homogeneity and race. Non-Latino Americans, and even some Latinos, think we constitute a homogeneous group. Non-Latino Americans themselves are diverse: Anglo-Saxons, Irish, Italians, Germans, Jews, Africans, and so on. Yet they have tried repeatedly to think of themselves as somehow homogeneous. For many this homogeneous paradigm is identified with the WASP, the White Anglo-Saxon Protestant, with cultural values added to a certain race. And others speak of the proverbial melting pot. Both stereotypes are inaccurate, but this has not stopped many from thinking of the American population in these terms.

American society is diverse and differences of many sorts remain in it, but the myth of its homogeneity continues, and it is helped by the view Latinos have of non-Latino Americans. Indeed, Latinos frequently think of non-Latino Americans also as 'one' in kind. Authors as distant in location as the Uruguayan José Enrique Rodó and the Mexican José Vasconcelos have thought of their neighbors to the north as a race, a group of people biologically unified who share common values that set them apart from Latinos. Non-Latino Americans are supposed to be uncharitable, exploitative, moved by economic desires, and dominated by technical advances. Is this true? Of course not! This is a caricature; it does not take much to see how wrong it is. And it is wrong for the same reason that the picture non-Latino Americans have of Latinos is wrong. Non-Latino Americans think of Latinos as a homogeneous group, a group whose members have the same characteristics. Milk is homogenized when it is submitted to a process that makes it to have uniform consistency. Are non-Latino Americans like homogenized milk? Are Latinos like homogenized milk? No, non-Latino Americans and Latinos are more like minestrone soup, with all sorts of different ingredients mixed together that preserve some of the original consistency. Minestrone can be made homogeneous, but in order to do so it has to be put through a blender. And in spite of all the efforts that have been undertaken to put non-Latino Americans and Latinos into cultural, or even racial, blenders, it has not worked. Both non-Latino Americans and Latinos remain diverse.

The homogeneous picture, however, has worked to this extent, that most non-Latino Americans *think* Latinos are homogeneous, and often Latinos also *think*, not only that we, but also that non-Latino Americans, are. So what does the stereotype tell that I am, qua Latino? Perhaps more than anything else, I am supposed to speak Spanish. This is not just a view present among common folks; it is a view voiced by many academics, and even by many Latinos. It so happens that I do speak Spanish, yet many Latinos do not. If Spanish is our language, where does that leave those Latinos who speak Portuguese because they come from Brazil? And what about those for whom Spanish or Portuguese is itself a foreign tongue? In Paraguay, 80 percent of the population does not have Spanish as their mother language. And presumably this is also true of some Paraguayans who have come to the United States. Their language is Guaraní, a language that has nothing to do with Spanish. Even Latinos who speak Spanish or Portuguese as native tongues vary in terms of accent, vocabulary, and syntax. An Argentinian traveling in Mexico sometimes has difficulty understanding what is said in the street, and the same happens to a Mexican who visits Buenos Aires. And many children of Latin American immigrants to the United States do not speak, or even understand, Spanish or Portuguese. Yet, the homogeneous linguistic model assumes they do.

As a Latino I am also supposed to eat tortillas and like hot food. I am of Cuban origin and I first tasted the Mexican tortilla in this country. For Cubans, a tortilla is an omelette. And hot food? That is not Cuban at all; it is not even Mexican everywhere in Mexico. I do like relatively hot food, but this is an acquired taste for me, as acquired as the taste for Beluga caviar. Neither is a staple of the Cuban cuisine. Food is, like language, a phenomenon where variety predominates among Latinos. Even in the same Latin American country, the predilection for local dishes is prevalent. *Chapulines* are rare outside Oaxaca and, although the sauce known as *mole poblano* has caught on in other places, it is in Puebla that it has its characteristic taste and is most appreciated. In all my travels throughout Latin America, I have not found anything quite like the Cuban diet outside Cuba. Cuban staples, such as fried plantain, are seldom eaten in most parts of Mexico and never, to my knowledge, in Chile. The Latin American elites who travel internationally know dishes from various parts of Latin America, but they seldom appreciate them as they are appreciated in the areas where they originate. Some Latin Americans do not actually like Argentinian *dulce de leche*, and years of trying have been fruitless in convincing my Argentinian wife that the Caribbean boiled *malanga* is close to ambrosia. I have yet to find an Argentinian, or Cuban for that matter, other than myself or my wife, who has eaten Maguey worms, grasshoppers, or ants eggs, delicacies in some parts of Mexico. Regionalism in food predominates in Latin America and among Latinos everywhere. There is no uniform cuisine in the place.

An even more controversial feature of the Latino stereotype than homogeneity is that we constitute some kind of race. The confusion between race and ethnicity is found everywhere in this country. We are asked to fill out forms in which 'white' and 'black' are listed next to 'Hispanic' and 'Cuban.' Since when is there a Hispanic or a Cuban race? Then these categories are used to disqualify people. I have been told that I am not really Cuban. Why? Because I do not 'look' Cuban. In fact, one of the first things that non-Latino Americans tell me when they meet me is that I do or do not look Cuban, or Latin American, or Latino, or Hispanic. The reason is that people belonging to these groups are supposed to have a certain look and if they do not, they are regarded as not being what they are supposed to be. It is like saying that Americans are supposed to be White, and Blacks do not qualify because they are not. Is someone still saying such things about Americans? Not many, but when it comes to Latinos, the racial stereotypes are being repeated by academics, government officials, and other members of the 'educated' public. I hear them in the media almost every day. Latinos are not a race. Some of us are Black, and some of us are White, although most of us are mixed. Now, mixture does not entail homogeneity. If this were so, we would look pretty much the same way. And what do we look like, those of us who are mixed? We look very different from one another, because miscegenation does not imply homogenization. We are not just like minestrone as a group; we are like minestrone even as individuals.

These examples illustrate the fact that to be Latino does not entail much that is generally associated with the stereotype. But why should this lumping and homogenization generate fear in the Latino population? Why do we find strident voices complaining and warning about this phenomenon? Because we worry that by being lumped together into one stereotyped group, the reality which we are will be misunderstood – we will be taken as what we are not and this can affect our lives in significant ways, some very nefarious to our well being. Homogenization becomes particularly dangerous in political contexts because the government often formulates and implements social policy based on stereotypes.

Apart from the worry about homogenization, there is also alarm within the Latino community at the particular labels used to refer to us. Some Latinos object to the use of the label 'Hispanic' for at least two reasons: First, it carries with it connotations of Spanish, bringing back all the abuses carried out by Iberians throughout the long period of colonial rule in Latin America; second, it neglects the reality that Latin America is a backward and marginalized part of the world, different from Europe and the United States. To speak of us as Hispanic is to miss that we live a reality very different from the reality of Spain and to miss the need to address it in unique terms.

The use of the Hispanic label has a political dimension insofar as the particular social plight of Latinos may be lost in the larger cultural understanding suggested by the label. For what does the situation of Latinos in this country have to do with the Hispanic culture, or with the situation of Hispanics in the Iberian peninsula, for example? The problems that we face here are particular to this society and are neither the product of Hispanic culture at large nor characteristic of other Hispanic groups around the world. We need to remove the label 'Hispanic,' so the argument goes, and use one that more accurately focuses attention on our situation in the United States, and not on our cultural traits.

But this is only one side of the story. Others object to the use of 'Latino,' which is the label most frequently proposed as an alternative. They point out that this term does not make sense etymologically, ignoring the history and culture that tie us together and missing the point that it is precisely that culture and that history that is at the bottom of our situation in the United States. 'Latino' means Latin and the Latins were the Romans and all those who are tied to the Latin language, thus including the French and also the Spaniards. The use of 'Latino' ignores that those of us presently here are products of a long history of colonialism, making us forget that it is precisely cultural characteristics that make other groups of Americans think we are different. Again, this has political implications, for if we forget our cultural roots, the country will also forget them, and our Latino culture and unity are threatened.

Let me recount the three factors I have mentioned as sources of fear concerning the Latino population in the American context: the extraordinary growth of Latino numbers in the United States, the stereotyping of Latinos, and the use of the general labels 'Latino' and 'Hispanic' to refer to the Latino population. All three factors have political and social dimensions. The first is seen as a challenge to Anglo Americans and African Americans, and the other two to the political needs and well being of Latinos.

But are the perceived threats real and the fear they generate justified? The most frequent approach to this challenge is through the social sciences. In this book, however, I turn to a generally ignored approach, the philosophical analysis of the concepts we use to think about Latinos and their place in American society. If the Latino threat and the fears it generates are thought to be real and they influence how some think and act, they are significant to the extent that they can have serious consequences. One important question, then, is not whether they are in fact real, but whether we should continue to think about Latinos in the ways that we have been doing so far. My answer is no. We need to change the way we think about ethnicity in general if we are going to deal rationally with the presence of ethnically diverse peoples in the United States, and we particularly need to change the way we think about Latinos.

The defense of this thesis is the primary purpose of this book. The task is accomplished in three parts, each divided in turn into three chapters. The first part goes to the source of misunderstandings concerning Latino identity, the problem of Latino identification, and the significance of the two general labels used to refer to Latinos. The second part explores the problems encountered by Latinos in American society in part as a result of the misunderstandings indicated in the first part, paying particular attention to the philosophy marketplace, affirmative action, and language rights. And the third part looks into who Latinos think we are by turning to Latino philosophy, its roots in Latin America, and the place it occupies in American and world philosophy.

Let me add some final comments about conventions and terminology. I will be using the term 'Latino' and its derivatives both in a narrow sense to refer to Latinos (and Latino matters) in the United States, and in a broader sense to refer to them in conjunction with Latin Americans (and Latin American-related matters). The context should make these uses clear, but it is also important to understand that I do not see clear ethnic boundaries between the categories of Latinos in the United States and of Latinos in Latin America; I see these as ethnically the same. I use terms such as 'Cuban' and 'Cuban American,' and 'Mexican,' and 'Mexican American,' in the same way: Cuban Americans are merely a subgroup within the more encompassing ethnic group of Cubans, and the same applies, *mutatis mutandis*, to Mexican American. I also make a distinction between the national use of such labels as 'Cuban' and 'Mexican' and their ethnic use. The term 'America' will be used in two senses: in one, I will be referring to the United States and in another to what is usually called 'the Americas,' that is, North and South America and the Caribbean. I shall have more to say in the body of the book about both senses of 'Latino' and 'America.' For the sake of aesthetics and parsimony, I use 'Latino' and 'Latinos' in the text, rather than 'Latino/a' and 'Latinos/as,' except in the titles of the three parts in which the book is divided. The first terms are intended to include both genders, in the way neutral terms do in Spanish, since they are in fact Spanish terms. Finally, I have tried to stay away from philosophical jargon and technicalities as much as possible, and I have used common and sometime humorous examples and personal anecdotes to lighten up the tone of the book and make the discussion more accessible.

Several chapters of the book are based on materials published previously as articles, although important modifications have been introduced in all cases, and the discussions have been integrated into the general framework and argument of this book. The pertinent texts are the following: 'Hispanics, Philosophy, and the Curriculum,' *Teaching Philosophy* 23, 3 (1999), 241–8; 'Hispanic/Latino Identity: Homogeneity and Stereotypes,' *Ventana Abierta* 2, 8 (2000), 17–25; 'Affirmative Action for Hispanics? Yes and No,' in Jorge J. E. Gracia and Pablo De Greiff (eds.), *Hispanics/Latinos in the United States: Ethnicity, Race, and Rights* (New York: Routledge, 2000), pp. 201–22; 'Sociological Accounts in the History of Philosophy,' in Martin Kusch, (ed.), *The Sociology of Philosophical Knowledge* (Dordrecht, Netherlands: Kluwer, 2000), pp. 193–211; 'Globalization, Philosophy, and Latin America,' in Mario Sáenz (ed.), *Globalization and Latin America: Ethics, Politics, and Alternative Visions* (Lanham, MD: Rowman & Littlefield, 2002), pp. 123–34; 'Minorities in the Philosophical Marketplace,' *Metaphilosophy* 33, 2 (2002), 535–51; 'Language Priority in the Education of Children: Pogge's Argument in Favor of English-First for Hispanics,' *Journal of Social Philosophy* 35, 3 (2004), 420–32; 'The History of Philosophy and Latin American Philosophy,' in Arleen Salles and Elizabeth Millán-Zaibert (eds.), *The Role of History in Latin American Philosophy: Contemporary Perspectives* (Albany, NY: State University of New York Press, 2005), pp. 21–42; 'A Political Argument for Ethnic Names,' *Philosophy and Social Criticism* 31, 4 (2005), 409–17; 'Individuation of Ethnic and Racial Groups: The Problems of Circularity and Demarcation,' in Jorge J. E. Gracia (ed.), *Race or Ethnicity? On Black and Latino Identity* (Ithaca, NY: Cornell University Press, 2007), pp. 78–100; and 'What Is Latin American Philosophy?' in George Yancy (ed.), *Philosophy in Multiple Voices* (Lanham, MD: Rowman & Littlefield, 2007), pp. 175–96.

I am grateful to the editors and publishers of these venues for the permission to use these materials. I am also grateful to many colleagues and friends who have commented and criticized my work at various stages of development, whether verbally or on writing. Among these, I am particularly indebted to: Linda M. Alcoff, Richard Bernstein, J. Angelo Corlett, Enrique Dussel, J. L. A. García, Robert Gooding-Williams, Iván Jaksić, Eduardo Mendieta, Walter Mignolo, Elizabeth Millán-Zaibert, Paula Moya, Susana Nuccetelli, Suzanne Oboler, Lucius Outlaw, Mario Sáenz, Arleen Salles, Ofelia Schutte, Ernesto R. Velásquez, George Yancy, the late Iris Young, and Naomi Zack. I am also deeply indebted to José Medina and Oscar Martí, who read the manuscript of this book carefully and offered extensive and invaluable advice. It would become tedious to recount all the places where his help was useful, so I hope this general acknowledgment is sufficient. Paul Symington offered some valuable comments on the manuscript and helped with the bibliography, and Susan Smith compiled the index. The interest and support of Jeff Dean was essential in making the publication of this book possible, and the expertise in production of his colleagues at Blackwell was most welcome. Finally, let me thank Carolyn Korsmeyer for a clever suggestion concerning the title.

Latino/a Identities

Identities: General and Particular

The difficulties raised by social identities are many, complex, and confusing. They have at least two sources: first, the very notion that there are overall and general social identities for groups at all; second, the fact that this kind of identity seems to dissolve into many other, more particular, identities. We are Latinos, but some of us are also Puerto Ricans or Mexicans. Can we make sense of this? Can we talk meaningfully about a Latino identity and Latino identities? These questions take on added significance when the social and political implications of the use of social identity labels is considered.

Two difficulties are particularly vexing. The first is a version of the old problem of the one and the many: How is it possible for someone to have an overall, general identity, such as Latino, and at the same time have other, less general ones, such as Mexican and Tarahumara? Does it make sense for the same person to have several social identities, and if so, how is this to be understood?

The second problem has to do with the question of what social identities entail. Does having these identities entail common properties that constitute the ground for the identities and distinguish between those who have the identities and those who do not? At first our intuitions seem to justify this idea, but upon reflection serious difficulties come up. For it is far from clear that the members of a group that signals a social identity of the sort Latino is, share any properties.

In this chapter, I suggest that the issue of identity among Latinos presents us with at least two major dilemmas. One is a choice between what I label *generalism* and *particularism*, and the other between *essentialism* and *eliminativism*. I argue that there is a third alternative to the second dilemma that favors neither essentialism nor eliminativism, and that there should be no need to choose between generalism and particularism, for both positions have something valuable to offer in context. In short, I reject the dilemmas and propose a more nuanced solution to the problem of identity among Latinos which should open the way for dealing with the social and political significance of Latino identities. I call this the Familial-Historical View of Latino identities.

The issue I take up here and the solution I offer to the difficulties it poses are closely related to two other topics that have received some attention recently. The first concerns the number and kind of identities that persons can have. The examples I have provided are of ethnic identities because our topic here is Latino identity and this is an ethnic identity. But ethnic identities, although extraordinarily important, both personally and socially, are only one kind of social identity. Other social identities frequently mentioned these days include racial, gender, sexual, religious, and national, to name just a few.

The second topic that is receiving considerable attention today is the way these various identities are related to each other and how they are negotiated by both individual persons and particular groups. What difference does it make personally and socially if a person is both Latina and female, or if she is Angla and female? And what of a man who is Anglo but gay and one who is Anglo but heterosexual? Even a superficial perusal of these cases indicate that there are differences, sometimes significant, because ethnic identities often include behavioral patterns and views about gender orientation and sexuality. And matters become even more complex when we consider national identities, particularly because in some cases the same terms used to refer to them are also used to refer to ethnic ones. 'Mexican' is used to talk about Mexican nationals and ethnic Mexicans whether they are also nationals or not. So how do these different identities function within an individual person and within society? This topic is some times discussed under the label 'intersectionality.'

Obviously, both the question concerning the number and kind of identities persons have, as well as the issue of intersectionality, are related to the questions I raise in this chapter, and whatever one concludes about them will affect the topic of the chapter. However, it would be impossible to give them the kind of treatment they deserve, and so I must put them aside for another time.[1]

---

[1] For recent discussions of intersectionality, see José Medina, "Identity Trouble: Disidentification and the *Problem* of Difference," *Philosophy and Social Criticism* 29, 6 (2003), 655–80; and Linda M. Alcoff, *Visible Identities: Race, Gender, and the Self* (Oxford: Oxford University Press, 2006). For a discussion of Medina's article, see the exchanges sponsored by the *Symposia on Gender, Race, and Philosophy* in May 2005 (http://web.mit.edu/sgrp).

I.   Two Dilemmas

Let me begin by formulating the two dilemmas. Here is the first:

> Either there is one general Latino identity or many particular Latino identities.
> If there is one general identity, then there cannot be many particular ones, and
> if there are many particular ones, then there cannot be one general identity.

According to this dilemma, we cannot maintain that I am both Latino and Cuban, for example. I am one or the other, and to be one precludes that I am the other. Let me call this conundrum the *Generalism vs Particularism Dilemma*. The idea is that more general identities preclude more particular ones, and vice versa, because one can have one and only one group identity of the sort we are talking about. In our especial case, the general Latino identity precludes more particular identities, such as Cuban or Mexican, and each of these particular identities precludes a general one. We must, therefore, choose one identity and discard the talk about the others.

The problem is that no matter which horn of the dilemma we choose, we end up dissatisfied. The rejection of an overall Latino identity appears to be as unsatisfactory as the rejection of particular identities, because we both understand and feel right when we are described as, say, Latino and Cuban, Latino and Mexican, or Tarahumara and Mexican. The second dilemma runs as follows:

> Either there is an essential set of properties entailed by an ethnic identity or there
> is not. If there is such a set, all those persons who instantiate the properties in
> the set also share in the Latino identity. But if there is no such a set of properties,
> then there is no group of persons who share the identity.

According to this dilemma, I cannot maintain that I am Latino or Cuban, or have the Latino or Cuban identity, unless I can point to a set of necessary properties that I share with other Latinos or Cubans. Let me call this the *Essentialism vs Eliminativism Dilemma*. The thought here is that an essence is necessary for the concept of a group identity. Latino or Cuban identities require essences, otherwise they do not exist. But this dilemma, just as the first, leaves us dissatisfied because neither of its horns is acceptable. The facts seem to contradict it: we seem not to share an essential set of properties with the other members of the social groups to which we belong, and yet we seem to have these identities.

A. Generalism vs particularism

Let's consider the Generalism vs Particularism Dilemma first. Latinos have clearly been concerned with both general identities, such as Latino or Hispanic, and particular identities, such as Mexican or Puerto Rican. We tend to be either generalists or particularists. In philosophy, the concern for a general identity reveals itself among Latinos in discussions about whether there is such a thing as a Latino philosophy and the kind of characteristics it has. The first attempt in this direction is found in Juan Bautista Alberdi's *Ideas para presidir a la confección del curso de filosofía contemporánea en el Colegio de Humanidades* (1842). And the project has continued among thinkers as diverse as Ernesto Mayz Vallenilla, Enrique Dussel, and Francisco Miró Quesada.[2] This effort has also extended beyond philosophy to peoples themselves; authors such as José Vasconcelos, Eduardo Nicol, and I have argued for overarching identities, Latino or Hispanic.[3]

The search for particular identities is evident in discussions of the character of various regional and national philosophies and of peoples from certain regions or nations. Philosophers have repeatedly addressed the identity of Mexican or Peruvian philosophy, or of the Mexican or Peruvian peoples, for example. Among those best known for their efforts in a general direction are Félix Schwartzmann and Leopoldo Zea.[4] And among those who have tried to find what is characteristic of particular peoples, is Samuel Ramos.[5]

It would be interesting to discover a pattern from the more general to the more particular, or vice versa, in these discussions of identity. Say that one

---

[2] Ernesto Mayz Vallenilla, *El problema de América* (Caracas: Ediciones de la Universidad Simón Bolívar, 1992; formerly published in 1969); Enrique Dussel, *América Latina: dependencia y liberación* (Buenos Aires: Fernando García Cambeiro, 1973); Francisco Miró Quesada, *El problema de la filosofía latinoamericana* (Mexico City: Fondo de Cultura Económica, 1976). For the pertinent texts of these and other authors, see Jorge J. E. Gracia and Iván Jaksić (eds.), *Filosofía e identidad cultural en América Latina* (Caracas: Monte Avila, 1988) – an updated and expanded edition of this work is in preparation.

[3] José Vasconcelos, *Obras completas*, 4 vols. (Mexico City: Libreros Mexicanos, 1957); Eduardo Nicol, *El problema de la filosofía hispánica* (Madrid: Tecnos, 1961), and Jorge J. E. Gracia, *Hispanic/Latino Identity: A Philosophical Perspective* (Oxford: Blackwell, 2000).

[4] Félix Schwartzmann, *El sentimiento de lo humano en América* (Santiago: Universidad de Chile, 1950); Leopoldo Zea, "En torno a una filosofía americana," *Ensayos sobre filosofía en la historia* (Mexico City: Stylo, 1948), pp. 165–77.

[5] Samuel Ramos, *El perfil del hombre y la cultura en México* (Mexico City: Universidad Nacional Autónoma de México, 1934 and 1963).

could find that discussions of more general identities occur first, chronologically speaking, and that it is only because of the difficulties associated with this enterprise that the discussion shifts to particular identities. Or alternatively, that discussions of more particular identities precede discussions of more general ones. But there appears to be no such a pattern. The search for more general identities does not always occur first, and it continues while the discussion of more particular identifies is under way: Ramos's emphasis on Mexicanity (*mejicanidad*) is balanced out by Nicol's emphasis on Hispanicity (*hispanidad*).[6] The reverse is also the case: Vasconcelos's interest in Latin America as a whole precedes the more nationalistic emphases of later thinkers.[7]

In this, the situation in Latin America is somewhat different from the situation we encounter in the discussion of identity in the United States. In this country, discussions of a more general identity, such as American identity, seem to occur first. The founding fathers and others made attempts to pin down an identity for the newly established country. But, more recently, the focus has shifted to other, more particular, identities: Black, African American, Latino, Hispanic, Puerto Rican, gender, gay, and so on. And even within these more particular identities, there has been a narrowing or particularization. In this connection, the case of Latinos is instructive, because the discussion seems to begin with a more general approach, such as Latino or Hispanic identity, but later we find challenges to this general concept and an emphasis instead on more particular identities, such as Puerto Rican, Cuban American, and Mexican American. Yet, this has not stopped the talk about more general identities in America. Indeed, if we look at analyses of Black or African-American identity, we see that it goes back a long way, well into the nineteenth century and the work of Alexander Crummell and W. E. B. Du Bois.[8] And the concern with a general American identity is still in full swing.[9]

---

[6] Ramos, *El perfil del hombre y la cultura en México*; Nicol, *El problema de la filosofía hispánica*.

[7] Vasconcelos, *Obras completas*.

[8] For Crummell, see Kwame Anthony Appiah, *In My Father's House: Africa in the Philosophy of Culture* (New York: Oxford University Press, 1992), ch. 1. For W. E. B. Du Bois see *The Conservation of Races*, The American Negro Academy Occasional Papers, No. 2 (Washington, DC: The American Negro Academy, 1897), pp. 5–15; rep. in Robert Bernasconi (ed.), *Race* (Oxford: Blackwell, 2001), pp. 84–92.

[9] See Suzanne Oboler, "It Must Be a Fake! Racial Ideologies, Identities, and the Question of Rights," in Jorge J. E. Gracia and Pablo De Greiff (eds.), *Hispanics/Latinos in the United States: Ethnicity, Race, and Rights* (New York: Routledge, 2000), pp. 125–46.

In spite of these differences, the logic of identity displays similarities in the United States and the Latino world. Perhaps the most important is that, no matter how the discussion begins, the tendency is to address issues that are both general and particular, although the authors engaged in these controversies are often polarized and opposed to each other. Concerns for identity in Latin America fall into two quite distinct groups: those that favor more general approaches and those that do not. There are some authors who go so far as to reject identity altogether except at the individual level, a development that mirrors the situation in the United States.[10]

The arguments proposed by generalists and particularists may be characterized in three ways: some are a priori, some a posteriori, and some pragmatic. The a priori argument is most commonly found in philosophy, the a posteriori argument is particularly evident among historians, and the pragmatic argument is often proposed by political scientists. Curiously, all three kinds of arguments are used by the two factions mentioned. For example, many philosophers who argue against the idea of a general Latin American philosophical identity, such as Risieri Frondizi, do so based on an a priori conception of philosophy.[11] They claim that philosophy, like physics and other disciplinary enterprises, is interested in truth, and truth has no national or ethnic alliances. It would be preposterous to argue that mathematics can be Latin American or French, in the sense that the mathematics done in Latin America or France are significantly different from the discipline practiced in Spain or Germany. Likewise, for these authors it makes no sense to claim any kind of identity, whether general or particular, for philosophy. This argument is a priori because its conclusion is derived from a presupposed conception of philosophy as a universal discipline which is not adopted on the basis of experience.

Those who oppose this point of view respond also based on an a priori, although different, conception of philosophy. They argue, as Leopoldo Zea does, that philosophy, unlike other disciplines of learning, has to do with particular cultural and historical points of view and, therefore, its conclusions are colored and affected by these points of view.[12] In this sense, philosophy develops an identity depending on the time and place in which it is practiced.

---

[10] For a discussion of this position see Jorge J. E. Gracia, *Hispanic/Latino Identity*, pp. 21–6. J. L. A. García rejects the use of identity in "Racial and Ethnic Identity?" in Jorge J. E. Gracia (ed.), *Race or Ethnicity? On Black and Latino Identity* (Ithaca, NY: Cornell University Press, 2007), pp. 45–77; see also David A. Hollinger, "From Identity to Solidarity," *Daedalus* (Fall 2006), 23–31.

[11] Risieri Frondizi, "¿Hay una filosofía latinoamericana?" *Realidad* 3 (1948), 158–70.

[12] See Leopoldo Zea, "Identity: A Latin American Philosophical Problem," *The Philosophical Forum* 20, 1–2 (1988–9), 33–42; and "En torno a una filosofía Americana."

Latin America, in virtue of its historical location, provides a unique vantage point that gives Latin American philosophy a particular identity different from other philosophies. Again, the argument is a priori in that it is based on a presupposed conception of philosophy not based on experience, but the conception in this case is particular and perspectival.

The a posteriori argument used to support general or particular identities argues from a consideration of observable facts. Interestingly enough, here also the same kind of argument is used to support the two conflicting points of view. For some the facts clearly preclude the notion of any kind of general identity, whereas for others they confirm it. Consider again the case of philosophy. Those who oppose the notion of a more general identity point to the enormous variety of philosophical styles and positions that Latino philosophers have adopted throughout history, asking rhetorically: What do they have in common? And more concretely, for example, what does scholastic philosophy have in common with positivism, or phenomenology with analysis, as these philosophical perspectives are found in Latin America?

At the opposite end we have those who find some unity in Latin American philosophy, for example. Some of them argue that there is a concerted effort in every period of development in Latin American philosophy to search for freedom and liberation, and that this search arises from the marginal and oppressed situation of Latin America.[13] This, they claim, not only gives unity to Latin American philosophy, but distinguishes it from other philosophies, such as French or German, which are philosophies of what Enrique Dussel has called "the Center."[14] Some also argue that Latin Americans in general display attitudes that distinguish them from, say, Anglo Americans, clearly indicating that there is an identity at play. Vasconcelos figures prominently among those who argue thus, and more recently, liberationists such as Dussel, as well as more traditional authors, such as Juan Rivano and Augusto Salazar Bondy, echo similar claims.[15] The argument is often made that these factual characteristics

---

[13]   See Dussel, *América Latina: dependencia y liberación*; Juan Rivano, *Punto de partida de la miseria* (Santiago: Universidad de Chile, 1965); Jorge J. E. Gracia, "La liberación como foco utópico del pensamiento latinoamericano," in *La utopía en América: Simposio internacional sobre el quinto centenario* (Santo Domingo: Universidad Autónoma de Santo Domingo, 1992); and "Zea y la liberación latinoamericana," in *América Latina: historia y destino. Homenaje a Leopoldo Zea* (Mexico City: Universidad Nacional Autónoma de México, 1992–3), vol. 2, pp. 95–105.

[14]   Dussel, *América Latina: dependencia y liberación*, ch. 1.

[15]   Vasconcelos, *Obras completas*; Augusto Salazar Bondy, *The Meaning and Problem of Hispanic American Thought*, ed. John P. Augelli (Kansas City: Lawrence Center for Latin American Studies of the University of Kansas, 1969); and the works of Dussel and Rivano cited earlier.

are the result of a history of colonization and exploitation common to all of Latin America.[16]

Finally, the pragmatic approach focuses on the advantages and disadvantages of the use of general notions to describe particular phenomena. Those who oppose such use bring out the counterproductive consequences of general approaches to situations marked by very different conditions at the local level.[17] One thing is to talk about economic development in Argentina, where the population is largely educated and European, and another to do it in Bolivia, where most of the population is uneducated and of pre-Columbian origin. Indeed, this applies even within the same country: one thing is to speak about the economic situation in Mendoza and another to do so about El Chaco, both provinces in Argentina. Differences in geography and natural resources make it difficult to apply the same economic analyses and measures in different locations throughout Latin America – the pampas are different from the Andes, the Amazonian basin from Patagonia. And what is true of economics is also true elsewhere.

On the other hand, those who argue pragmatically in favor of a general Latin American identity point out, for example, that there is a common history to Latin America, as well as many cultural threads in its population. How can we ignore that most of Latin America was conquered and subjugated by Spain and Portugal? Aren't Spanish and Portuguese the predominant languages in the area? Don't the overwhelming religious leanings toward Roman Catholicism count for anything? One need only look at the architecture of the region to see common elements. And the history of colonial oppression serves to create a common experience. To ignore these facts, they argue, is to ignore the Latino reality.

Who is right? In thinking about the Latino world, should we take the particular route and discard the general, or should we take the general and discard the particular? This is the dilemma, and one that stirs the passions. Proponents of either side are adamant about how wrong the other side is. Just as happens between proponents of general Latino or Hispanic identities in the United States and those who oppose them in favor of such identities as Dominican or Venezuelan, there seems to be no meeting point, no compromise, acceptable to the opposing sides. Generalists are wrong, according to particularists, and particularists are wrong, according to generalists. And that puts an end to the

---

16 Walter Mignolo, "Latinos (and Latino Studies) in the Colonial Horizon of Modernity," in Gracia and De Greiff (eds.), *Hispanics/Latinos in the United States: Ethnicity, Race, and Rights*, pp. 99–124.

17 Eduardo Mendieta, "The 'Second Reconquista,' or Why Should a 'Hispanic' become a Philosopher?" *Philosophy and Social Criticism* 27, 2 (2001), 11–19.

discussion. Of course, the real conundrum is that the arguments offered for these positions, whether a priori, a posteriori, or pragmatic, are evenly divided. But do we have to take sides? Is there any way to mediate what appear to be two irreconcilable views?

Before we can answer these questions it is helpful to take a look at the assumptions made by generalism and particularism. Indeed, it is my claim that these assumptions set up the logic of the Generalism vs Particularism Dilemma and are responsible for the apparent irreconcilability of these positions. These assumptions are revealed by the second false dilemma mentioned earlier: Essentialism vs Eliminativism.

B. Essentialism vs eliminativism

Essentialism is the view according to which things have essences and essences consist of sets of properties that characterize the things that have those essences. In common philosophical jargon: sets of necessary and sufficient conditions. Thomas Aquinas was an essentialist with respect to human nature, for example, because according to him, human beings share a set of properties specified in a definition that expresses their essence: humans are rational animals. If one is an essentialist with respect to Latino identity or Mexican identity, one holds that there is a set of such properties that characterizes anyone who is Latino or Mexican.

At the opposite end of the spectrum we have the view that there are no essences. Jean-Paul Sartre was an eliminativist with respect to human essence. His position is known as existentialism rather than eliminativism, because he argued that humans exist (whence the term existentialism), but what they are (their essence) is the result of their individual free choice. I prefer to call it eliminativism in this context, rather than existentialism, for two reasons: its negative claim about essence and the fact that this term is used in the recent literature concerned with social identities.[18] According to Sartre, we are free to choose what we want to be, and there is no set of properties that we necessarily share. When this view is applied to our question, the answer is that there is no such a thing as a Latino, or even a Mexican identity, for there is no essence to them. There are only individual identities forged by individual humans.

The kinds of arguments given for essentialism and eliminativism duplicate to a great extent the arguments given earlier for generalism and particularism and so there is no need to repeat them. Some are a priori, some a posteriori, and some pragmatic. It is not difficult to find them in the literature on identity

---

[18] See Howard McGary, "Racial Assimilation and the Dilemma of Racially Defined Institutions," in Gracia (ed.), *Race or Ethnicity?* pp. 155–69.

produced in Latin American countries, and certainly they are frequent in the philosophical literature in this country. A similar situation to the one described earlier ensues: a sharp disagreement which appears unresolvable. On the one hand, some authors favor identity at group level, whether general or particular, and on the other, some object to any identity except at the individual level.

What are we to do, then? The a priori arguments mentioned would take us into the murky waters of the very foundations of philosophy. There is no point in even trying to pursue this line of thinking because philosophers are quite divided about these issues. The a posteriori arguments seem to lead nowhere, in that it is not the facts that are disputed but which facts are considered relevant. Again, this seems to lead us to presuppositions that it would be too difficult to evaluate except by going into areas that are too far from our topic. Finally, the pragmatic arguments do not seem to be convincing insofar as, again, the advantages and disadvantages emphasized by the opposing factions seem to be rather selective and depend on pre-established goals. Are we at an impasse, then?

Here is a suggestion for getting out of the situation, in three parts: first, the dichotomies on which the contrary positions examined are based are misguided; second, the first dichotomy, between generalism and particularism, is based on the second, that is, that between essentialism and eliminativism; and third, the second dichotomy, between essentialism and eliminativism, relies on a misguided notion of identity. In short, I claim that the alternatives from which to choose are not just essentialism and eliminativism, or generalism and particularism, but that there is a third alternative to essentialism and eliminativism, which if adopted also opens a third alternative to generalism and particularism. The notion of identity does not require that one subscribe to essentialism or that identities be exclusive of each other. It is possible for the same person or persons to share a variety of identities, some of which are more general and some less general. One can be Latino, Mexican, and Tarahumara. But how is this possible? By taking into account the relational, contextual, and historical nature of identity.

II.   Four Basic Questions about Identity

One way to make this point clear is by asking four questions:

1   How do identities function?
2   How do identities arise?
3   How do identities endure?
4   What does having an identity entail?

The first question is intended to ask for the use we make of identities. Let's look at a concrete case, say, me. I am Cuban, but I am also considered to be Latin American and Latino. It would be difficult to contradict anyone who says that I am one of these, and in fact I feel quite comfortable when I am described in these ways. I was born in Cuba, of Cuban parents. When I hear Cuban music I have difficulty keeping my feet still. I love hot weather, the beach, the sweet/sour humor from the island, and the easy-going, friendly attitude of Cubans. When I encounter a group of Cubans at a gathering, I tend to gravitate toward them because I feel comfortable in their company, never mind their political allegiance. And a few years ago, when I decided that I was going to collect art, I decided to do it with Cuban-American art. And what kind of pieces do I collect? All sorts, but some of them clearly have a connection to my particular Cuban experience. One example is Alberto Rey's painting of *El Morro*, one of the architectural icons of Havana. El Morro is a fortress that guards the port of Havana, and is the first and last thing one sees when arriving or departing by boat from the Havana harbor. Rey's painting is done mono-chromatically in shades of grey, which is exactly what I saw in 1961 when I was leaving the port at dusk on my way to West Palm Beach. Would I have acquired the painting if I were not Cuban and not had the experience of leaving? Perhaps, because it is a stunning rendition of an impressive structure. But the fact that I am Cuban and the painting arouses certain feelings and memories surely had something to do with it.

But I am also Latino, am I not? I feel that way in particular when I travel to Europe, or when I am in the company of Anglo Americans. I am not part of them in some significant ways – I am from another part of the world. And they agree. For some Spaniards, those with stereotypical ideas and prejudices against Latin Americans, who indiscriminately lump all of us together, I am a Sudaca (even if coming from Cuba), and for Anglo Americans I am a Hispanic. Moreover, I share a strong kinship with the places I have visited in Latin America. I have traveled almost everywhere in Mexico – indeed, I know Mexico better than most Mexicans. I can identify with the food, the music, the courtesy of the Mexicans. I am married to an Argentinian (yes, they are Latinos too, in spite of what many of them think). So I have learned to cook *bife a la plancha*, and *dulce'e leche* sends me to Olympus (it is almost as good as *dulce'e guayaba*).

And I feel Latino. I have strong ties to other Latinos in the United States and elsewhere, and with them I feel something different from what I feel when I am with Latinos who live in Latin America. And I also act Latino. Indeed, I was the founding member and first chair of the American Philosophical Association Committee for Hispanics in Philosophy, so I have been committed to a certain course of action, promoting the interests of Latinos for some time.

Whenever possible I try to help Latino graduate students and young philosophers in their careers, and often I encourage them to learn something about their intellectual heritage.

These examples illustrate both feelings of solidarity and certain actions I take. I feel Cuban, Latin American, and Latino, but I also act in certain ways, gravitating toward Cubans at parties, collecting Cuban-American art, visiting Latin American countries, eating certain foods, and promoting the interests of other Latinos and of Latino cultures. Let me summarize the point by saying that I both *feel* and *act* in accordance with my Cuban, Latin American, and Latino identities. These are two major functions of identities: they generate feelings of solidarity with certain people and they give rise to certain actions that otherwise would probably not take place.[19]

Now for the second question: How do identities arise? Well, how did I become Cuban and Latino? Surely the factors involved are many and variegated. The tendency these days is to focus on one factor to the exclusion of others. I constantly hear the mantra that the United States government created Hispanic identity – this in spite of the fact that the term 'Hispanic' was in use long before United States bureaucrats adopted it to refer to people like me and that it was picked by United States bureaucrats precisely because it was available. I also hear that United States international policies created Hispanic identity – and this in spite of the fact that Latinos were talking about themselves as a group long before there was a United States at all. The first distancing and contrast developed in Latin America was not between Latin America and the United States, but between *criollos* (descendants of Iberians born in Latin America) and *peninsulares* (born in Iberia), although the membership of these divisions fluctuates from place to place. I have not yet heard that Cuban identity was created by anybody, but perhaps some will argue that it is the United States again that is responsible for it. If this were true, then I really would be a rather curious artifact, created by the United States. Am I? Just tell the father of the Cuban nation, José Martí, that he was a United States created artifact! He talked about Hispanics and "our America" long before United States bureaucrats thought of putting all of us together under a label.

Do I want to deny that there is some truth to the claims concerning the influence of the United States on Latino identities? Of course not. American foreign policy, American bureaucrats, and the United States government have had to do with the creation of much that I am. But, contrary to what many believe, the United States is not as powerful as it thinks. Indeed, it has proven to be very ineffective insofar as it often fails to accomplish much that it tries to do in the world. And although it is true that the United States may have

---

[19] See Kwame Anthony Appiah, "Does Truth Matter to Identity?" in Gracia (ed.), *Race or Ethnicity?* pp. 19–44.

been responsible to some extent for the creation of some Latino countries and United States bureaucrats have helped consolidate a Hispanic identity in this country, it is just not the case that this extends to all countries of Latin America or makes the United States government and its bureaucrats solely responsible for Latino identities in the United States or elsewhere.

My identities are not the result of an act or acts of political or economic fiat, whether American or otherwise. There is more to their origin than this. Any one-sided attempt to analyze the origin of my identities, and for that matter of any other identities, is simply inaccurate. Identities are the result of complex historical processes that shape us individually and as groups. Isolation contributes to them, provided that there is also some other identity with which they can be contrasted. Being on an island is certainly a major factor in the development of a Cuban identity. Particular events tie people in certain ways and separate them in others. A war, a dispute, a treaty, a natural disaster, topography, an invasion, government actions, migrations, economic forces, the publication of a book, all these are important factors in the construction of identities. Some of these factors do not consist in conscious efforts to create identities, and indeed most of them do not. The formation of identities involves both conscious and unconscious factors. In the contemporary philosophical jargon, identities, including social ones, are the result of both "internal" (what we think) and "external" (causes other than our thought) factors. This is the answer to the second question concerning how identities arise.

And what are we to say to the third question: How do identities endure? Well, how is it that I personally endure as Jorge Gracia? We must acknowledge that the key to the answer is that I change and yet remain the same. Certainly I am not the baby that wet its diapers in the early forties. I might get to the stage of wetting diapers again, if I live long enough, but somehow that situation will not be the same as it was in the early forties. I remain the same while I also change. Change is of the essence when it comes to endurance, and this applies to social identities. Cuban identity has changed and has been affected by events during the past one hundred years, and the same could be said about Latino identity. This very discussion might affect Latino identity insofar as it might modify how some of us think about it and promote events – publications, discussions, and so on – that will influence not only our feelings, but also our actions.

Change is of the essence for certain identities; survival requires adaptation, and adaptation involves change. Consider the need for change in organisms. Evolution has demonstrated that change is necessary for the survival of species, and the same could be said when it comes to organic individuals. We survive because we adapt to new circumstances. How is it that some species have endured whereas others have been annihilated? How is it that I am still alive while many of my friends from high school are dead? Without change, most species and individuals would die out in time as a result of the challenges they have to face in their environment.

Now let me turn to the fourth and crucial question: What does having an identity entail? We know that an identity is a source of feelings and actions, it originates through conscious and unconscious historical processes, and it is subject to change. If this is so, then it would seem that the two dichotomies we considered earlier fail to explain what Latino identity, or for that matter any other group identity, is. Essentialism appears misguided insofar as it does not allow for change. If an identity entails a fixed number of unchanging properties, then endurance is doubtful. Yet, the fact that an identity is a source of feelings and actions points to its existence, so eliminativism cannot be right either. Indeed, the discussion of the various identities that have a claim on me, some more general (Latino) and some more particular (Cuban), indicate that the generalism vs particularism dichotomy also does not work. But, then, in what does an identity consist, and what does it entail?

Clearly, it cannot consist in a set of unchanging, essential properties. Identities need to be conceived as flexible, contextual, historical, and relational. The position I propose, the Familial-Historical View, satisfies these conditions. I have discussed it in greater detail elsewhere in the context of Hispanics in particular and ethnic groups in general, and therefore here I limit the presentation to its fundamental tenets in order to avoid duplication. Let me apply it to the case of Latinos.

III.   The Familial-Historical View of Latino Identities

Alexander Crummell and W. E. B. Du Bois were the first to make use of the notion of a historical family to explain the unity of social groups, but they did it in the context of race. The former gives only a sketchy idea of what he has in mind, and therefore is of no help to us here. Du Bois is more specific. After rejecting the nineteenth-century biological view of race, he presents his sociological position in an often quoted passage:

> the history of the world is the history, not of individuals, but of groups, not of nations, but of races. . . . What then is a race? *It is a vast family of human beings,* generally common blood and language, *always common history, traditions and impulses,* who are both voluntarily and involuntarily striving together for the accomplishment of certain more or less vividly conceived ideals of life.[20]

---

[20]   Du Bois, *The Conservation of Races*, p. 74. My emphasis.

A race is a family that always has a common history, traditions, and impulses, although other things, such as language and blood, also enter into the mix. Elsewhere Du Bois returns to the kinship provided by history:

> [O]ne thing is sure and that is the fact that since the fifteenth century *these ancestors of mine and their descendants have had a common history*; have suffered a common disaster and have one long memory. The actual ties of heritage between the individuals of this group vary with the ancestors that they have in common with many others. . . . But the physical bond is least and the badge of color relatively unimportant save as a badge; *the real essence of this kinship is its social heritage* of slavery; the discrimination and insult; and this heritage binds together not simply the children of Africa, but extends through yellow Asia and into the South Seas.[21]

This is still not enough for our purposes, because Du Bois does not sufficiently dwell on what he takes a racial family to be, or specify what he means by history and the pertinent aspects of it for his view. The vagueness of this position has led to a number of criticisms and interpretations. Is he an essentialist or a non-essentialist? He seems to waver.[22] If his view is essentialistic, then it would be of no help to us insofar as we need an alternative to essentialism. And if it is not essentialistic, then we need more than he has given us in order to apply the view to Latinos.

I propose, instead, to use the version of the Familial-Historical View I have defended elsewhere and apply it to Latinos.[23] It is more developed, containing some of the specific elements missing in Du Bois, and can effectively answer the objections based on the difficulties posed by the individuation of races and ethne to be discussed in chapter 2. Here is the formula:

> Latino identities are identities of Latino ethne, and Latino ethne are sub-groups of individual humans that satisfy the following conditions: (1) they belong to many generations; (2) they are organized as families and break down into extended families; and (3) they are united through historical relations that produce features which, in context, serve (i) to identify the members of the groups and (ii) to distinguish them from members of other groups.

---

[21]   W. E. B. Du Bois, *Dusk of Dawn: An Essay Toward an Autobiography of a Race Concept* (New York: Harcourt, Brace and Co., 1940), p. 117. My emphasis.

[22]   See Appiah's discussion in *In My Father's House*, ch. 2.

[23]   As developed in Jorge J. E. Gracia, *Hispanic/Latino Identity* and *Surviving Race, Ethnicity, and Nationality: A Challenge for the Twenty-First Century* (New York: Rowman & Littlefield Publishers, Inc., 2005).

The fundamental tenet of this formulation is that ethnic groups, such as Latinos, Mexicans, or Dominicans, are best conceived as constituting extended historical families whose members have no identifiable properties, or set of properties, that are shared by all the members throughout the existence of the familial groups, but that the historical connections that tie them give rise to properties which are common to some members of the groups and, in context, serve to distinguish them from other social groups. The lack of common properties accounts for the lack of agreement concerning any particular conditions, or even kinds of conditions, that are necessary and sufficient for Latino identity in general, or any Latino identities in particular. Even the most superficial consideration of available research points to difficulties in the identification of any such conditions. According to the Familial-Historical View of Latino identities, then, we must abandon the project of trying to develop essentialistic conceptions of those identities. And the relations that tie Latinos as well as the properties some of us share account for both our individuation and identification.

The common properties that this view rejects are significant first-order properties. I am not speaking about trivial properties such as the property of belonging to the group, or second-order properties such as identity. I mean primarily phenotypical or genotypical properties, such as skin color and capacities, or cultural properties, such as tastes and values, frequently associated with ethne. This means, in turn, that in order to be Latino or Puerto Rican it is not necessary that one share a first-order property (or set of properties) with other members of the group.[24] Latinos may lack Spanish fluency and be Latinos, just as Jews may be atheists and be Jews. Indeed, contrary to what some philosophers and sociologists think, it is not even necessary that Latinos name themselves in particular ways or have a conscious sense of belonging to the group of Latinos. Some of them may in fact consider themselves so and even have a consciousness, or sense, of themselves as a group, but it is not necessary that all of them do. After all, Latino children and people suffering from Alzheimer's disease cannot be expected to have a sense of Latino identity and yet their identity is not questioned for that reason, and the same applies to Latino groups, such as Puerto Ricans or Dominicans. I return to this point in chapter 2.

Latinos and Latino groups are tied by the same kind of thing that ties the members of a family. We are related, as a mother is to a daughter, and grand-

---

[24] This explains why, in his attempt to characterize ethnicity, Max Weber concluded that it is not feasible to go beyond vague generalizations. Max Weber, "What Is an Ethnic Group?" in M. Guibernau and J. Rex (eds.), *The Ethnicity Reader: Nationalism, Multiculturalism and Migration* (Cambridge: Polity Press, 1997), pp. 22 and 24.

parents to grandchildren. The notion of family does not require genetic ties. One does not need to be tied by descent to other members of a family to be a member of the family.[25] Indeed, perhaps the most important foundation of a family, namely marriage, takes place between persons who are not related by descent but by contract. In-laws become members of families indirectly, again not through genesis. And the same applies to Latinos: it is not necessary that one share a property or set of properties with others who also have Latino identity. Are all Latinos conscious of a Latino identity? Do all Mexicans have a sense of themselves as Mexican? How about the *campesino* lost in the ravines of the Copper Canyon? How about the descendants of the Maya living in isolation, somewhere in Yucatan? This extends to knowledge of the group's history. Being Latino or ethnically Mexican does not entail knowing anything about Latino or Mexican history, and even less having an accurate knowledge of those histories.

History generates relations that in turn generate properties among Latinos and serve to unite us among ourselves and to distinguish us from others in particular contexts. The use of the Spanish language is one of the properties that unites many Latinos and can serve to distinguish us from other ethnic groups in certain contexts. Some Latinos in the southwest are united by their knowledge of Spanish and this serves also to distinguish them from most Anglos who live in that part of the country. They speak Spanish as a result of certain historical events, such as the invasion and colonization of the southwest by Spaniards in the sixteenth century. Had these events not occurred, these Latinos would not know any Spanish, but they would still be Latinos if the southwest had been invaded and colonized by the Portuguese.

The same could be said about a Mexican identity. Do all Mexicans have to share something that characterizes them? Do they have to share values, a bio-logical feature, a physical mark, or even a cultural trait? There seems to be nothing like that which ties all Mexicans, and this in spite of the strong efforts of the Mexican government at ethnic homogenization for the purpose of nation building. Mexicans share a history, a past, and certain relations that tie them in various ways. Factors such as territory, religion, political organization, and values need not be common to everyone who shares in the Mexican iden-tity. But everyone who shares in this identity must be tied in some ways to other people who share in it. The ties, however, can be different, and they can also change throughout time and location. Identities are messy, just like reality.

---

[25] Some have argued for necessary genetic ties among members of ethnic groups, particularly Latinos. See J. Angelo Corlett, *Race, Racism and Reparations* (Ithaca, NY: Cornell University Press, 2003), chs. 2 and 3. For a criticism of this position, see Gracia, *Surviving Race, Ethnicity, and Nationality*, ch. 3.

There are no Euclidean triangles in the world, the Euclidean triangle is an idealization. Yet, the notion of a triangle is of much use to us. Likewise, it is not necessary that there be neat, clear, and fixed boundaries between Latinos and non-Latinos, or between Cubans and Mexicans, just as there are no such boundaries between families.

Although historical events and relations tend to generate common properties in ethne, such properties are usually restricted to certain periods, regions, or subgroups within an ethnos. Latino identity entails both unity and distinction in a world of multiplicity such as ours, and unity and distinction are easily understandable when there are properties common to all the members of a group, but such properties are not necessary. The unity and distinction of Latinos can be explained as long as there are relations or properties that tie each member of the group with at least one other member without assuming that there are common properties to all members. Of course, in most cases the tie will not be with just one member, but with several, as happens with families. Indeed, the number of members involved is not as important as the various ties and whether these ties are significant for the ethnic group. Elsewhere I have argued that it is not possible to establish what these ties are for all ethnic groups, but that the particular group and its historical reality determine what they are in each case, and so they may vary substantially. The single most important factor for Jews to be Jewish is that their mothers be Jewish. But other ethnic groups emphasize the relationship with the father, and many do not have this kind of genetic requirement, but are more concerned with other human relations and with culture.[26]

The unity of Latinos, Cubans, Argentinians, Brazilians, and Tarahumara does not involve commonality; it is a familial-historical unity founded on historical relations and the properties they generate in context among members of the group. This is one reason why membership in the groups that share identities is neither permanent nor closed. Latino identities, like all identities, are fluid, open, and changing; those who share in them come and go, enter and leave, as they forge new relations, among themselves and with others, which depend on particular and contingent circumstances.[27] If we use the

---

[26] Gracia, *Surviving Race, Ethnicity, and Nationality*, ch. 3.

[27] The fluidity of ethnic groups has been frequently recognized. See, Joan Vincent, "The Structuring of Ethnicity," *Human Organization* 33, 4 (1974), 376; E. P. Thompson, *The Making of the English Working Class* (New York: Pantheon Books, 1963), p. 9; Richard Jenkins, "Ethnicity Etcetera: Social Anthropological Points of View," in Martin Bulmer and John Solomos (eds.), *Ethnic and Racial Studies Today* (London: Routledge, 1999), p. 90; and Corlett, *Race, Racism, and Reparations*, chs. 2 and 3.

Familial-Historical View of Latino identities, we can understand how these identities do not require that we subscribe to essentialism. There is no essential core of properties required for an identity of the sort Latinos share. But the lack of an essence does not entail the lack of an identity; it does not entail eliminativism.

The view I propose recognizes that when the classification of particular persons comes up, there will be some cases in which classification is clear and some in which it is not. A Cuban American who came from Cuba last year, does not know English, and lives immersed in a Cuban-American environment is surely Cuban American. And I think I have shown above that I am obviously Latino: I act Latino, I feel Latino, both Latinos and Anglos think of me as Latino, and I was born in a country that is part of Latin America. On the other hand, Bill Clinton is not Latino. He does not think of himself as Latino, he does not act Latino, others do not think of him as Latino, and he was born in the United States and from non-Latino ancestry. So it seems that the cases of the Cuban American mentioned, of Bill Clinton, and of myself are clear and decidable. But not every case is like this. What do we make of my granddaughter Clarisa. Her mother is my daughter, but her father has pure English ancestry and was born in Canada, and she takes after her father's family in looks and temperament. Is she Latina? And what will we make of her children if she turns out to marry another Anglo, and they never have any contact with Latinos? These are cases in which Latino identity is up for negotiation, but this should not militate against the idea of a Latino identity. That the case of my great grandchild is difficult to decide, or perhaps even impossible, or that the decision needs to be made contextually and in terms of negotiation, does not alter the fact that I am Latino and Bill Clinton is not.

Elsewhere I made this point clear by noting that many of our concepts have members that clearly belong, some that clearly do not belong, and others that are unclear.[28] A mistaken assumption about ethnic categories is that they must have clear and strict boundaries so that their membership is never in doubt. This is quite out of step with the conditions under which we accept many of our most valued categories and concepts, so there is no reason why we should impose on ethnicity, conditions without which we are willing to do in other cases.

Consider, for example, as common a concept as "most of the X's," as we use it when we say "Most of the students who are taking my course in ethnicity this semester will pass it." Everyone understands what this means, but when one looks at the situation more closely, it is clear that the membership of the category is clear in some instances but not in others. Say that the course

---

[28] Gracia, *Surviving Race, Ethnicity, and Nationality*, pp. 59–60.

has 20 students enrolled. In this case, it is clear that "most of the students" does not refer to 1, 2, 3, 4, 5, 6, 7, 8, 9, or 10 students, for these would not be most of the students. Nor is it 20, for that would be all of the students. It is also clear that most of the students would cover 19, 18, and 17. But once we get below 17 questions arise. Can one consider 11, 12, 13, 14, 15, and 16 to constitute most of the students? Interestingly enough, the total number of students affects also the numbers in doubt. If the course has an overall enrollment of 10, then clearly 1 through 6 and 10 are not most of the students; 9 and 8 do constitute most of the students; but what do we make of 7? Here it is only one number that seems to be in doubt, rather than the six numbers in the case of 20. Now, if we increase the number of students to 50, then we will find that the number in doubt is even larger than in the case of 20.

Two things are clear from this example. First, the category "most of the X's" has members that are in doubt and members that are not. Second, the exact number of members that are in doubt depends very much on the particular number that constitutes the totality, which means that it results from contextual factors particular to the situation. None of this, however, stands in the way of our using the concept "most of the X's," and certainly we do not think any less of the category to which this concept refers because of it. There is no reason, then, to assume that, because a particular category has an undetermined membership, it is useless or must be abandoned. And this applies obviously to the category of Latinos.

The Familial-Historical conception of Latinos serves to explain in particular how the same person can share in different identities, for the conditions of one identity need not preclude another. I can be Latino and Cuban. If there is no fixed necessary set of properties that I have to have for membership in each of these groups, the grounds for incompatibility between these identities diminishes considerably. There is always the possibility of accommodation and negotiation, particularly when change is essential for identity preservation.

Finally, the adoption of this position makes clear that the use of more general labels to describe more general identities does not entail rigid parameters of homogenization, nor does it exclude the use of less general labels to indicate more particular identities. This is important insofar as a great objection against all talk about general identities is precisely that they homogenize and preclude the use of more particular ones. If I have to choose between being Latino and being Mexican, someone says, I prefer being Mexican, for that is closer to me. But if we adopt the Familial-Historical View of Latino identities, this kind of conflict and choice is not inevitable. For each of these labels indicates something about me that is important, and this is not a set of properties that defines and confines me.

A Latino identity is a historical marker. It tells me that I am here and I am now a part of a group within which I fit in many ways. It does not tell me that

I am like everyone else in the group and different from everyone else who does not belong to the group, or that I have been and will continue to be what I am. Rather, it tells me that I am part of the group because I am related in various ways to other members of the group and that I have properties that these relations generate in context with some members of the group, and that all these relations and properties set me and other members of the group apart from other groups. I am not part of those other groups because either I have no relations with their members or because the relations I share with them do not justify membership and thus identity, or even because I do not share with them certain properties that in context identify the groups that have them. Clearly I am not Jewish – I share no history with the Jews and there are no properties resulting from that history that I also have. And the citizenship relation I share with other Americans does not warrant Latino identity, because citizenship is not an ethnic marker for Latinos. This reference to nationality and its close relation to ethnicity requires that I say something about it in passing.[29]

IV. Ethnicity and Nationality

In the discussion of ethnic identities I have frequently used terms that can also refer to national identities and I have used examples of national identities to make a point about the relationship between different identities. But national-ity and ethnicity should not be confused. A nation is a voluntary political organization of people based on a system of laws devised for the regulation of the relations and governance of the members of the group of people who accept it in a certain territory with the aim of ensuring justice and the good of all members. Belonging to a nation is ultimately a matter of political will, laws, territory, justice, and the well-being of its members, whereas this is not the case with ethnicity. Ethnicity has to do with historical relations of various sorts that contingently tie people.

The identification of nationality and ethnicity, however, is widespread.[30] Its origin goes back at least to the eighteenth century.[31] It has at least three sources. One is that nations require some foundation. The glue that binds nations

[29] I say much more in chapters 5 and 6 of *Surviving Race, Ethnicity, and Nationality.*

[30] J. Llobera, *The God of Modernity: The Development of Nationalism in Western Europe* (Oxford: Berg, 1994), p. 214; M. G. Smith, "Pluralism, Race and Ethnicity in Selected African Countries," in J. Rex and D. Mason (eds.), *Theories of Race and Ethnic Relations* (Cambridge: Cambridge University Press, 1986), p. x.

[31] Anthony D. Smith, "The Problem of National Identity: Ancient, Medieval, and Modern," *Ethnic and Racial Studies* 17 (1994), 382.

together is the political will of a people to live under a system of laws that regulate the relations of the members of the nation, and this in turn involves a certain degree of self-identification of the members with the group. But this also requires that there be some common background to the members of the group. If they are going to self-identify with the group and accept certain laws, there must be some common values and shared assumptions. Moreover, self-identification requires symbols through which the members of the group can unite, such as flags, celebrations, anthems, and particularly traditions.[32] Naturally, these could also be part of the ethnicity of the members of the group, and can be easily considered ethnic elements because ethnicity tolerates all kinds of features, and particularly cultural ones. So this leads some to think that a nation is, after all, an ethnos. The mistake here is that the requirements for nationality are minimal if compared with the requirements for ethnicity. Agreement about living together under certain laws is not enough to constitute an ethnos. More is required. The foundational structure of nationality is too basic and skeletal to sustain an ethnos. This is in fact a substantial advantage, for it makes possible for nations to be constituted by many ethnic groups.

A second reason why ethnicity is frequently identified with nationality is that, just as in the case of race, nationality can give rise to ethnic features. If the key to ethnicity is the historical relations among members of a group, then a nation constitutes a powerful factor of ethnicity generation. Nations force their members to deal with each other, consign them to a territory helping develop their relations further, and bring them together in all sorts of ways. Moreover, isolation from other nations and groups helps the process. And, as is well known, nations often try to promote the ethnic (and even racial) homogenization of their members in order to create stronger national bonds and make governing easier.[33] Indeed, in some cases attempts have been made

---

[32] For the role of tradition in the identity of groups, including national ones, see Jorge J. E. Gracia, *Old Wine in New Skins: The Role of Tradition in Communication, Knowledge, and Group Identity*, 67th Marquette University Aquinas Lecture (Milwaukee, WI: Marquette University Press, 2003).

[33] M. Guibernau, "Nations without States: Catalonia, a Case Study," in M. Guibernau and J. Rex (eds.), *The Ethnicity Reader: Nationalism, Multiculturalism and Migration* (Cambridge: Polity Press, 1997), p. 5 and *Nationalisms: The Nation-State and Nationalism in the Twentieth Century* (Cambridge: Polity Press, 1996), p. 11. Indeed, Thomas Hyland Eriksen, in "Ethnicity, Race, and Nation," in Guibernau and Rex (eds.), *The Ethnicity Reader*, p. 35, points out that the distinguishing mark of nationalism is the view that "political boundaries should be coterminus with cultural [i.e. ethnic, for him] boundaries."

to make a certain ethnicity a condition of membership in certain nations.[34] And it is often the case that, even after the dissolution of a political group, an ethnic feeling remains in the group.[35] But, again, this does not mean that we need or should conflate the notions of ethnos and nation. It only means that one can contribute to the origin of the other in particular circumstances and that the categories can overlap or even coincide in certain contexts.

A third reason why nationality is often conceived in ethnic terms has to do with the legitimate complaints of ethnic groups in states in which they are oppressed. The Kurds in Iraq felt for long time that their only way to terminate the oppression they have suffered in the Iraqi state because of their ethnicity was to liberate themselves and form a sovereign state themselves. Obviously, their experience of ethnic discrimination led them to think that the only way to avoid it is by forming an ethnic state of which they are the nation.[36] Oppression, however, is not a sufficient reason for the ethnic understanding of nations insofar as there are other ways of doing away with such oppression without incurring the problems that result from the creation of ethnic states.

We need, then, to keep in mind that, although closely related, the notions of nationality and ethnicity are not the same. Moreover, as I explain in chapter 3, some pernicious consequences often follow in countries where ethnicity and nationality are not distinguished. In the present context the confusion does not rise with the Latino ethnos, for there is no such nation as the Latino or Latin American nation. But when we use terms such as Mexican or Cuban, we must be clear as to whether we are using the terms for ethne, nations, or a combination of the two.

V.   Latino Identities

In conclusion, to reject essentialism does not force us to reject Latino identities, and to accept the value of particular identities does not, prima facie, preclude

[34]   Guibernau, "Nations without States," p. 6. See also Will Kymlicka, "Ethnicity in the USA," in Guibernau and Rex (eds.), *The Ethnicity Reader*, p. 240.

[35]   Weber, "What Is an Ethnic Group?" in Guibernau and Rex (eds.), *The Ethnicity Reader*, p. 19.

[36]   Many authors argue that this aim to create a state that represents the nation is essential to nations and a nationalist spirit. See, for example, Dan Smith, "Ethical Uncertainties of Nationalism," *Journal of Peace Research* 37, 4 (2000), 494. Allen Buchanan, *Secession: The Morality of Political Divorce from Fort Summers to Lithuania and Quebec* (Boulder, CO: Westview, 1991), pp.152–3, has proposed a list of conditions in which ethnic groups seek secession from a state. See also Anthony Smith, *The Ethnic Origins of Nations* (Oxford: Blackwell, 1986).

general identities. That Latinos share no essence does not mean that we do not share a general identity. And the same applies to more particular identities such as Mexican or Dominican. Moreover, that we are Latinos does not entail that we reject the Mexican identity some of us have, or vice versa. We do not need to choose between generalism and particularism. We can be Latinos and Mexicans or Quechua. General and particular identities can, and do, coexist. The Essentialism vs Eliminativism Dilemma and the Generalism vs Particularism Dilemma are based on a misguided conception of identity. If we adopt the Familial-Historical View of Latino identities, the dilemmas disappear. So, yes, I am Latino and Cuban, among many other things, and all these identities serve to describe me, give rise to particular feelings in me, and function as sources of action for me. In the next chapter I examine two key objections that can be brought against this view in relation to individuation.

Individuation: Circularity and Demarcation

Can Latinos be effectively individuated? Contradictory answers to this question abound in the literature about both Latinos in particular and ethnic groups in general: yes, Latinos can be effectively individuated; no, they cannot. The affirmative answer is particularly common among those who subscribe to an essentialistic and realistic conception of these groups. By essentialistic, as noted in chapter 1, I mean that the members of the groups are taken to have common properties that function as necessary and sufficient conditions of group identity and membership. By realistic I mean that both, groups and their properties, are considered to be real entities in the world, not mere concepts or imaginings. In the case of races, the properties of the racial groups or their members are frequently taken to be physical or mental, whether involving gross morphology or intellectual capacities.[1] Blacks, for example, are thought

---

[1] For the discussion of these views, see: L. L. Cavalli-Sforza et al., *The History and Geography of Human Genes* (Princeton, NJ: Princeton University Press, 1994), p. 17; Stanley M. Garn, "Modern Human Populations," in *The New Encyclopedia Britannica* (Chicago, IL: Encyclopedia Britannica, Inc., 1993), p. 844; M. Guibernau, *Nationalisms: The Nation-State and Nationalism in the Twentieth Century* (Cambridge: Polity, 1996), p. 86; W. E. B. Du Bois see *The Conservation of Races*, The American Negro Academy Occasional Papers, No. 2 (Washington, DC: The American Negro Academy, 1897), pp. 5–15; Bernard Boxill, "Introduction," in Bernard Boxill (ed.), *Race and Racism* (Oxford: Oxford University Press, 2001), p. 7; Pierre L. van den Berghe, *Race and Racism: A Comparative Perspective* (New York: Wiley, 1967), pp. 9–10, and "Does Race Matter?" in Boxill (ed.), *Race and Racism*, p. 104. Among important historical figures who have held views of this sort are Hegel, Blumenbach, Kant, Voltaire, de Gobineau, and Bernier.

to have a certain skin color, hair texture, and intellectual capacities. In the case of ethnic groups, the properties that mark membership have been sometimes understood to be physical, but most often they involve cultural differences, such as values and attitudes.[2] Latinos are often thought to have darker skin than Anglo Saxons, and to put a special value on the family. From the essentialist/realist perspective, the affirmative answer to the question of individuation of Latinos is given in terms of these properties. Latinos are individuated either by certain physical features, such as skin color, or by cultural characteristics, such as an emphasis on family values.

The negative answer is particularly common among those who conceive racial and ethnic groups as "imagined communities," to use a favorite expression in the literature.[3] There is no fixed set of properties belonging to an ethnic group or their members. Rather, there is a sense of group identity that has developed among members of the groups themselves, or that has been imposed on them by others.[4] No fact of the matter characterizes these groups or serves

[2] For discussions of these views, see Anthony Appiah, " 'But Would That Still Be Me?' Notes on Gender, 'Race,' Ethnicity, as Sources of 'Identity,' " *Journal of Philosophy* 87 (1990), 498; Clifford Geertz, "The Integrative Revolution," in Clifford Geertz (ed.), *Old Societies and New States: The Quest for Modernity in Asia and Africa* (New York: Free Press, 1963); William Peterson, "Concepts of Ethnicity," in William Peterson et al. (eds.), *Concepts of Ethnicity* (Cambridge, MA: Harvard University Press, 1982); Nathan Glazer and Daniel P. Moynihan (eds.), *Ethnicity: Theory and Experience* (Cambridge, MA: Harvard University Press, 1975), p. 4; Audrey Smedley, *Race in North America: Origin and Evolution of a World View* (Boulder, CO: Westview Press, 1993), p. 30; Fredrick Barth (ed.), *Ethnic Groups and Boundaries: The Social Organization of Culture Difference* (Oslo: Universitetsforlaget, 1969); Thomas Hyland Eriksen, *Ethnicity and Nationalism: Anthropological Perspectives* (London: Pluto Press,1993), pp. 10–12; Richard Jenkins, "Ethnicity Etcetera: Social Anthropological Points of View," in Martin Bulmer and John Solomos (eds.), *Ethnic and Racial Studies Today* (London: Routledge, 1999), p. 88; and van den Berghe, *Race and Racism*, pp. 9–10 and "Does Race Matter?" p. 104.

[3] Benedict Anderson, *Imagined Communities: Reflections on the Origin and Spread of Nationalism* (London: Verso Edition, 1983; rev. ed. 1990).

[4] For discussions of this position, see: Harold R. Isaacs, "Basic Group Identities," in Glazer and Moynihan (eds.), *Ethnicity: Theory and Experience*, pp. 34–5; Talcott Parsons, "Some Theoretical Considerations on the Nature and Trends of Change of Ethnicity," in Glazer and Moynihan (eds.), *Ethnicity: Theory and Experience*, p. 56; Donald L. Horowitz, "Ethnic Identity," in Glazer and Moynihan (eds.), *Ethnicity: Theory and Experience*, p. 113; Milton Gordon, *Assimilation in American Life* (New York: Oxford University Press, 1964); Anthony Smith, "Structure and Persistence of *Ethne*," in M. Guibernau and J. Rex (eds.), *The Ethnicity Reader: Nationalism,*

the purpose of determining membership. Latinos have no essence and there is no reality that corresponds to the ideas of the group or its presumed common properties. Latinos, like other ethne, are mere concepts resulting from social construction – whence the term 'conceptualism' used to describe this position. From this perspective, individuation becomes difficult, if not impossible, and many of those who agree with this judgment go on to argue that efforts in this direction are futile and must be abandoned.[5]

Recently, the tide of scholarship has favored the negative answer. Essentialism and realism with respect to ethnic groups has been on the defensive, if not altogether vanquished. Genetic discoveries seem to support the flimsiness of a biological conception of race, a fact which has also helped erode the essentialistic and realistic view of ethne.[6] Some go so far as to question the cogency of the concept of ethnos. And yet, talk about ethne is common not just in ordinary discourse, but also among academics of various stripes.[7] Moreover, this talk is not just general, that is, about ethnicity as such, but particular, about

---

Multiculturalism and Migration (Cambridge: Polity Press, 1997), p. 27; and Michael E. Brown, "Causes and Implications of Ethnic Conflict," in Guibernau and Rex (eds.), *The Ethnicity Reader*, pp. 81–2.

[5] See, for example, the sustained argument of Kwame Anthony Appiah, "Race, Culture, Identity: Misunderstood Connections," in Kwame Anthony Appiah, and Amy Gutmann, with an Introduction by David B. Wilkins, *Color Conscious: The Political Morality of Race* (Princeton, NJ: Princeton University Press, 1996).

[6] For discussion of this view, see Kwame Anthony Appiah, "The Uncompleted Argument: Du Bois and the Illusion of Race," *Critical Inquiry* 12 (1985), 23ff., and "But Would That Still Be Me?" 496–7; Bob Carter, *Realism and Racism: Concepts of Race in Sociological Research* (London: Routledge, 2000), p. 157; Michael Omi and Howard Winant, *Racial Formation in the United States: From the 1960s to the 1990s*, 2nd ed. (New York: Routledge, 1994), pp. 56ff.; David Brion Davis, "Constructing Race: A Reflection," *William and Mary Quarterly* 54 (1997), 7; R. C. Lewontin, "Race," in *Encyclopedia Americana*, vol. 23 (Danbury, CN: Grolier), pp. 116–22; Cavalli-Sforza et al., *The History and Geography*, pp. 19–20; and Naomi Zack, "Race and Philosophic Meaning," in Boxill (ed.), *Race and Racism*.

[7] Indeed, the controversy about whether the scientific talk about race makes sense or not goes on. For some recent discussions, see: Robin O. Andreasen, "The Meaning of 'Race': Folk Conceptions and the New Biology of Race," *Journal of Philosophy* 102 (2005), 94–106; and "A New Perspective on the Race Debate," *British Journal for the Philosophy of Science* 49 (1998), 199–225; Joshua M. Glasgow, "On the New Biology of Race," *Journal of Philosophy* 100 (2003): 456–74; Philip Kitcher, "Race, Ethnicity, Biology, Culture," in Leonard Harris (ed.), *Racism*, (Amherst, NY: Humanities Press, 1999), pp. 87–120; and Michael O. Hardimon, "The Ordinary Concept of Race," *Journal of Philosophy* 100 (2003), 437–55.

such ethnic groups as Jews, Latinos, and Puerto Ricans. If in fact the individuation of these groups is not possible, what sense can this talk have? Could the
concepts that are supposed to correspond to the linguistic terms in question
have any value when the entities to which they refer cannot be effectively individuated? Add to this that many social and political projects depend on the
effective individuation of these groups and identification of their members.
Affirmative action policies, for example, do not seem to be able to be effectively
implemented otherwise. Indeed, as Angelo Corlett has pointed out, such policies require that we "provide means by which persons can identify themselves
accurately."[8]

It would appear, then, that only if there are acceptable alternatives to essen-
tialism/realism and non-essentialism/conceptualism can we hope to account
for the individuation of ethnic groups. Essentialism/realism can account for
individuation, but it is a discredited view, and non-essentialism/conceptualism
appears to be unable to account for individuation.

I made one such attempt in chapter 1, with the Familial-Historical View of
Latino identities.[9] However, two important objections have been proposed
against this particular theory. Both question the effectiveness with which the
theory accounts for the individuation of social groups such as races and ethne.
I call the first argument the *Circularity Objection*. It has been proposed by
Anthony Appiah against the use of the theory in connection with racial groups,
but what it says about race can be easily applied to Latinos.[10] I call the second
argument the *Demarcation Objection*. It has been advanced by Richard Bernstein against the use of the theory specifically in the context of Hispanics and
can be applied to Latinos as well.[11]

These two objections are important in the current philosophical conversation because they arise within two different, but significant, philosophical

---

[8]   J. Angelo Corlett, *Race, Racism and Reparations* (Ithaca, NY: Cornell University
Press, 2003), p. 16.

[9]   I first defended this view in the context of ethnicity in Jorge J. E. Gracia, *Hispanic/
Latino Identity: A Philosophical Perspective* (Oxford: Blackwell, 2000), ch. 3, and I
further elaborated on it and developed it in the context of race in *Surviving Race,
Ethnicity, and Nationality: A Challenge for the Twenty-First Century* (New York:
Rowman & Littlefield Publishers, Inc., 2005). A familial version of race has been
defended by Anna Stubblefield in *Ethics Along the Color Line* (Ithaca, NY: Cornell
University Press, 2005), ch. 5.

[10]   Kwame Anthony Appiah, "The Uncompleted Argument," integrated, with the title
"Illusions of Race," as ch. 2 in *In My Father's House: Africa in the Philosophy of
Culture* (New York: Oxford University Press, 1992).

[11]   Richard Bernstein, "Comment on *Hispanic/Latino Identity* by J. J. E. Gracia,"
Philosophy and Social Criticism 27, 2 (2001), 44–50.

traditions – analytic and Continental – and yet they express related concerns. Their proponents are distinguished philosophers whose opinions carry considerable weight within the American academy and their criticisms have had an impact on recent discussions of group identity.

My purpose here is to show that the Familial-Historical View of Latino identities is in fact immune to these objections. My aim is quite limited. I do not present a full defense of it against other kinds of objections that can be, or have in fact been, brought up against it.[12] Nor do I make a full case for the way in which the theory accounts for the individuation of Latinos. To do these things would require much more space than I have available here.[13]

I. Circularity and Demarcation Objections

A. Circularity

The Circularity Objection is presented by Appiah in the context of his criticism of Du Bois's view of race. As we saw in chapter 1, the core of Du Bois's position is that races are like families and need to be understood historically. A history is the key to racial identity, the distinctions among races, and racial group membership.

To this, Appiah objects that this claim is circular insofar as the individuation of a race by its history presupposes the individuation of the history by the race. He puts it thus:

> [W]hen we *recognize* two events as belonging to the history of one race, we have to have a criterion for membership in the race at those two times, independent of the participation of the members in the two events. To put it more simply: sharing a common group history cannot be a criterion for being members of the same group, for we would have to be able *to identify* the group in order to identify *its* history. . . . Du Bois' reference to a common history cannot be doing any work in his *individuation* of races.[14]

---

[12] For answers to some other objections, see Jorge J. E. Gracia, *Hispanic/Latino Identity: A Philosophical Perspective* (Oxford: Blackwell, 2000).

[13] There have been various interpretations and discussion of these objections in the literature. For a recent attempt to answer the Circularity Objection, see Paul Taylor, "Appiah's Uncompleted Argument: W. E. B. Du Bois and the Reality of Race," *Social Theory and Practice* 26 (2000), 103–28. Taylor's strategy is to argue that Appiah's objection is unsuccessful as long as history is not understood globally, as the history of a race, but individually, as the history of the individuals who compose the racial group.

[14] Appiah, "The Uncompleted Argument," 27. My emphasis, except on 'its.'

B.   Demarcation

The Demarcation Objection is raised by Bernstein in his criticism of my view
of Hispanic identity, but it can easily be adapted to Latino identity, so from
now on, I speak of the second identity rather than the first in order to maintain
the connection to what is said in other parts of this book.[15]

The difficulty concerns demarcation, that is, the way to determine who
qualifies as Latino. The Familial-Historical View, Bernstein claims, does not
provide sufficient guidance in this respect. He frames the argument in terms
of the use of history my theory makes.[16] History, he objects, is not specific or
particular enough to be able to distinguish Latinos from other ethnic groups.
History is general: it can be your history or mine, this history or that. So the
view that historical relations individuate (or "particularize," as he puts it)
Latinos and account for membership in the group fails.

Bernstein is aware that when I apply the Familial-Historical View to Latinos,
I speak not of history in general, but of "our history," that is, of the history of
Latinos. But he argues that I need to point to something that turns "history"
into "our history," and that the Familial-Historical View does not effectively
do this because it denies that there are common properties to the group of
Latinos and the notion of family it uses to further clarify the issue is ineffective
without such properties.

From this it would seem that Bernstein's objection is similar to Appiah's:
History cannot individuate ethnic groups, because history itself needs to be
individuated. However, Bernstein's argument is not the same as Appiah's. His
objection is not that the Familial-Historical View is circular, for he believes it
need not be, provided that one identifies a group's sense of history as what
individuates the history of the group. In short, he accepts the Familial-
Historical View's tenet that ethnic groups are individuated by their history,
but he objects that this view as articulated by me does not identify a sense of
history as the individuator of Latino history.

Do the Circularity and Demarcation Objections defeat the Familial-
Historical View of Latino identities? Before we can answer this question, we
need to make sure that we understand the exact force of the objections. One
major difficulty with this is the vagueness of the notion of individuation. Both
objections use this notion, but we are not quite sure of what is meant by it.
The reason is that individuation is not only frequently debated, but also under-

[15]   Bernstein, "Comment on *Hispanic/Latino Identity*," 44–50.
[16]   Ibid., P. 49.

stood in different ways in the literature. This lack of uniformity generates ambiguities that we need to avoid.[17] So let me briefly turn to individuation.

II. Individuation Clarified

Individuation is frequently understood in at least two ways.[18] In one, it has to do with the conditions that must be satisfied for something *to be* individual. This is a metaphysical understanding of it, so let us call it "metaphysical individuation." In this way, we speak of the individuation of this 2 × 4 card as the process involved in the satisfaction of certain conditions that establish the card's individuality.

In a second sense, individuation is used to refer to conditions that must be satisfied for something *to be known* as individual. This is an epistemological understanding, so let us call it "epistemological individuation." In the case of this 2 × 4 card, the pertinent conditions that have to be satisfied refer to the knowledge that someone may have about the card's individuality.

The difficulties with figuring out what is meant by the individuation of ethnic groups do not end here, however, for the notion of individuation is parasitic on the notion of individuality, and individuality too is a contested notion.[19] There are in fact many understandings of it, but it suffices to point to two frequently found in the literature that are particularly pertinent for present purposes. The first conceives individuality as a second-order property of things that are non-instantiable instances of instantiables, so let us refer to

---

[17] Apart from the sources to which reference will be made later, see Ofelia Schutte's comments in her discussion of racial and ethnic identity in "Negotiating Latina Identities," in Jorge J. E. Gracia and Pablo De Greiff (eds.), *Hispanics/Latinos in the United States: Ethnicity, Race, and Rights* (New York: Routledge, 2000), pp. 61–76. Several other articles in the same collection illustrate the variety of uses to which the term 'individuation' is put in the context of races and ethne in particular.

[18] In a third way, individuation is understood, linguistically, to refer to conditions that govern the effective use of language to pick out individuals. This is irrelevant for present purposes, although I discuss the meaning and reference of ethnic terms in general, and 'Latino' in particular, in chapter 3.

[19] The notions of racial and ethnic groups themselves are also contested, but for the sake of brevity I assume that we all have some understanding of what these expressions mean when we say that Blacks constitute a racial group and Latinos constitute an ethnic group.

it as "non-instantiable individuality."[20] In this sense, "this 2 × 4 card" is individual, but "card" is not, for "this 2 × 4 card" is an instance of "card" that cannot itself be instantiated into other cards. "2 × 4 card," on the other hand, is not individual, for there can be instances of it, "this 2 × 4 card" and "that 2 × 4 card" being two of them. In another way, individuality is conceived as a second-order property of things that are different or distinct from all other things.[21] We might say that this is a conception of individuality as uniqueness, so let us call it "uniqueness individuality." In this sense, "this 2 × 4 card" is individual in that it is in some sense different or distinct from everything else, such as "that 2 × 4 card," "that human being," and "the table."

There are at least two common senses of "uniqueness," however, that we also need to make explicit. According to one, uniqueness is a second-order property of a thing that is one of a kind. The last Dodo bird is unique in the sense that there can be only one of its kind (when the kind is taken precisely as "the last Dodo bird"). But when the kind is taken to be just "Dodo bird," then the last Dodo bird is not unique, for there are many other individual animals that qualify as Dodo birds.

There is, however, another, weaker sense of uniqueness. In this way, a particular Dodo bird is unique in the sense that there is no other bird, or any other being for that matter, that happens to be in fact quite like it, even if there are other entities that are also birds, or even Dodo birds. This is the result of the particular properties that the Dodo bird in question happens to have. Being born at a certain place, of certain parents, at a certain time, having lived in certain places and certain times, and having associated with certain other birds, eaten certain foods, and so on, make this Dodo bird to have a set of properties that is not shared by any other bird, or any other being for that matter. So, it is not that the Dodo bird in question is one of a kind, for all Dodo birds belong to the kind "Dodo bird," but that it enjoys a unique, albeit contingent, set of properties that renders it different from everything else, including other Dodo birds, in particular circumstances. This is the sense of 'uniqueness' that is used in the subsequent discussion.

[20] For a defense of this view, see Jorge J. E. Gracia, *Individuality: An Essay on the Foundations of Metaphysics* (Albany, NY: State University of New York Press, 1988), pp. 43–56.

[21] For a very early understanding of individuality in this way, see Boethius, *De Trinitate* I, in *Theological Tractates*, ed. and trans. H. F. Stewart and E. R. Rand (Cambridge, MA: Harvard University Press, 1968), p. 6. For a contemporary criticism of this kind of view, see Héctor-Neri Castañeda, "Individuation and Non-Identity," *American Philosophical Quarterly* 12 (1975), 131–40. For other conceptions of individuality, see Gracia, *Individuality*, ch. 1.

If we combine the two conceptions of individuality and the two conceptions of individuation we have distinguished, and apply this schema to ethnic groups, we get at least four possible ways of understanding the topic that concerns us here:

1 Metaphysical individuation of the non-instantiability of ethnic groups.
2 Metaphysical individuation of the uniqueness of ethnic groups.
3 Epistemological individuation of the non-instantiability of ethnic groups.
4 Epistemological individuation of the uniqueness of ethnic groups.

In (1), the issue involves the conditions that need to be satisfied for a group to be non-instantiable. What are the conditions that make it impossible for Latinos, considered as a group, to be instantiable into other groups of Latinos? In (2), the conditions apply to the uniqueness of the group. In this case the question has to do with what makes a group contingently different, as a group, from all other groups. What makes Latinos different or distinct from all other groups? And in (3) and (4), the question involves the conditions governing the knowledge of such non-instantiability or uniqueness. How can we know that Latinos constitute a group that is non-instantiable or unique?

III.   Back to Circularity and Demarcation

A.   Circularity

Applying the scheme developed above about individuation to Appiah's objection in the context of the Latino ethnos, we can surmise that it concerns individuation understood as uniqueness rather than as non-instantiability. He is concerned with what makes the group the same as itself and different from other groups. Still, the objection could be formulated in at least two ways, depending on whether one takes him to be speaking about metaphysical or epistemological uniqueness. There is room in his text for both interpretations insofar as Appiah speaks both of the sameness of the group (metaphysics) and our ability to identify it (epistemology). So here are two likely formulations of the argument as applied to Latinos, whether to the ethnos as a whole or to particular Latino ethne, such as Mexican or Tarahumara:

Metaphysical formulation

1 The Familial-Historical View of Latino identities proposes that Latino ethne are unique because they have unique histories.

2   But the histories of Latino ethne are unique because they are the histories of those unique ethne.
3   Therefore, Latino ethne cannot be unique because they have unique histories.
4   Therefore, the proposal of the Familial-Historical View of Latino identities fails when applied to Latino ethne.

Epistemological formulation

1   The Familial-Historical View of Latino identities proposes that Latino ethne are known to be unique because they are known to have unique histories.
2   But the histories of Latino ethne are known to be unique because they are known to be the histories of Latino ethne.
3   Therefore, Latino ethne cannot be known to be unique because they are known to have unique histories.
4   Therefore, the proposal of the Familial-Historical View of Latino identities fails when applied to Latino ethne.

Put in these terms, the objection at first appears to be impregnable. Indeed, we could illustrate Appiah's point by putting it linguistically in this way: The claim, "The history of an ethnos individuates the ethnos," and in our case "Latino history individuates the Latino ethnos," is circular because a reference to the ethnos is already contained in the subject of the sentence.

I submit, however, that Appiah's objection is not impregnable. One weakness in it is that Appiah equivocates on the meaning of 'the history of an ethnos.' This expression can have at least three senses. In one, it refers to the history of the ethnos once the ethnos is constituted, that is, the history that follows the constitution of the ethnos. In another sense, it refers to the history within which the ethnos becomes constituted. And in a third sense, it refers to the history that precedes the constitution of the ethnos.[22] Ethne, just like other social groups, are established in time and under particular circumstances, and there is a history that precedes them, a history in which they develop, and a history that follows them. The history that precedes them consists of the set of events that happens before the ethne are constituted. The history in which they develop consists of the events that directly or indirectly affect the ethne throughout the process of its constitution and thereafter. And the history that

[22]   One can also speak of the history that follows the disappearance of an ethnos, but it would be hard to construe this as in any sense being "the history of the ethnos."

follows the ethne consists of the events that follow after the ethne has been constituted.

It might be helpful to present the three cases I have suggested schematically in reference to Latinos, where 'L' stands for a Latino ethnos and 'E_1 E_2 E_3 E_4' stand for (the events that constitute) a history, as follows:

1   The history of a constituted Latino ethnos:

   L E_1 E_2 E_3 E_4

2   The history within which a Latino ethnos is constituted:

   E_1 E_2 L E_3 E_4

3   The history preceding the constitution of a Latino ethnos:

   E_1 E_2 E_3 E_4 L

Sense 1 of history refers to the series of events (E_1 E_2 E_3 E_4, all coming after L) that occurred after the Latino ethnos became distinct from other social groups. Sense 2 of history refers to the series of events (E_1 E_2 E_3 E_4, where L is between E_1 E_2 and E_3 E_4) within which the Latino ethnos became distinct from other groups. And sense 3 refers to the series of events (E_1 E_2 E_3 E_4, coming before L) that preceded the distinction of Latinos as an ethnos. Keep in mind that by 'history' here I mean a series of events and not a narrative about the series. The term 'history' has both meanings and I am adopting the first without prejudice against the second.[23]

Now, it makes sense to argue that an ethnos could not be individuated by the history that follows the constitution of the ethnos, for that history presupposes the ethnos. However, the history that is regarded as individuating in the Familial-Historical View need not be this history, but rather it can be the history that precedes the constitution of the ethnos or even the history within which the ethnos develops. The history that precedes an ethnos is not contingent on the ethnos, and can be described without reference to it, so the problem of circularity does not arise concerning it. That history can be individuated, both in the metaphysical and epistemological senses, without reference to the ethnic group that follows it, by referring to such things as other

23   For more on this, see chapter 1 of Jorge J. E. Gracia, *Philosophy and Its History: Issues in Philosophical* Historiography (Albany, NY: State University of New York Press, 1992).

events, other entities, and so on. The history that precedes the Latino ethnos can be distinguished by reference to the events that constitute it, for example, and not the group of Latinos. So, it is possible to claim that history individuates the ethnos without falling into circularity in that it is in the context of certain events in that history that the ethnos emerges. Something similar could be said about the understanding of the history of an ethnos as the history in which the ethnos develops. A developing ethnos may not yet be considered to be an ethnos, and so the factors involved in its individuation do not appear to require the ethnos as fully constituted. But this case is not as clear as the previous one.

There is surely a time at which Latinos did not exist. Indeed, before 1492 there was no such a group of people. What was there? In the Iberian peninsula there were Catalans, Spaniards, Galicians, Portuguese, Basques, and Andalucians. Some of these groups had political independence – the Portuguese, for example – but most of them did not. In pre-Columbian America also there were many groups of indigenous people: the Maya, Aztec, Inca, and so on. And so there were in Africa before Africans were abducted and brought to the Americas as slaves. Surely, then, before 1492, there was a history. Events were happening in Iberia, Africa, and pre-Columbian America. There were wars, invasions, and the formation of political units among many other happenings, and these events were individual and can also be identified and distinguished from other events.

For example, the marriage of Ferdinand and Isabella brought the kingdoms of Castile and Aragon together. Montezuma became the king of the Aztecs. And the Portuguese made important nautical discoveries. These events were historically unique and could be identified as such by any observer who had access to them. But neither the individuality nor the identification of these events require a reference to the future that is Latin America or the group we know as Latinos. Yet, these very events, as well as others, set the stage for the encounter between Iberia and pre-Columbian America and the introduction of Africans as slaves in the Americas. And this encounter, or encounters, as I have argued elsewhere, generated events that slowly created the conditions for the development of the group of people we now refer to as Latinos.[24] Latinos are certainly not Iberians, but they are not pre-Columbians or Africans either. So much for the history that preceded them.

Now let us consider the history within which the Latino ethnos emerged. This is the history that begins in 1492 and continues to this date. At first there were no Latinos, but slowly, as a result of many events there came to be. And this happened in different places, contexts, and circumstances. In this history,

---

[24] Gracia, *Hispanic/Latino Identity*, ch. 5.

there are events that can be identified without reference to Latinos. For the formation of this group is not uniform in every place. So there may be places where historical events may be individuated and we can identify them as such without reference to Latinos. In other places, however, there are events tied to the group because the group has already emerged. So the history within which Latinos arise is sometimes dependent on the group but at other times it is not. This makes possible reference to some of this history, or part of it, without involving the group, and therefore precludes circularity.

Finally, there is the history that follows the group's formation. This one clearly is tied to the group. Yet even here one could speak of this history as molding and changing the group and thus as influencing it. Consider a natural disaster in Mexico that elicits a sense of solidarity throughout Latin America. The national disaster can be indicated without reference to Latinos, or even Mexicans, but it can be a force in the formation of a feeling of solidarity between the people directly affected by the disaster in Mexico and the people not affected by it in Chile, thus strengthening Latino ties.

Metaphysically, then, the Circularity Objection fails. But does it fail also epistemologically? I do not see why not, as long as the mentioned senses of history are kept separate. In principle one can speak of the events that preceded 1492 and of the knowledge we have of them. And we can speak of those events as narrowing down and preparing the conditions for the emergence of Latinos as well as establishing the conditions for knowing the group. We can speak of the historical events that preceded the Latino ethnos, but we only *know* that it is their history once the group has been established. More on this later.

B.   Demarcation

When the schema of individuation presented earlier is applied to Bernstein's objection, it becomes clear, as it was with Appiah, that Bernstein is not interested in individuality taken as non-instantiability. He is not concerned with the fact that the group of Latinos is not instantiable into other groups of Latinos. If the group of Latinos is composed of 400 million individual persons, the group of these persons is not instantiable into groups of 400 million individual persons. This is just as happens with this cat: it is not instantiable into other cats. Bernstein's concern is with individuality conceived as uniqueness, that is, with what makes the group of Latinos unique, in a similar way in which Napoleon was unique. In this, the issue Bernstein addresses is similar to Appiah's. But to know this, as was also the case with Appiah, is not enough to understand the full impact of Bernstein's objection insofar as we still have to establish whether he frames the issue in metaphysical or epistemological terms.

A point to consider is that Bernstein makes the suggestion that the Familial-Historical View can be rendered effective in accounting for individuation when a sense or consciousness of history as "ours" is added to it. By consciously appropriating history, by identifying ourselves with certain events, he holds, we can effectively particularize history and demarcate the ethnic group to which we belong. This seems to suggest that Bernstein's claim is epistemological insofar as the individuation factor to which he refers is our consciousness. But in fact, from something else he tells us, we can surmise that it is in fact metaphysical. In a pertinent text he states that "there must also be a sense of one's identity and pride *in being* [Latino]," for Latinos to constitute a group.[25] This suggests that Bernstein has in mind a sense of identity ("pride in being"), or we might say self-identification, here, but this pride functions metaphysically – it is what unifies and distinguishes Latinos, what makes them *be* Latinos. History individuates groups, but it is history made uniquely "ours," as he puts it, through self-identification. It is history as we know it and appropriate it that is pertinent for uniqueness, not history independently of our knowledge of it. Knowledge of our history makes us who we are.

One way to render Bernstein's argument is as follows:

1   For Latino ethne to be unique, they have to have unique histories.
2   But for Latino ethne to have unique histories, their members must know the groups' histories.
3   But according to the Familial-Historical View of Latino identities, members of Latino ethne do not have to know the groups' histories.
4   Therefore, the Familial-Historical View of Latino identities fails to account for the uniqueness of Latino ethne.

Again, as with Appiah's argument, this objection appears very strong, maybe even impregnable. The key to it is the second premise, for Bernstein can claim good company. Indeed, Searle has argued along similar lines concerning the reality of social groups.[26] Still the argument is not convincing and its main weakness is precisely found in the second premise. This claim can be challenged on at least four grounds.

First, the members of ethnic groups do not need to know the histories of the groups. Ethnic groups function as such even when their members lack a

---

[25]   Bernstein, "Comment on *Hispanic/Latino Identity*," p. 49. My emphasis. Note the similarity between this view and Paula Moya's position in "Why I Am Not Hispanic: An Argument with Jorge Gracia," *The American Philosophical Association Newsletter on Hispanic/Latino Issues in Philosophy* 2 (Spring 2001), 100–5.
[26]   John Searle, *The Construction of Social Reality* (New York: The Free Press, 1995).

sense of themselves, in that self-identification is a long and protracted process which often depends on conditions external to a group and takes a long time to emerge. How long has it taken Latinos in the United States, for example, to have a sense of themselves? Indeed, some even dispute they have such a sense now! Besides, even if a sense of themselves was required, this does not necessarily entail knowledge of the group's history.

Second, people can be taught to think of themselves in ways that are contrary to the facts; they can be indoctrinated, and facts can be covered up or misrepresented. Consider that children may grow up thinking they are natural offsprings of their parents when in fact they are adopted. What members of an ethnic group may think is their history is not always an accurate reflection of that history. Indeed, there is much about Latino history that is pure fabrication, or dependent on a certain take on the facts determined by ideological commitments.

Third, Bernstein's claim can be taken to refer to all members of ethnic groups or just to some members of the groups. If all, then clearly this is false insofar as children and incompetent persons may not be able to know about the history of the groups to which they belong, and even among those members of the groups who are competent to know it, it might happen that they do not know it for a variety of contingent reasons. Many members of ethnic groups in the United States, for example, have an underprivileged status that prevents them from learning about their historical roots. When one is concerned with putting bread on the table, it is difficult to think about one's heritage. And if it is only some members of the groups that need to know about the histories of the groups, how are we to identify them and on what basis are we to legitimize their authority in this matter? Who among Latinos has been "appointed" to this task? Academics? Hardly, they disagree among themselves. So, to whom do we turn? These are tough questions to answer for anyone who holds the view Bernstein favors.

Last, even if one were to accept that knowledge of history is required for the individuation of groups on historical grounds, it would not be necessary that such knowledge be found in the group, it could be found in members of other groups. And, indeed, it is often the case that what others think is as important, or even more important, for group identity than what the group itself, or its members, think.

This does not mean that self-identification and group identification cannot be part of the conditions that play a role in Latino ethnic unity, or that the appropriation of history by Latinos does not play a role in Latino self-identification. They certainly can and do. The knowledge of a fact does not alter the fact, although it may (1) produce other facts which otherwise would not have been produced and (2) modify certain facts which otherwise would not have been modified. My knowledge of who hit me over the head may alter my future conduct, but that knowledge cannot alter the hit or the identity of the person who did it. This is a distinction that is often missing in discussion of these issues.

IV.   Individuation of Latino Ethne

So much for the failure of the Circularity and Demarcation Objections to undermine the Familial-Historical View of Latino identities by attacking its effectiveness in accounting for individuation. This is as much as can be accomplished here. To hope that we can go beyond this and establish the conditions of effective individuation of Latinos is unrealistic. It is not possible for us to determine what things, or even what kinds of things, whether properties or relations, make Latinos unique and account for their particular ethnicity. Nor can we expect to establish the causal genesis of Latinos, that is, how the group has been formed and the sorts of things that are responsible for its creation rather than the creation of some other kinds of groups. Such tasks would require a detailed presentation and discussion of the Familial-Historical View. Nonetheless, we can learn something from these objections and the answers that we have given to them that will allow us to say something useful here about the individuation of Latinos. Although the objections turn out to be ineffective as formulated, their consideration brings to the fore some aspects of the individuation of ethnic groups that merit attention and help in determining the parameters of an effective view.

The Circularity Objection reveals the need to take into account various senses of history and to understand the history of social groups in concrete terms. One of the problems with this objection is that it looks at ethne as fixed groups of people already constituted, without taking into account their context, development, and changing character. Another is that it ignores the variety of histories that affect these groups.

The Demarcation Objection, on the other hand, by emphasizing the sense of history, uncovers the need to consider significance an important factor in the constitution of ethnic groups, although it makes the mistake of restricting significance to mere awareness. Such individuating factors as the number of people involved and the unique spatio-temporal location of these individuals are not sufficient to account for the uniqueness of ethnic groups. These groups increase and decrease, and they cross spatio-temporal boundaries.

With this in mind, we can turn to the two pertinent questions for us in this context: first, what makes Latinos of various stripes unique if one adopts the Familial-Historical View of Latino identities? And second, how do we know they are unique at any particular time? The first question is metaphysical, the second epistemological.

A.   Metaphysical uniqueness of Latinos

The uniqueness of ethnic groups results from the bundle of properties, including relations, which in turn arise from historical events and apply to their members at any time during, and cumulatively throughout, their existence. These groups are unique but contingently so, because history is the key to their uniqueness, in that history generates the properties that distinguish them in context. History is contingent; things could have been otherwise. It is possible that Latinos could not have existed. What if the Spaniards had decided that San Salvador was not India and therefore had turned back to Spain? After all, the Vikings seem to have done something like this, and nothing came of their landing on North America. Or what if Cortés had not burned his ships? Or what if Montezuma had not been captured and the Spaniards that invaded Mexico had been killed? If any of these events had happened, history could have been very different. Perhaps pre-Columbian America would not have been unified under two empires – the Spanish and Portuguese. Perhaps the British would have invaded instead. Perhaps many nations would have developed without common languages and history. And perhaps there would never have been any Latinos!

From the answer to the Circularity Objection we know that the history in question is complex. First, there is the history that precedes the constitution of the groups; second there is the history within which the groups develop; and third, there is the history that follows their constitution. The first two of these histories contribute to the individuation of the groups, that is, to making them unique and thus different from other entities in context. But, of course, this by itself does not explain why groups actually become constituted as unique. So what is it in history, or what is necessary in history, to accomplish this? At least three factors need to be considered:

1   Historical events that affect certain people directly and not others.
2   A substantial number of events – a few isolated events cannot compare to chains or clusters of many events.
3   The significance of the events.

An example might help. Consider Latinos and the historical factors that in particular have helped constitute them into a specific ethnos. First, the initial encounter between the sailors aboard the Castilian ships and the natives of San Salvador affected both groups of people directly in rather obvious ways, but it did not directly affect Russian peasants or Chinese bureaucrats living in Russia and China at the time. Second, the Viking landing in Newfoundland, for example, produced only a few events, whereas the landing of the Castilian ships in San Salvador unleashed a chain of events of enormous proportions. And, third, the Spaniards did not just give a few colored beads to the natives, but rather proceeded to change their way of life in significant ways, imposing a foreign model of government and a different religion, among other things, on them, while at the same time incorporating much from them into their own culture.

The three factors mentioned, when taken together, illustrate how certain historical events effectively tie some people, while at the same time separating them from others and rendering the group in question unique through the relations in which they are embedded and the properties that these relations generate. The relations and properties in question vary, depending on the circumstances. Often they involve experiences of particular sorts, whether positive or negative. Indeed, negative experiences, such as those associated with domination, colonization, and marginalization, are frequently cited as particularly significant.[27]

This is similar to what happens with a family: marriage unites certain persons and separates them from others. History becomes ours, as Bernstein would put it, precisely because of the kind of history it is. It creates us as groups, by uniting us and by generating relations and properties that, in context, separate and distinguish us from others.

The Familial-Historical View, then, allows for the consideration of historical conditions and properties of ethnic groups at particular times and places in spite of its rejection of the need for common group properties. There is no reason why, for example, we cannot speak of certain properties of these groups at certain periods. We can speak of Latino philosophy or thought in the nineteenth century, as will become clear in chapter 7. It also allows for the discussion of criteria of identity within a historical context. But all this has to be understood within a relational and non-essentialist metaphysical framework. This is why we can, without contradiction, discuss particular properties of Latinos in context.[28] To make this, or any other property associated with *some* members of the group, part and parcel of the nature of *all* members of the group, is to fall back into the kind of essentialism that distorts ethnicity and is responsible for much oppression and discrimination in human history. On the

---

[27]   See, for example, Walter Mignolo, "Latinos (and Latino Studies) in the Colonial Horizon of Modernity," in Gracia and De Greiff (eds.), *Hispanics/Latinos in the United States: Ethnicity, Race, and Rights.*

[28]   I have done something like this with Hispanics and *mestizaje*, in Gracia, *Hispanic/Latino Identity*, ch. 5.

other hand, to reject the metaphysical framework is to give up on understanding ethne and how they work. It condemns us to a kind of superficial, and culturally biased, description of ethnic phenomena without a foundational understanding of them, or to the kind of description that is more properly undertaken in fields such as sociology and cultural anthropology.

B.   Epistemological individuation of Latinos

Can we effectively account for the identification of Latinos? Surely the answer is yes, provided we have access to the unique bundle of properties and historical relations that apply to them, for these distinguish them from other entities we know and tie Latinos throughout their histories. Of course, we cannot account for the uniqueness of the groups merely *qua* ethne, for as such they are not unique. An ethnos, *qua* ethnos, is not unique and cannot be known to be unique insofar as there is a plurality of ethne. Rather, Latinos are known to be unique *qua* Latinos. And how can we know our unique sets of properties and histories? By the relations that can be established between Latinos and an observer. It is by considering Latinos in a historical grid in relation to an observer that their identification is possible.

This is not very different from the way I know you as a unique and different human being. How do I do it? Because you are located in a grid of which I am part and that is centered on me. I function as an absolute point of reference in it. You are right in front of me, or to my left, or to my right. And you are related to me in certain ways, as my friend, or a stranger, or my daughter. And you have certain characteristics that are evident from my perspective: a certain height, a certain shape, and so on.[29] And so it is with groups. A group is nothing but its members, and I can identify it through them. Of course, there are questions about how to identify members I do not presently see, but there are ways to do it, just as I can identify members of families that I do not see. "Do you know my cousin Peter? No. Well, he is very tall, and . . ." This kind of talk makes perfectly good sense, although there is much more that needs to be said about this, but the saying will have to wait for another time.

My claim does not mean that there may not be disputable cases. But don't most of our concepts tolerate disputable cases? This applies to even a common notion such as "most of," which I brought up in chapter 1. In a group of 50, does 26 qualify as most of the group? How about 251 in a group of 500? And what of 1,000,001 in a group of 2,000,000? "Most of" is not equivalent to "the majority," or "to half plus one," so the issue is controversial. But this does not entail that the concept of "most of" is senseless or unusable. It only means that this concept, like some others, does not stipulate strict boundaries. This is

---

[29]   Gracia, *Individuality*, ch. 5.

precisely the case with ethnic groups in general and with Latinos and Latino groups in particular.[30]

V. Individuation of Latinos

I began this chapter by briefly presenting two contrary and defective answers to the problem of the individuation of ethne. Next I introduced the Familial-Historical View adapted to the case of Latinos, and formulated two objections to it: the Circularity Objection in the version adopted by Appiah in his criticism of Du Bois's view of race, and the Demarcation Objection, in Bernstein's formulation used against my view of Hispanic identity. The Circularity Objection argues that the Familial-Historical View cannot explain the metaphysical or epistemological uniqueness of ethne in general, and therefore neither of Latino ethne in particular, because it falls into circularity. The Demarcation Objection argues that this view cannot explain the metaphysical uniqueness of these ethne because it fails to make reference to the sense of history necessary for history to be considered particular to an ethnic group. This led me to introduce some distinctions between four different conceptions of individuation which I subsequently used to understand the Circularity and Demarcation Objections. I concluded that both objections are concerned with individuality understood as uniqueness, taken broadly and contingently.

I argued that both objections are ineffective: the first, because it fails to distinguish several senses of history and, the second, because its assumption about the need for a sense of history for ethnic groups to exist as such is misguided. However, I found that the consideration of these objections proved useful in establishing some parameters for an effective view of the individuation of ethnic groups in general and Latinos in particular, although I did not attempt to provide any list of necessary or sufficient conditions for them here. Indeed, I did not say anything either about the kind of history that generates ethnic groups or Latino identities as opposed to other social groups, although I added some general conditions concerning the relevance of the events in question. This is an important issue, but one that will have to wait for another occasion. If the argument of this chapter is right, then Latino identities can be effectively conceived in terms of the Familial-Historical View and Latinos and Latino groups can be effectively individuated both metaphysically and epistemically. The most common way we signal epistemic individuation is through language, so in the next chapter I turn to the controversial issue of the terms we use to do so.

[30]   Gracia, *Surviving Race, Ethnicity and Nationality*, ch. 3.

Labels: Politics and Names

Two questions are fundamental when we turn to ethnic names in general and to names such as 'Latino' in particular. One has to do with the relation of these names and politics. This is particularly important for ethnic names because they are found most frequently in a context where political agendas are at play and the way the terms function is closely related to these agendas. Names like 'Latino' and 'Hispanic' are used to classify people and make decisions about their education, economic well-being, affirmative action, and so on. They also carry with them various connotations, some of which are pejorative, and this affects how people called by these names are treated. The use of these terms often carries political and social baggage, giving the question of the social and political dimension of their use substantial importance.

The second question has to do with the meaning and reference of these names. Meaning has to do with the properties associated with the things called by the names. The meaning of 'triangle' is a geometrical figure with three angles. And the same applies to 'cat,' whose meaning includes having fur and the capacity to meow. Reference has to do with the things picked by the name. 'Cat' picks my cats Hunter and Peanut, as well as any other things that are cats, and 'triangle' picks anything that is a triangle. So what is the meaning and reference of ethnic names like 'Latino'? What does being Latino involve? And what people does the name 'Latino' pick? The question of meaning and reference is not frequently explicit in the context of ethnic names, as it is discussed almost exclusively in the broader context of names in general. But the way the question is formulated and answered is important for understanding ethnic names, how they function, and how they are used.

I begin by examining the relation of ethnic names and politics in the context of 'Latino' and 'Hispanic,' two labels that are frequently interchanged.[1] Then I turn to the meaning and reference of 'Latino.' Note that I use the term 'name' instead of 'term' to talk about words such as 'Latinos' and 'Hispanics.' I prefer this terminology not only because of a long tradition in the philosophy of language that discusses theories of names, both proper and common, but also because my arguments in the second part of this chapter in particular rely on that discussion. I also think that the meaning of 'term' is too broad and may create unnecessary vagueness, insofar as it includes such categories as syn-categorematic terms. However, readers should be aware of the fact that some recent discussions of these issues use instead 'ethnic-group terms.'[2]

I.   Latinos and the Politics of Ethnic Names

Should ethnic names be used at all? If so, which ethnic names should be used for particular ethnic groups? And how can the use of ethnic names in general, and of some ethnic names in particular, be justified? These questions are attracting increasing attention in the United States. A few years back, they were completely ignored. Indeed, if one scans the pertinent literature, only very few social scientists have been concerned with them.[3] Current population pressures in the United States, however, have brought increasing attention to issues of ethnicity among sociologists, psychologists, and anthropologists, although philosophers continue to have relatively little to do with these issues.[4] Still the

---

[1]   Although the official adoption of 'Hispanic' for purposes of affirmative action at the Federal level seems to have taken place in the mid seventies, the term was in circulation long before then to refer to the people, speech, or culture of Spain, Portugal, and Latin America. See 'Hispanic' in *Webster's Third New International Dictionary* (Chicago: Encyclopaedia Britannica, Inc., 1966). Something similar can be said for the use of 'hispánico/a' in the Iberian peninsula and Latin America. See, for example, Miguel de Unamuno, "Hispanidad," in *Obras completas* (Madrid: Exelsior, 1968; first published in 1927), vol. 4, p. 1081.

[2]   Susana Nuccetelli, "Reference and Ethnic-Group Terms," *Inquiry* 6 (2004), 528–44; and José Medina, "*Latinidad*, Hispanicity, and Ethnic-Group Terms," in Susana Nuccetelli, *Blackwell Companion to Latin American Philosophy* (Oxford: Blackwell, forthcoming).

[3]   For a rare example, see R. E. Brewer and M. B. Brewer, "Expressed Evaluation toward a Social Object as a Function of Label," *Journal of Sociological Psychology* 84 (1971), 257–60.

[4]   As far as I know, the first published general discussion of ethnic names from a philosophical point of view is found in Jorge J. E. Gracia, *Hispanic/Latino Identity: A Philosophical Perspective* (Oxford: Blackwell, 2000), ch. 2, in the context of 'Hispanics/Latinos.'

attention is often centered on particular ethnic groups and their names, and for good reasons; these ethnic groups are perceived to pose serious challenges to the country in general. Among these, perhaps the one that has received most attention recently is the group often referred to as "Latinos" or "Hispanics."[5] In philosophy, even this area has received scant attention.[6] The general questions raised above can be formulated in this case as: Should names such as 'Latinos' or 'Hispanics' be used?; Which of these two names is more appropriate for the ethnic group in question?; and, How can the use of 'Latinos' or 'Hispanics' be justified?

Elsewhere I have presented an extended analysis of the arguments that are often given against the use of (1) ethnic names in general, or (2) 'Hispanics' and (3) 'Latinos' in particular, but I followed it with a familial-historical defense of the use of 'Hispanics.'[7] My view has been criticized for a variety of reasons, to which I have responded elsewhere.[8] However, none of these criticisms has involved a defense of the use of 'Latinos,' except for that provided by Alcoff in a recent article.[9] The arguments she presents are both novel and intriguing, deserving careful attention. I cannot do complete justice to them here, but nonetheless I try to point out some of their most obvious strengths and weaknesses. My aim, however, will not be merely to evaluate Alcoff's view; I also make a proposal of my own about the use of 'Latinos,' namely, that this

---

[5]   See, for example: H. H. Fairchild and J. A. Cozens, "Chicano, Hispanic or Mexican American: What's in a Name?" *Hispanic Journal of Social Behavioral Sciences* 3 (1981), 191–8; Martha Giménez, " 'Latino?/Hispanic?' Who Needs a Name? The Case Against a Standardized Terminology," *International Journal of Health Services* 19, 3 (1989), 557–71; David E. Hayes-Bautista and Jorge Chapa, "Latino Terminology: Conceptual Bases for Standardized Terminology," *American Journal of Public Health* 77 (1987), 61–8; G. Marín, "Stereotyping Hispanics: The Differential Effect of Research Method, Label and Degree of Contact," *International Journal of International Relations* 8 (1984), 17–27; Suzanne Oboler, *Ethnic Labels, Latino Lives: Identity and the Politics of (Re)Presentation in the United States* (Minneapolis, MN: University of Minnesota Press, 1995); and Fernando Treviño, "Standardized Terminology for Hispanic Populations," *American Journal of Public Health* 77 (1987), 69–72.

[6]   The first philosophical discussion of this topic is found in chapter 1 of Gracia, *Hispanic/Latino Identity*. Some other issues related to the topic of names have since been explored by Susana Nuccetelli and others, as we shall see below.

[7]   Gracia, *Hispanic/Latino Identity*, chs. 1 and 3.

[8]   See the articles in *Philosophy and Social Criticism* 27, 2 (2001) by Richard Bernstein (44–50), J. L. A. García (29–43), Robert Gooding-Williams (3–10), Gregory Pappas (20–8), and Eduardo Mendieta (11–19), and my response in the same issue (51–75).

[9]   L. Alcoff, "Latino vs. Hispanic: the Politics of Ethnic Names," *Philosophy and Social Criticism* 31, 4 (2005), 395–408.

name has connotations that are different from those of 'Hispanics,' but is nonetheless quite useful in a variety of discourses.

A.   Political argument for 'Latino'

Alcoff's argument begins by claiming that "the choice of [ethnic] names is inherently political," although she qualifies this statement by adding that "[t]he process of choosing a[n] [ethnic] name cannot be reductively political or opportunistic, as if these concerns trump any considerations of descriptive adequacy, because the political effects that a name has depends heavily on its capacity for descriptive adequacy, its ability to gel lived experience, to sound right, to make sense of things."[10] Still, she adds, "there is always more than one story that can be given that gels to some extent with the diversity of lived experience," and this "both calls for a political solution and makes a political solution possible in the sense that it makes a space to interject political considerations in the discussion, as one consideration whose importance will vary depending on the strength of other factors."

In this carefully crafted statement, Alcoff tries to strike a middle ground between a strict political constructionist view of ethnic categories and one that allows for some non-political considerations and applies it to the use of ethnic names. Still, one problem with the statement is its vagueness, for it leaves us without guidance when it comes to what "the strength of other factors" means. What are these other factors first of all, and second, how can we measure their strength so as to use them to modify and change the political factors that Alcoff claims are inescapable when it comes to the formation of ethnic categories and the corresponding choice of ethnic names? This is an initial question that needs to be answered. Rather than dwelling on it, however, let me turn to the particular political argument Alcoff gives in favor of the use of 'Latino' rather than 'Hispanic,' for this constitutes the core of her article and is particularly pertinent here.

The argument has two parts. The first presents the advantages of the use of 'Latino'; the second points to the disadvantages of the use of 'Hispanic.' The first begins by noting that "the term Latino signifies and is itself marked by that moment of crystallization [i.e., 1898] in the colonial relation between, not Spain and Latin America, but the USA and Latin America." And she adds: "this historical genealogy of the term brings to the fore the idea that present-day Latinos are those peoples who have been constituted largely in and through a colonialism that has not yet left us."[11] The point I think is clear. We should

[10]   Ibid., P. 400.
[11]   Ibid., P. 402.

use 'Latino' rather than 'Hispanic,' because the former term has a connotation of colonialism missing in the second. This colonialism contrasts one group of people, Latinos, with another group of people, Anglo-Saxons, and by implication Latin America and the United States.

The second part of the argument argues specifically against the use of 'Hispanics,' taking us to "1965, when the new immigration law ended the previous quotas on immigration to the United States" from Latin America. This opens the way for the later introduction of 'Hispanics' by the United States Census bureaucracy to encompass peoples from different countries from Latin America residing in the United States. Alcoff goes on to claim that 'Hispanic' is a cultural, rather than a national term, and it is one that links those named by it to Spain. This is an important step in the argument, for, as a consequence of these events, Alcoff argues that this group of people have been de-nationalized, de-linked to the multi-national region of the world that represents their group history, and, arguably, group interests, in favor of a term that places the emphasis on culture, on language, and that, to the extent it reminds us evocatively of a colonialism, it reminds us of that older, previous, historically impotent colonialism of Spain rather than the one that is all too potent even in our own present day.[12]

B. Evaluation of the political argument

Let me respond to the first part of Alcoff's argument first and separately, before I turn to the second, which is more complex. I have several objections against this first part, but let me just mention two here: One, the choice of 1898 as the significant year for the "gelling" of the colonial mind set that bears on the use of 'Latino' is based on one of Walter Mignolo's highly interpretative and polemical claims.[13] But to base a claim such as Alcoff makes on a separate, borrowed thesis that is as controversial as Mignolo's weakens Alcoff's inference.

Second, as Alcoff acknowledges, 'Latino' is a term of French institution, and France was a colonial power at the time it coined the term, and continued to be so for years afterwards. But Alcoff and Mignolo should keep in mind that the introduction of the term by the French was political, and the aim was not to underscore any kind of pernicious colonialism, but rather to advance the very colonial interests of France in North and South America. The historical

---

[12] Ibid., P. 404.

[13] Walter D. Mignolo, "*Local Histories/Global Designs: Coloniality, Subaltern Knowledges, and Border Thinking* (Princeton, NJ: Princeton University Press, 2000), pp. 32–3.

record suggests that 'Latino' was introduced to emphasize a religious and legal tradition, to support the unity of Roman-derived Continental European Law in opposition to Anglo-Saxon, non-Roman derived, Common Law, first of all. It was also used to underscore the Roman Catholic unity of certain parts of the world as opposed to the Protestant religious affiliation of others.[14] And all of this with the aim of making room for France's colonial interests. Frankly, I think Mignolo, and Alcoff, insofar as she relies on Mignolo, have put on the choice of the term 'Latin' to refer to Latin America, a historical interpretation that the facts cannot bear, precisely because of a pre-determined, but post-facto, political agenda. I need to see the historical facts before I can agree to this, and I have not seen them yet. Indeed, my reading of the sources of the period support just the opposite interpretation.

In short, I find the support Alcoff offers for the use of 'Latino' to be at least historically suspect and probably groundless. This does not mean that we should not use the term, but only that Alcoff's argument for its use is ineffective. Now let me turn to the second part of Alcoff's argument, the one in which Alcoff argues against the use of 'Hispanic.'

The argument here is quite complex. I see at least four different reasons why Alcoff thinks 'Hispanic' should not be used, although further analysis might reveal more. Let me summarize the ones I see as follows. The use of 'Hispanic' is to be avoided because:

1   It is not a national name and national names are to be preferred.
2   It separates certain people from their common history as Latin Americans.
3   It is a cultural term that refers to a colonial culture, that of Spain.
4   In evoking Spain, the term draws attention away from present-day United States colonialism, which is the real one we must fight today.

My response to (1) – that 'Hispanic' is not a national name and national names are to be preferred – can be made in terms of a question: Why? It is true that 'Hispanic' is not a national name, like 'Cuban' or 'Mexican,' but why should one hold that national names are better than non-national ones particularly when the terms are used to pick ethnic, rather than national groups? Is this judgment based on political, historical, or moral considerations? The reason most favored by those who use this kind of argument is political, and this is consistent with Alcoff's general approach. But national names can be as polit-

---

[14]   Francisco García Calderón, *Las democracias latinas de América* (Caracas: Biblioteca Ayacucho, 1979; first published in French in 1912), pp. 154–5.

ically oppressive as ethnic ones, and indeed, often they are more so because they are based on the self-interested choices of the powerful. Think about Chiapas, where a largely Mayan minority has been oppressed by a *mestizo* majority that considers themselves "true Mexicans."

Moreover, there are dangers in confusing nationality and ethnicity. The view that nations are the same as ethne turns all relations between nations into ethnic ones. Thus, national conflicts become conflicts between ethnic groups, fueling their virulence and lending support to the position that only the complete extermination of one of the nations in conflict can solve the problem. Disputes about territory, resources, and influence, which in other contexts are subject to compromise, now become conflicts about values, ethnic characteristics, and cultures, which are regarded as not negotiable. Whereas losing a war between nations not understood ethnically may simply mean that one nation loses some territory, when nations become identified with ethne, the loss of a war presents itself as an opportunity to eliminate a way of life or even to commit genocide in order to prevent future conflicts. Indeed, is not the expression "ethnic cleansing" a commonplace these days? For as long as something of the original ethnos remains, there is the possibility of strife.

This is the problem seen from without, as it were. But internally also the consequences of the identification of nations with ethne are pernicious, for no state is in fact ethnically homogeneous. This means that a nation that identifies itself with one ethnos, leaves other ethne out. The nation becomes an institutionalized place of privilege for some and oppression for others.[15] Examples of this phenomenon have been so common in recent history that little has to be added; we need only look at recent events in Afghanistan and India, and to the history of the United States.

The alternative view, that ethne are in fact nations, also has disastrous consequences. Considering them to be nations leads immediately to the desire for ethnic political independence, regardless of whether the group in question has been oppressed or not. The result is the generation of conflict and the implementation of terrorism as a way to fight for ethnic independence. This is the case of Spanish Basques. But we may ask, how far can we divide the world to make national lines correspond to ethnic ones? How far do ethnic groups go? We have witnessed recently the division of Czechoslovakia into two states as a response to the desire to separate two nations ethnically conceived. But this is not sufficient, for one of the resulting divisions, the Czech Republic, contains

---

[15] David Copp, in "Democracy and Communal Self-Determination," in Robert McKim and Jeff McMahan (eds.), *The Morality of Nationalism* (Oxford: Oxford University Press, 1997), pp. 277–300, has argued that for culturally unified groups to have the right of self-determination, i.e., of forming states, is anti-democratic.

at least three ethnic groups – Bohemians, Moravians, and Salesians. Is a further division necessary, then? And would this be enough? Since there are no countries today that correspond exactly to ethnic boundaries, should every nation on earth be broken up and new political borders drawn? Imagine the disruption, and the possible conflicts that would arise! Finally, how much peace have divisions of this sort brought about in the past? The track record is dismal, so optimism in this direction is unwarranted.

But this is not all. The reality is that human ethnic populations are mixed all over, so where are we to draw the lines? These divisions, as is clear from the case of India and Pakistan, lead to endemic conflicts because there are bound to be disagreements about the boundaries and resentment resulting from the resettlement of people away from places they regard as their home. And how is such an idea to be implemented in a place like the United States, in which ethnic and racial groups are mixed over the entire national territory? Are we to ship all African Americans to Africa and all Latinos to Latin America? Are we to send all Arab Americans to the Middle East, all Cuban Americans to Cuba, and all Irish Americans to Ireland? The same would have to happen in Spain, where all Catalans would have to go back to Catalonia, all Basques to the Basque Country, and all Castilians to Castile. Does anyone really think this is possible, or desirable? It is as crazy an idea as humans have come up with, and one that encourages a kind of strife that cannot end in peace and harmony. Indeed, it only postpones the need to grapple with the real issue, which is to find a political solution to the survival of humankind that takes into account the variety of ethnic groups of which it is composed.

Finally, 'Latino' itself would fail the test of being a national term, and thus preferable to cultural ones, because Latin America is not a country or a nation, but a region of the world without political unity. Indeed, as many questions have been raised concerning the validity of using this term as against the use of 'Hispanic.' Mignolo himself has recently questioned the whole idea of Latin America.[16]

Argument (2) – that the use of 'Hispanic' separates people from their common history as Latin Americans – is historically inaccurate to this extent: after 1492, Latin America has no *common* history to speak of separate from the history of the colonial powers that invaded it. Indeed, Latin America had no common history even before then. Pre-colonial Latin America was composed of many different peoples separated in various ways, and sometimes quite isolated from each other. Even after the independence of most parts of Latin America from Iberia in the nineteenth century, there is no substantial *common*

---

[16] Walter D. Mignolo, *The Idea of Latin America*, Blackwell Manifestos (Malden, MA: Blackwell, 2005).

history to Latin America. There are national and regional histories, but no overall Latin American history that one can easily identify. Nowhere is this more obvious than in the history of philosophy, for so far Latin American philosophy has been no more than a minor – and generally regarded as marginal by both Latin Americans and non-Latin Americans alike – footnote to European and American philosophy. I return to this point in later chapters.

Even to this day, Argentinians consider themselves to have more in common with Europe than with their Latin American neighbors, and often have closer economic, political, and cultural relations with European countries than with other Latin American countries. But even leaving Argentinians out, what do Mexicans have to do with Chileans? How do events in Chile affect Mexico? Indeed, it appears that the history of Mexico is more closely tied to the history of the United States than to the history of most other countries – perhaps all – from Latin America. And something similar can be said, *mutatis mutandis*, about other Latin American countries.

Argument (3) is that 'Hispanic' is a term that refers to the colonial culture of Spain and this poses a problem in that it privileges the culture of a past foreign oppressor. To this I have two responses. First, it is not quite accurate to say that 'Hispanic' connotes only what has to do with Spain. The original Latin term *Hispania* was not the Roman name for what we today know as Spain, but for the entire Iberian peninsula, and the denotation of *español*, or 'Spanish,' to this day includes such people as Catalans, Basques, Galicians, and others. It is true that 'Spain' is a corruption of *Hispania*, and that the political unit we know by that name has claimed right to it, as the United States has claimed right to the term 'America.' But the use of 'Hispanic' exclusively for what is Spanish should be resisted, as some Latin Americans resist the use of 'America' for the United States and of 'American' for what pertains exclusively to the United States.

My second response is that, the Spanish component of the cultures of parts of Latin America is undeniable. Can I deny that Spanish is my native tongue? Can I deny that some of my ancestors were Spanish? Can Alcoff deny similar facts? When I travel throughout Latin America, I see a mixed reality, culturally, racially, and politically. And I see a reality that to this day makes no sense considered apart from historical ties to the Iberian peninsula. Based on fact, I can make very little sense out of anything south of the United States border without reference to the Iberian peninsula at the present moment; the future, of course, is something else, for Spain and Portugal are turning toward Europe, and this may sever some of the ties that have to this day united Iberia with Latin America. In short, even though the term 'Hispanic' has a cultural connotation of Spanish in some contexts, this is not exclusive and therefore it need not deter us from using it in other ways, as in fact I have proposed elsewhere.

In *Hispanic/Latino Identity*, I argue that the term should be used to refer to a cultural complex which incorporates both Latin America and Iberian elements.

Finally, in argument (4), Alcoff claims that the connotation of Spain and Spanish colonialism of the term 'Hispanic' draws attention away from the real culprit of present colonialism, that is, the United States, while presumably 'Latino' does not. This is the most intriguing and original of Alcoff's arguments. It is original because, although there have been other attacks on the use of 'Hispanic' and defenses of the use of 'Latino,' they generally are based on other considerations. For example, some authors have argued that 'Latino' is a grassroots term arising from a choice by the Latino community in the United States, rather than a bureaucratically imposed term, like 'Hispanic.'[17] But I need not go into other justifications. Let it suffice to point out that Alcoff's argument for 'Latino' and against 'Hispanic' does not follow the usual routes. The question that matters is whether this argument is sound or not. Is Alcoff right in proposing that the use of 'Hispanic' is counterproductive because it detracts attention form the present "colonial" condition of Latinos, whereas the use of 'Latino' is not insofar as it helps to focus attention on that condition?

Two considerations may be brought forth in favor of a negative answer to this question. The first is that, if 'colonialism' is taken in its strict sense, the present relation between the United States and Latin America cannot be regarded as colonial. Colonialism is a primarily political relation which has also important social, economic, and cultural implications. It is certainly the kind of relation that Spain had with respect to the territories it conquered in Latin America. But it is misleading to talk about United States colonialism in the region today; for the United States has no colonies in Latin America (except

---

[17]   This is mistaken on two grounds. First, it is not some Americans that first decided to call themselves "Latinos." This term is used in Latin America and this use antecedes its use in the United States. It takes only crossing the border and visiting various Latin American countries, from Mexico to Costa Rica, to realize this fact. Indeed, the use of *latino/a* as an adjective is frequent. One finds *tiendas latinas, restaurantes latinos, comida latina,* and so on, throughout Latin America. The attribution of the creation of the term, or its use, to some segment of the American community is one more instance of the provincialism and distorted sense of importance that many of those who live in the United States have, including Latinos. The second ground on which it is mistaken to hold that 'Latino' is a grassroots term chosen by the Latino community in the United States is that not every member of the presumed Latino community in the United States, or anywhere else for that matter, has chosen to be called Latino/a. Many people favor national names instead, and others favor 'Hispanic.'

perhaps, some would argue, for Puerto Rico and the Virgin Islands). Yes, there is exploitation of natural resources; yes, there is political manipulation; yes, there is cultural influence; and so on. But strictly speaking, there is no colonialism. To describe the relation between Latin America and the United States as involving colonialism is a metaphorical use of language in which the meaning of the term and its derivatives is stretched beyond usual boundaries. This is counterproductive to the extent that it introduces imprecision in discourse and results in confusion. This kind of metaphorical stretching of word meanings in the political arena is popular in postmodernist discussions of these issues, but I find it unhelpful, although it is frequently quite effective rhetorically and serves well some pre-established ideological purposes. With characteristic sense and evenhandedness, Alcoff stays away from these excesses in her article, but she lapses into this approach when she uses 'colonialism' loosely and metaphorically.

One of the objections Alcoff voices against the use of 'Hispanic' is its cultural connotation, the fact that it distracts us from political considerations by echoing culture. But certainly it would be very difficult to defend a view that 'Latino' does not have important cultural connotations of its own. Indeed, the term is frequently used as an adjective in both Spanish and English to qualify such things as music, food, restaurants, art, and so on. So clearly the term has a strong cultural connotation, perhaps as strong as the term 'Hispanic.' If having a cultural connotation is a factor that can be used against the use of 'Hispanic,' it could also be deployed against the use of 'Latino.'

However, this is not the whole story. Although these two considerations undermine Alcoff's last argument, there are at least two other considerations that support her conclusion. The first is that 'Latino' does have, unlike 'Hispanic,' a regional connotation which has to do with Latin America in particular and which excludes Spain and Portugal. This is rather rough and found in both Spanish and English. 'Latino' is used to refer to people or things that are part of the region known as Latin America or originate there in some way rather than elsewhere. Thus we speak, both in English and Spanish, of people, foods, artifacts, and so on as Latinos/as and we mean by it things such as Mexican tortillas or the tango.

Second, 'Latino' also has a connotation of being backwater, marginal, unimportant, and poor. This connotation is not unique; it is shared by other regional terms as well, such as 'African.' Language studies confirm this connotation of 'Latino' in the United States. But even in Latin America, to qualify certain cultural endeavors as *latino* is deprecatory. This is quite clear in the case of philosophy. Latin American philosophy (*filosofía latinoamericana*) in Latin America is taken to be inferior, weak, and derivative, in comparison with European or American philosophy, as we shall see later.

This means that, after all, one can construct a political argument for the use of 'Latino' that does not apply to the use of 'Hispanic' based on these two reasons, without having to resort to the controversial notion of colonialism. If 'Latino' has a regional connotation which also involves marginality, lack of importance, and so on, then there is a place for it in political discourse insofar as its use brings to the fore the disadvantaged condition of a certain group of people and helps in the development of an effective political strategy to address their grievances. Moreover, not using it might cause us to overlook this condition and, therefore, prevent legitimate redress.

The political advantages of the use of 'Latino,' however, should not militate against the use of 'Hispanic,' as long as there are also advantages to the use of the latter term. And indeed there are, as I have extensively indicated elsewhere.[18] These advantages are not political, but have to do with the understanding of the culture and history of Latin America, Iberia, and their peoples. My argument is that in the context of certain cultural phenomena such as philosophy, the use of the term 'Hispanic' makes sense because it allows us to see historical connections that otherwise we would miss. Iberian philosophy has been closely tied to Latin American thought and this tie runs the risk of being missed if a term that gathers both Iberian and Latin American thought is not used. On the other hand, the use of 'Latino' also brings to the fore elements that would be missed if the term 'Hispanic' were to be used exclusively. For example, we would neglect the long history of ideological confrontation between Latino thought and qualities emphasized by Latin American philosophers such as José Vasconcelos, José Enrique Rodó, Carlos Vaz Ferreira, and Antonio Caso on the one hand, and Anglo-American thinking on the other.

Let me conclude, then, by summarizing my main points. First, the political advantages of the use of 'Latino' are founded on the actual connotation of the term as used in common discourse both in the United States and Latin America, and not on some presumed relation of colonialism between the United States and Latin America. Second, the use of 'Latino' should not conflict with the use of 'Hispanic,' for both are effective for bringing into focus some aspects of the condition of a group of people that are important for our understanding of the present situation in the United States. And finally, Alcoff is right in trying to bring attention to the political advantages of the use of 'Latino' and the lack of these advantages in the case of 'Hispanic.' But discarding 'Hispanic' altogether, in favor of 'Latino,' is a mistake, because the use of ethnic names should not exclusively obey political considerations.

[18]   Gracia, *Hispanic/Latino Identity.*

I agree with the substance of Alcoff's claim about 'Latino,' although not with its justification; and I disagree with both the substance and justification of her claim against 'Hispanic.' There is room for both 'Hispanic' and 'Latino' in our discourse, although neither terms do not function in the same way and there are objections one can bring up against the use of either one. This is one reason why, having provided a justification for the use of 'Hispanic' in another book, I have here chosen to speak of Latinos instead. The argument of this book is presented in a social context where 'Latino' is more appropriate than 'Hispanic.'

The political dimension of the use of 'Latino' and 'Hispanic' is only half of the topic that we need to deal with, however, if we are concerned with the labels used to refer to Latinos. We also have to account for the nature of ethnic names and how they function, and the way this applies to 'Latino.' This is the topic of the second part of this chapter.

II. Names, Sense, and Reference

In ordinary discourse, we approach issues of identity and identification of individuals with questions like: Who am I? Who are you? and Who is Fox? When I am asked "Who are you?" the most frequent answer I give is: "Jorge Gracia." That is, I state my proper name. But I could also say something like: "The living son of Ignacio Gracia" or "the oldest member of the Department of Philosophy at the University at Buffalo who is a native speaker of Spanish." In the last two cases I give what philosophers call definite descriptions, that is, the kind of description that begins with the definite article and is supposed to apply only to the referent of the question. Likewise, when someone asks "Who is he?" or "Who is Bolívar?" the answers are usually given in terms of proper names in the first case or definite descriptions in the second. Sometimes we also ask this kind of question of groups, and again the answer can take the form of some name or definite description. Who are they? English, Papists, the people of the Book, or what have you. Or we might ask: What are they? And we answer: French, the people of God, or the damned.

The case of re-identification is slightly different, for here we usually ask something more concrete: Is he Jorge Gracia? Are they the people of the Book? That the question in this case contains the proper name or the definite description for what is wanted is a confirmation that someone at a particular time is the same at some other time, and this assumes a certain degree of identity and identification.

These questions and answers have to do with identity because they concern the conditions that must be satisfied for someone to be whoever he or she is.[19] What is it that makes me who I am? But they also have to do with identification because they involve the conditions that must be satisfied for us to know what or who someone is. What is it that makes me, or others, know who I am? Presumably, these conditions are specified through the names and descriptions we use in answering these questions. Names and descriptions are important in that they appear to tell us something fundamental about the persons we name with them; they seem to make explicit the conditions that must be satisfied for us to be who we are and they allow us to pick their referents. But, is this correct, and what do we make of ethnic names, such as 'Latino' or 'Puerto Rican'?

A.   What is an ethnic name?

Names come in two basic sorts: common and proper. Common names generally apply to more than one thing and are often taken to indicate common features in the things to which they apply. Some of these features are instantiated only by individuals that exist or can exist by themselves. 'Cat,' 'tree,' 'human,' and 'mother' are of this sort because cats, trees, humans, and mothers exist by themselves. Other features are instantiated by individuals that do not exist by themselves. 'Strong,' 'red,' and 'virtuous' indicate such features, because this or that red, or this or that virtuous, do not exist by themselves, but rather in this or that thing which is red or this or that person who is virtuous.

Proper names, on the contrary, are supposed to apply only to one thing and the thing in question is usually a person, an animal, or a likeness of these; these names are called proper because they belong to someone (and sometimes to something, such as a sword or a place). 'Jehovah,' 'Rigoberta Menchú,' 'Hernan Cortés,' and 'Peanut' are all proper names. The first applies to the Judeo-

---

[19]   The first one to see the relevance of a theory of names for group identity was Appiah, in "Race, Culture, Identity: Misunderstood Connections," in Kwame Anthony Appiah and Amy Gutmann, with an Introduction by David B. Wilkins, *Color Conscious: The Political Morality of Race* (Princeton, NJ: Princeton University Press, 1996), pp. 32ff. He was concerned primarily with racial terms. Since then Susana Nuccetelli, in " 'Latinos,' 'Hispanics,' and 'Iberoamericans': Naming or Describing?" *Philosophical Forum* 32, 2 (2001), 175–88, and "Reference and Ethnic-Group Terms," *Inquiry* 6 (2004), 528–44, and I, in Gracia, *Hispanic/Latino Identity*, and *Surviving Race, Ethnicity, and Nationality: A Challenge for the Twenty-First Century* (New York: Rowman & Littlefield Publishers, Inc., 2005), have discussed related issues concerning ethnicity.

Christian God, the second and third to individual historical persons, and the fourth to one of my cats. Of course, some proper names, like 'Mary' or 'Patrick,' apply to more than one person, but this is just a coincidence, in part the result of the lack of linguistic imagination humans have. It is possible to conceive a world in which a proper name would apply only to one individual. In any case, proper names, unlike common ones, have often been understood not to indicate anything common between things, but rather to pick out what is unique and unshareable in their bearers. Indeed, some philosophers have gone so far as to argue that proper names do not have any descriptive function at all.

The position that draws a drastic distinction between the function of common and proper names has come under heavy criticism recently. Some philosophers argue that there is no significant difference between the way proper and common names function, but I do not address this question here because our business is much narrower – with groups of people. Many kinds of names are used to talk about groups of persons. Indeed, every common name applied to persons can in principle serve to name a group, namely, the set of persons of whom the name is truly predicated. 'Strong' can be used to talk about the group of all strong persons; 'just' for the group of all just persons; 'Roman Catholic' for the group of all those who belong to the Roman Catholic Church; 'philosopher' for the group of all philosophers; and so on. We say things like: "The just shall inherit the Earth" and "Roman Catholics believe in the infallibility of the Pope." For our present purposes, however, only ethnic names are of interest, because we are concerned with 'Latino.'

In this context, there are at least three important questions for us:

1   What names are ethnic names?
2   What kind of names are these names?
3   Do these names have sense in addition to reference?

The first question is important in this context because ethnic names are frequently confused with other kinds of names. For example, ethnic names are frequently taken to be racial, and racial names are taken to involve ethnic elements, reflecting the general confusion about the categories they name.[20] 'Latino' is often interpreted as a name of a racial category, and 'Black' is often assumed to connote more than racial features; Latinos constitute a certain kind of race, and Blacks constitute a certain kind of ethnos. Indeed, some philosophers have argued explicitly for the racial understanding of ethnic names and

---

[20]   See Gracia, *Race, Ethnicity, and Nationality*, chs. 3 and 4.

the ethnic understanding of racial names.[21] Finally, ethnic names and national names seem to be interchanged often. We speak of Poles and Cubans, for example, without attempting to distinguish the senses in which an ethnic Pole is different from a Polish national, and an ethnic Cuban is different from a Cuban national.

If one adopts the Familial-Historical View of ethnic identity proposed in chapter 1, then ethnic names, when used *qua* ethnic, should not generally be used to connote race or nationality, although they could do so in particular cases. Terms such as 'Polish' or 'Italian,' when used to designate United States citizens, should not refer to a race or the nation to which these persons belong. Of course, as these two examples indicate, often the same name is used both nationally and ethnically. 'Polish' can be used to designate a citizen of Poland, in which case it is being used nationally, or it can be used to designate an American citizen, in which case it is being used ethnically. And sometimes the same name is used racially and ethnically. This is the case with 'African,' 'Latino,' and even 'Black.' Indeed, because the conditions for belonging to ethne are not uniform and depend on social and historical factors, both race and nationality can and sometimes do play a role in the identities of particular ethne.

Ethnic names, or ethnically used names, are also very often believed to refer to common cultural traits, but this is misleading. Something that seems quite clear, however, is that these names serve to identify, both in the epistemological sense of revealing and in the metaphysical sense of establishing, ethnic identity.[22] Given our present purposes and the fact that I have dealt extensively with this issue already elsewhere, I ignore it here.[23] Let me, then, propose the following formula in answer to the question, What names are ethnic?

---

[21]   See, for example: David Mason, "The Continuing Significance of Race: Teaching Ethnic and Racial Studies in Sociology," in Martin Bulmer and John Solomos (eds.), *Ethnic and Racial Studies Today* (London: Routledge, 1999), p. 21; S. Wallman, "Ethnicity and the Boundary Process Context," in J. Rex and D. Mason (eds.), *Theories of Race and Ethnic Relations* (Cambridge: Cambridge University Press, 1986), pp. 296–313; Michael Omi and Howard Winant, *Racial Formation in the United States: From the 1960s to the 1990s*, 2nd ed. (New York: Routledge: 1994); L. Gordon, *Bad Faith and Antiblack Racism* (Atlantic Highlands, NJ: Humanities Press, 1995), pp. 119, 130–1; L. Alcoff, "Is Latina/o Identity a Racial Identity?" in Jorge J. E. Gracia and Pablo De Greiff (eds.), *Hispanics/Latinos in the United States: Ethnicity, Race, and Rights* (New York: Routledge, 2000); and David T. Goldberg, *Racist Culture: Philosophy and the Politics of Meaning* (Oxford: Blackwell, 1993).

[22]   Harold R. Isaacs, "Basic Group Identities," in Nathan Glazer and Daniel P. Moynihan (eds.), *Ethnicity: Theory and Experience* (Cambridge, MA: Harvard University Press, 1975), p. 50.

[23]   Gracia, *Hispanic/Latino Identity* and *Surviving Race, Ethnicity, and Nationality*.

A name is ethnic just when, in its singular form, it is used distributively to refer to individual members of an ethnos *qua* ethnos and, in the plural, to refer to more than one of the members of the ethnos. 'Latino' functions as an ethnic name when it is used to refer to Petra, Serafín, me, any other Latino, or to the entire group of Latinos. It is possible for other names, including racial and national names, to be used to refer to members of an ethnic group, but even if they are, they do not need to function ethnically insofar as they do not need to refer to the group or its members *qua* ethnic. Two terms or descriptions may have the same extension, that is, refer to the same things and not share the same intension, that is, not connote the same set of properties. For example, the descriptions 'the husband of Norma' and 'the grandfather of Eva' refer to me, but do not connote the same properties.

B.   What kind of name is an ethnic name?

Our second pertinent question asks: What kind of name is an ethnic name? For our purposes the two categories of names mentioned earlier are pertinent: proper names and common names. So the question amounts to asking whether a name like 'Latino,' or 'Latinos,' is proper or common.

The answer is by no means obvious, for ethnic names appear to function both as proper and common names. 'Latino' is a name that applies to many individual persons and, insofar as it does, it appears to function like a common name, such as 'woman,' which is predicable of Mercedes, Leonila, and Clara. At the same time, the plural form, 'Latinos,' applies to an individual group of persons that does not constitute a natural kind, unlike women or cats. In this, it is very much like 'Gracia,' which is supposed to apply to members of the Gracia family. This suggests that, just like 'Gracia,' it is a proper name, not a common one. Ethnic names, or labels, as some sociologists refer to them, appear to function as common names in that they apply to several persons and are generally treated as if they were imposed on the basis of some feature common to the persons in question; and they appear to function as proper names in that they apply to groups of persons treated as unique, and the name is frequently given in a way similar to that in which a proper name is given. This means that much of what one can say about both common and proper names applies also to ethnic names.

In a 2001 article, Susana Nuccetelli argues in favor of conceiving 'Latino' exclusively as a proper name.[24] Indeed, her answer to the question of whether ethnic names have sense in addition to reference is given via her understanding that they are proper names, for she applies John Stuart Mill's Referential

[24]   Nuccetelli, " 'Latinos,' 'Hispanics,' and 'Iberoamericans.' "

Theory to them: proper names tell us nothing about the things they name. Referentialists present their view in terms of the notions of reference (or denotation) and sense (or connotation). The sense of a name is the set of properties the named thing is supposed to have; the reference of the name is the thing or things named.[25] This view claims that a proper name, such as 'Perón' for example, does not have sense, but only reference.[26] If 'Perón' had sense, the sense would consist of the properties that characterize Perón, such as, for example, that he was Argentinian and the husband of Evita, had an aquiline nose, was president of his native country, and so on. The reference of 'Perón,' by contrast, is the individual person we call Perón. A proper name like 'Perón,' according to this view, does not really tell us anything about Perón; it merely picks him out.

In contrast, the use of descriptive terminology is intended to do something else, namely, to describe or identify the type of individual person in question. This is reflected in the structure of certain questions, which instead of being of the form "Who did X?" ("Who spilled the milk?") are usually such as, or can be translated as, "What kind of Y did X?" ("What kind of individual spilled the milk?"). The question "What kind of individual spilled the milk?" can be answered satisfactorily with a description such as 'a playful cat' or 'a reckless animal.' Of course, one could still answer by saying 'Peanut,' but in this case the proper name would be used elliptically for something like 'a cat of the sort Peanut is,' 'a cat with features such as Peanut has,' and the like.

I do not find the arguments that Nuccetelli musters in support of her contention convincing. The reason is that they appear to beg the question. Let me explain. Nuccetelli gives two arguments to buttress her claim. The first argument is that ethnic names are frequently used as proper names and therefore should be considered to be proper names. Thus, for example, originally an

---

[25] I do not assume that reference involves or requires existence, although some philosophers hold that it does: e.g., Alfred North Whitehead and Bertrand Russell, *Principia mathematica to *56* (Cambridge: University Press, 1962; abridged edition of "Principia mathematica," 2nd ed., Cambridge, 1927), p. 66.

[26] See: John Stuart Mill, *A System of Logic* (London: Longman, 1872), p. 21; Bertrand Russell, *Logic and Knowledge, Essays 1901–1950*, ed. R. C. Marsh (London: Allen and Unwin, 1956), pp. 200–1; Ludwig Wittgenstein, *Tractatus logico-philosophicus*, trans. D. F. Pears and B. F. McGuiness (London: Routledge and Kegan Paul, 1961), § 3.203; Peter Strawson, "On Referring," *Mind* 59 (1950), 320ff. The key point to what has come to be called "the theory of direct reference" is the denial that the conceptual content associated with a name secures its referent. Nathan Salmon, "Names and Descriptions," in D. Gabbay and F. Guenthner (eds.), *Handbook of Philosophical Logic*, vol. IV: Topics in the Philosophy of Language (Dordrecht, Netherlands: D. Reidel, 1989), p. 445.

ethnic name, such as 'Turk' or 'Gringo,' is "transformed and used, affection-ately, as the proper name of a person."[27]

The problem with this argument, even if we were to strengthen it by talking about an ethnic name taking the place and functioning as a proper name – something that Nuccetelli does not do – is that it begs the question insofar as one could always argue that the name in question, say 'Turk' or 'Gringo,' is actually being used ethnically, and not as a proper name, in cases in which Nuccetelli thinks it is being used as a proper name. In short, the example, taken by itself, cannot help us determine what is at stake, and can be used to illustrate two different theories because it is not neutral with respect to interpretation and, therefore, cannot definitively support one theory rather than the other.

The second argument Nuccetelli gives is that ethnic names do not have a set of properties they always connote. One can use these names effectively even if the descriptions associated with the names fail to apply to the referents of the names. And, Nuccetelli argues, this shows that these names must be proper names, for this is what characterizes proper names, presumably, in contrast to common names.[28]

The problem with this argument is that, as the previous one, it begs the question. Nuccetelli believes that it is characteristic of proper names not to be descriptive, that is, not to have sense, so she argues that because ethnic names do not have sense, they must be proper names. But surely she must first prove that proper names do not have sense in order to argue that ethnic names, because they do not have sense, are proper names. Further, the notion that non-proper names always involve a description that applies to the things to which they refer is questionable. Indeed, many philosophers these days claim that, in this respect, common names are not different from proper ones.

Still, Nuccetelli is right about her conclusion that ethnic names are like proper names rather than like common ones, even if the reasons she gives for it are unsound. And here I must also disagree with Nuccetelli's more recent article in which she changes her mind and argues that "words such as 'Eskimo,' 'Inuit,' and 'African-American' [and other 'ethnic-group terms'] function pri-marily as general terms and only derivatively as names of people."[29] Her change of mind is in the wrong direction, for although one might be able to argue that when terms like 'African American' and 'Eskimo' are used racially they func-tion like natural and biological terms used to refer to kinds, I do not see that the case can be made for properly ethnic names. 'Latino' does not function like 'water' or 'tiger,' but more like a familial name, such as Gracia or

[27] Nuccetelli, " 'Latinos,' 'Hispanics,' and 'Iberoamericans,' " p. 177.
[28] Ibid., p. 178.
[29] Nuccetelli, "Reference and Ethnic-Group Terms," 528.

Nuccetelli. When discussing this issue, one needs to keep clear the distinction between racial terms and ethnic ones, because race is a different case, even if frequently confused with, ethnicity.[30]

Let me suggest a reason that I think explains why, contrary to Nuccetelli's most recent claim, ethnic names do function like proper names. Proper names are characterized by the fact that, contrary to common names, they name individuals or groups of individuals, not kinds of individuals or groups of individuals. When I say, "Hunter," I am talking about one individual cat, but when I say "cat," I am talking about a kind, even if I am using the term to say something about one or more individual cats. When I say, "Cicero is Tully," I am merely establishing an identity between the referents of the terms 'Cicero' and 'Tully,' but when I say "Cicero is a man," I am saying that Cicero belongs to a kind, namely man. The issue is not one of description versus non-description; the issue has to do with the kinds of things to which these names apply.

One might want to object that this would make indexicals, such as 'this' and 'that,' also proper names. And the answer is that, indeed, they are proper names of a sort, that is, they are terms that are used as proper names in very particular contexts. 'This' functions like 'Hunter' when used in appropriate circumstances because it is intended to pick one and only one individual. But what about definite descriptions? Aren't they also names of individuals? I do not think so. 'The last Dodo bird' is a name for a kind, the kind of Dodo bird that was last. It so happens that there is only one such bird, but this makes no difference: the name is a name of the kind, not of the single individual that belongs to the kind. To be an individual is to be a non-instantiable instance of an instantiable. Individual is contrasted with universal, which is to be an instantiable. Cat is universal because it is instantiable; this cat is individual because it is not instantiable into other cats.

The reason that ethnic names are wrongly taken to be common names is that they apply to more than one person. If Linda, Susana, and Jorge are Latinos, some authors reason, 'Latino,' like other ethnic names, must not be proper, but common. The mistake in this inference is to think that, because ethnic names apply to several individuals, they are common. What makes a name common is not that it applies to several individuals, but rather that it names a kind or is applied to an individual to say that it belongs to a kind. Proper names surely apply to several individuals as well. Consider the name 'Gracia.' This is a proper name that does not apply to just one person, but rather to various members of the Gracia family, and this does not make it common.

[30] I explain some of the distinctions between these two concepts in Gracia, *Surviving Race, Ethnicity and Nationality*, chs. 3 and 4.

According to the Referential Theory of names, the issue at stake is whether or not terms such as 'Latino' have sense in addition to reference. If they do, then they are common names, but if they do not, then they are proper ones. However, we have seen that the issue of reference and sense can be raised both about proper and common names, so an answer to it in the case of ethnic names does not help us to settle the matter.

C.   Do ethnic names have sense in addition to reference?

Even if we accept, as I have proposed, that ethnic names are proper, this is not enough for our purposes, for we still do not know whether their function is to pick out or to signify, that is, whether they are intended to refer or to cause an understanding. Two views I have defended elsewhere are pertinent for answering this question: the first is the notion of individual, already mentioned above. If we use proper names to refer to individuals, then it is essential that we be clear that an individual is a non-instantiable instance of an instantiable. Cat is not individual because it can be, and in fact is, instantiated, but Hunter is individual because there can be no instances of him. And the same can be said about individual groups, such as the Kennedy family.

The second view is what I called elsewhere the *Tripartite Theory of Names*. According to it, we need to distinguish among three questions:

1   What is the function of proper names?
2   How are proper names established?
3   How do language users learn to use proper names effectively?[31]

Each of the three theories of names most frequently defended today provides an effective answer to one of these questions, but, when it attempts to answer the others, problems arise. All three theories have something important to contribute to an overall theory of proper names, but none of them by itself and without some modifications is sufficient to answer the three questions raised. The Referential Theory provides an appropriate answer to the first question: The function of proper names is to refer to individuals. The Causal Theory gives a convincing response to the second question: Proper names are established through a kind of baptism. And the Descriptivist Theory solves the problem suggested by the third question: Language users learn to use proper names through descriptions. The Referential Theory, however, fails to appreciate sufficiently that descriptions do play a role in any complete account of

---

[31]   Jorge J. E. Gracia, *Individuality: An Essay on the Foundations of Metaphysics* (Albany, NY: State University of New York Press, 1988), ch. 6.

proper names; the Causal Theory fails to recognize the full force of descriptions in learning to use proper names effectively; and the Descriptivist Theory misunderstands the key role that descriptions play with respect to proper names. Let me explain.

The arguments commonly used by those who favor the Referential Theory aim to support the view that the function of proper names is to refer to individuals, but we need not repeat them since I have discussed them at length elsewhere.[32] Let me instead call attention to a factor that accounts for the fundamentally referential character of proper names: the primitive character of individuality. Individuality is a fundamental or primitive notion that corresponds both to a basic datum of experience as well as to a basic building block of reality. Accordingly, an individual's individuality cannot be analyzed into a set of properties expressed by a description, and referring must consist in an act in which a sign is used to stand for an individual. Therefore, the sign used to refer to an individual does so, not in virtue of any sense it has, but simply because it stands for a non-instantiable instance. When this is applied to proper names, we see not only that proper names need not be descriptive in any sense in order to have referents, as Descriptivists believe, but also that it makes sense to consider them primarily non-descriptive and therefore as devoid of sense. Now, insofar as the primary motive for attaching sense to proper names has to do with explaining how they refer, and this motive is baseless, there is no need to hold that proper names have sense in addition to reference.

The Referential Theory of proper names captures correctly the primary function of proper names. What it does not do is explain successfully (1) how it is that proper names are established, and (2) how we learn to use them effectively. This is the contribution of the Causal and Descriptivist Theories. Proper names, according to the Causal Theory, are established in a kind of baptism where an individual is given the name. The name is given to the individual in its fundamental character as individual, and not to an individual that necessarily satisfies a particular description. This is why the individual may turn out to be different than it was originally thought to be and still retain the name. We could say, then, that the baptism ties a name to an individual in its character as non-instantiable and not necessarily to a particular description of one sort or another. This is revealed in the language used in ceremonies in which proper names are given. When the priest says, "I baptize thee 'X,' " there is no description involved. 'Thee' is used in its referential capacity as ostensive and not as standing for a set of features that could be captured in a description. Not even relations are involved. The name is not imposed on "the son of so

[32]   Ibid.

and so" or "the fat baby with big eyes," but rather on "thee." It is a mistake to think that the reference of proper names at the baptism is determined by a description of the individual named.[33] To grant this would be precisely to acknowledge that reference is related to sense and, therefore, that the function of proper names involves more than reference,[34] for in such a case, the very imposition of the name would have to be related essentially to the description of the referent. This makes the theory subject to the kind of objections to which the Descriptivist Theory is generally liable.

In order to avoid both the criticism of Descriptivists and the difficulties associated with Descriptivism, the imposition of a proper name must not be regarded as necessarily involving description. This applies not only for what might be called "accidental" or "extrinsic" descriptions, but also must extend to "natural kind" descriptions. We must allow for the possibility, however remote, that the bearer of the name is of a different natural kind than we think even at the moment of baptism. Indeed, it is in the realm of possibility that the baby of our example is not a human baby at all but rather a god, a devil, an extraterrestrial, or even a robot.

In short, the primary function of proper names is to refer, and they are established through an act of baptism. But, we still need to ask how one learns to use them effectively. This is where the Descriptivist Theory plays an important role, for we learn to use proper names effectively in a variety of ways, but often we do so through descriptions. This is particularly the case when we are not directly acquainted with the bearer of the name. When we are introduced to a stranger, we are told something like, "Let me introduce you to Mr Silva," or "This is Mr Silva," or "I would like you to meet Mr Silva," and in each case there are some bodily movements that aim to show you who Mr Silva is.

This procedure is similar to the baptismal ceremony in that a name is ostensibly related to an individual. The difference is that in the baptismal ceremony the name is given, whereas in the introduction the name and its relation to the individual bearer are communicated to someone. The identity of that someone, to whom the name and its relation to the individual bearer are communicated, is of no consequence, of course. Such communication could even be directed to the bearer of the name, although then the procedure would probably not be called an introduction. Persons who have had bouts of amnesia, for example, could be told their name by their family, and small children are likewise told that they are called such and such. But when we are not acquainted with the bearer of a name, the way to learn the name and use

[33] Saul Kripke, *Naming and Necessity* (Oxford: Blackwell, 1981), p. 96.
[34] John Searle, *Intentionality: An Essay in the Philosophy of Mind* (Cambridge: Cambridge University Press, 1984), p. 241.

it effectively is through descriptions. We learn who is called "Socrates" by learning that he is the main speaker in the *Symposium* as well as Plato's teacher, and that he was married to a scold. Thanks to these descriptions we are able to use the name 'Socrates' effectively in communication.

All this is consistent with the view that, although individuality, conceived as non-instantiability, is primitive and therefore cannot be analyzed in descriptive terms, it is also true that belonging to a kind is a necessary condition of it. There can be no individuals that are not instances of some universal, and, consequently, their description in terms of those kinds should be possible. Indeed, it is through features that individuals are often discerned, and thus a theory of reference to individuals needs to incorporate a descriptive component. But no particular description specifying the features of a thing is necessarily tied to the name. This is possible because, although belonging to a kind is a necessary condition of individuality, and we discern individuals through their features, no specific kind is required for individuality, and, therefore, no description can be necessarily tied to an individual *qua* individual. A description involving a kind property may be used for fixing the reference even though ostension at the point of baptism does not necessarily tie the name to the description, for the description plays an epistemic role that may be effective in fixing the reference in context, but nevertheless not be necessarily tied to the individual.

The mistake of Descriptivists is to try to give the same answer both to the question as to how we learn to use a proper name and to the question as to what the function of a proper name is. Likewise, referentialists attempt to answer both questions with the same answer, although they adopt a different view from that of Descriptivists. Finally, the Causal Theory of names, although more effective, tries to resolve the impasse by combining these views in a way that neglects the role descriptions play in determining reference after baptism.

Part of the problem that gives rise to the three theories of reference of proper names and that later undermines them, is the failure to distinguish clearly between the three questions mentioned earlier, which is in turn a consequence of a more basic failure to distinguish between epistemic, logical, and metaphysical issues. If the distinction among these questions is maintained, many of the puzzles that prompted the three theories can be avoided.[35]

For our present purposes, it is important that some of what has been said concerning proper names has also been applied by some authors to common

[35] For some possible objections to this conclusion and their answers, see Gracia, *Individuality*, pp. 221–6.

names such as 'cat' or 'dog.' In particular, it is important for us to note that some of these authors hold that common names function as proper names in that they have no sense because the features that the bearers of the names have, can, and often do, change. Indeed, some of those who favor this view argue that there is no way to fix the features of anything, for there are no such things as essences, that is, sets of properties that always belong to certain kinds of things. Things change, and yet we can still refer to them with the common names we have given them, which means that the names in question are not necessarily tied to any particular property or set of properties. Tigers do not have to have stripes – we could always find one that does not – and dogs do not necessarily have the capacity to bark – aren't there in fact some dogs that cannot bark?[36]

All this sounds quite reasonable, and yet we do learn common names through descriptions of some kind. Moreover, when we use them, we think about certain properties of the objects we name with them, just as we do with proper names. What I have said so far does not necessarily go against the theory that names, whether proper or common, are never associated with necessary sets of properties that are found in the things that we name through them. One can hold that names function effectively even when there is no such necessary set of properties, because there is always a set of properties to which those who use the name can appeal, in context, in order to communicate effectively about the bearers of the names. Users of a name learn to use it based on a set of properties, although not all those who learn to use the name have the same set of properties in mind when they learn to use it. As long as there is some link between what the speakers that use a name think at a particular time, and something common between what they think and what other speakers think, communication may effectively occur.

Consider the following case. Say that Isabelita thought of Perón both as the husband of Evita and as the president of Argentina; that Evita thought of Perón both as her husband and a general in the Argentinian army; and that I think of Perón both as a general in the Argentinian army and the husband of Isabelita. It is quite obvious that the features that Isabelita and I attribute to Perón are different. Yet Isabelita and Evita claim that they are talking about the same individual, and Evita and I claim that we are also talking about the same individual; and even Isabelita, Evita, and I claim that we are talking about the same individual, for although when I think of Perón, I think of nothing Isabelita thinks about, Evita functions as a bridge between Isabelita and me.

[36] Kripke, *Naming and Necessity*, pp. 48 and 109.

D.   Names, sense, and reference

In short, although a name tells us something, what it tells us is subject to the contingencies of history. Now let us go back to the three questions we asked about proper names and apply them to ethnic names: (1) What is the function of ethnic names? (2) How are these names established? and, (3) How do language users learn to use ethnic names effectively?

The answers appear to be quite straightforward. The answer to the first is that these names are used primarily to pick out either individual ethnic groups or the individual members of ethnic groups. In this, they are similar to proper family names like 'Silva' or 'Medici.' Generally, these names are not used to describe or convey information about groups of people, but rather to refer to them, although in particular circumstances, in contexts where some description has been given or is accepted as attaching to the members of the group, the names are used to recall that description. If we were to agree that Latinos are lazy, we could very well, in the context of a discussion in which laziness is involved, and in answer to a question whether such and such a person is lazy, say: Well, after all he is Latino!

The answer to the second question, about how these names are established, is that these names are established through a kind of baptism. At some place and time, there is one person or persons who decide to call a group of people by the ethnic term. This, again, is similar to what happens with families. Someone gets the name at some point and at some time. And whoever gets the name – whether it is an individual person in the case of a family name, or a group of people as is the case with an ethnic name – is an individual person or group of persons with particular characteristics that in context separate them from others. I call you "Gracia" or "Latino" here and now, as you are, with whatever features you have. The baptism in the case of ethnic names occurs at one time, when the term is first used by one person to refer to the ethnic group in question, but its acceptance by others, whether within or without the group, is a progressive matter; it occurs over time, just as happens with family names.

The answer to the third question, about the way we learn to use ethnic names effectively, has to do with descriptions in context. Note that I am not talking about how the reference is secured, that is explained by the Causal Theory. I am talking about how I, here and now, learn to use the term 'Latino.' The description through which we learn to pick out members of the group at any one time and learn the use of the name, is a contingent matter that changes. This fits the Familial-Historical View of ethnic identity, for the features that characterize Latinos, say, are contingent and depend in turn on particular historical relations.

This view also explains how ethnic names can be applied to new persons, for these names apply to the group and are, for that reason, transferred to its members. As long as the synchronic and diachronic identity of the group can be accounted for, new members of the group acquire this denomination without difficulty.

III. Politics and Names

The first part of this chapter discussed the politics of ethnic names. It argued against Alcoff's view concerning the use of 'Latino' in place of 'Hispanic' on the basis of political considerations. Instead, I claimed that both 'Latino' and 'Hispanic' are helpful when thinking about various dimensions of the Latino experience, because each brings out something the other misses and therefore helps to increase our understanding. 'Latino' connotes the marginal and colonial situation of Latinos, whereas 'Hispanic' brings out the historical and cultural connections between Iberia and Latin America. Both are helpful for understanding who we are, but the first is most important in a political context.

In the second part of the chapter, I raised the question of whether ethnic names, such as 'Latino,' are common or proper, and I distinguished between three standard theories of proper names, Referential, Descriptivist, and Causal. All three have strengths and weaknesses. Instead of adopting one of them, I reformulated the issue in terms of three questions: Which names are ethnic? What names are ethnic? and, Do these names have sense in addition to reference? I answered the first question in terms of usage: ethnic names are names used to refer to ethnic groups as such, or to the members of the groups. 'Latino' refers to the group of Latinos, and also to Jorge and María. I answered the second question by saying that ethnic names are proper names. 'Latino' is like 'Jorge Gracia.' Finally, I applied the Tripartite Theory to 'Latino.' The function of 'Latino' – and the same can be said about 'Puerto Rican' or 'Cuban' – is primarily to pick certain persons and groups of persons; the term goes back to a baptismal event; and we learn to use it through descriptions.

The position I have defended should clarify how ethnic names in general, and Latino identity names in particular, are used to stereotype and homogenize, in spite of the fact that the realities to which they refer are not homogeneous and do not generally tolerate uniform descriptions. They do because, although as proper names their function is referential – say, to pick the group of Latinos and also the members of the group – we learn to use them through descriptions which can be used to stereotype and homogenize. Finally, the position is consistent with the view of Latino identity presented earlier and thus strengthens the overall theoretical framework for which I argue in this book. The conception of ethnic names as proper names allows flexibility concerning the descriptions through which we learn to use them, and takes into account particular situations and conditions. There is no description that always applies, and this is consistent with the idea that Latinos, as other ethnic groups, are like families, whose identity is historical and contextual. Past history cannot change, but future history is open and can change the view of past history, even if not what actually happened.

The clarification of the obscurities concerning identity, individuation, and naming in the context of Latinos we have discussed in the first part of this book is only a first step in understanding Latinos and the challenges we face in American society. Three challenges are especially critical and serve as good examples: economic survival and intellectual flourishing, full participation in American society, and linguistic rights. These are the topics of Part II.

Latinos/as in Society

Marketplace: Survival and Flourishing

Economic survival has to do with finding adequate means of support and intellectual flourishing has to do with enjoying appropriate conditions for mental development. Perhaps no other profession and no other social group illustrate these challenges better than philosophy and Latinos. The picture that a survey conducted in the year 2000, concerning the situation of Latinos/Hispanics in the philosophy profession by the American Philosophical Association Committee on Hispanics/Latinos, is very bleak, to the point of being hopeless. Here is what the Committee states:

> Of the 140 graduate departments responding to the survey (which is a response rate of better than 75%), 58, or about 41%, reported having any Hispanic faculty, graduate or undergraduate students, or recently completed Ph.D. students. In these departments, there was a total of 19 tenured faculty, 13 untenured faculty, 37 recent Ph.D. recipients, 30 Ph.D. students, and 30 M.A. students. Given that the total number of faculty in the graduate departments that responded to the survey is 2,367, we can calculate that in these graduate departments, only 1.3% of the faculty are Hispanic, with .8% holding tenure and .5% without tenure.
>
> The total graduate student population in the U.S. is roughly 3,000, which means that (assuming all of these are in fact in the U.S. rather than Canada), only 2% are Hispanics. To compare, a similar survey conducted in 1992 established that the percentage of Hispanic graduate students was 1.9%. This statistic is perhaps the most disturbing of all, because it provides no reason to expect the future to change.[1]

---

[1] APA Committee on Hispanics, "Report on the Status of Hispanics in Philosophy," posted on the APA webpage, (http://www.apaonline.org/apa/).

In response to this situation, I propose two theses. The first is that many of the sociological factors endemic in the American philosophical community function as barriers to the recruitment of Latinos in the profession and to their functioning as spokespersons in the social arena, that is, as public intellectuals. The division into familial groups, the fights for security and success, and the weakness of the federal organization of the American Philosophical Association (henceforth APA) contribute to this effect. The second thesis is that sociology has a place in philosophy, even though it should not be confused with it. Not paying attention to sociological matters, as is frequently the case in the philosophical profession, contributes to the lack of recognition of the problems Latinos face in the philosophical community.

This discussion is not intended as technically philosophical; indeed, one could argue that it is not at all philosophical insofar as it does not address some particular philosophical problem or apply some particular philosophical principle, or even talk about how philosophers have tried to do so. Rather, the chapter discusses the profession of philosophy as practiced in the United States today and points to some areas in which this practice affects Latinos. In a sense, my topic is sociological rather than philosophical. I make this distinction because I am a believer in keeping things clear and I think too often philosophy is confused with other enterprises. Indeed, there is a group of philosophers today that argues for a sociological conception of philosophical knowledge.[2] According to some of them, philosophical knowledge, including knowledge of the history of philosophy, makes no sense apart from an understanding of the sociological factors that play a role in its development. This is not a unique position to philosophy; similar claims have been made about the sciences and about humanities other than philosophy. I do not endorse these claims, but I do not reject them out of hand either. In my view, although philosophy is not sociology and sociology is not philosophy, sociology has a role to play in philosophy. And indeed, a corollary of the sociological analyses I provide here is the philosophical claim that sociology does have a role to play in philosophy, even if sociology can and should be distinguished from philosophy.

---

[2] See: Martin Kusch, *Psychologism: A Case Study in the Sociology of Philosophical Knowledge* (London: Routledge, 1995), and the articles in Martin Kusch (ed.), *The Sociology of Philosophical Knowledge* (Dordrecht, Netherlands: Kluwer, 2000). Among other philosophers who have discussed the sociology of philosophy are: Lucius T. Outlaw Jr, *On Race and Philosophy* (New York: Routledge, 1996), and A. J. Mandt, "The Inevitability of Pluralism: Philosophical Practice and Philosophical Excellence," in Avner Cohen and Marcelo Dascal (eds.), *The Institution of Philosophy: A Discipline in Crisis?* (La Salle, IL: Open Court, 1989), pp. 77–101.

These issues are important for at least two reasons. First, Latinos constitute an increasing proportion of the American population and it is a matter of both justice and social stability that they be encouraged to play a role in the intellectual life of a nation that considers itself to be both democratic and representative. I explore this reason in more depth in chapter 5. Second, the public issues that affect Latinos cry out for the voices of Latino intellectual leaders, including philosophers, to be heard. Anything that prevents either the effective participation of Latinos in the life of the nation, or the points of view of Latino leaders being taken into account, should be brought into the open with the aim of eliminating it.

I begin with a discussion of philosophical goals in general. Then I turn to the American philosophical community, its current situation, and how it pursues the goals in question, as well as certain consequences of all these. Finally, I examine how the ways in which this community functions negatively affects Latinos who wish to practice philosophy or become public intellectuals.

I.   General Philosophical Goals

What is it that moves philosophers? What is it that makes them act? What are their primary concerns and aims? These questions are not directed toward the identification of particular interests or personal objectives, but rather toward what moves *most* philosophers, or perhaps just *many* of them. Nor am I concerned with philosophers, philosophical issues, or philosophical aims broadly understood. Taken broadly, anything that leads to a deep understanding of the world is often considered philosophical and anyone who is instrumental in achieving such an understanding may be called a philosopher. I have no objection against this broad view of philosophy, but here my interest is narrower. The question of motives I seek to answer concerns only professional philosophy and philosophers. Philosophy in this restricted sense refers to a professional enterprise, and a philosopher is someone who earns a living, or aims to earn a living, by being engaged in this enterprise.

Clearly, one of the things that moves professional philosophers is the practice of the discipline itself, whatever that may entail. I am not going to try to define philosophy here, because if I did we would never be able to go beyond that point. Philosophers are not known for their agreement concerning the nature of the discipline they practice. Some philosophers talk about truth, some about criticism, some about justice, some about edification, some about revolution, some about enlightenment, some about power, some about the satisfaction of curiosity, some about service to religion, and some about just having fun, to mention just a very few of the goals that are often identified for the discipline. I think we must take for granted that most philosophers do have one or more of these goals in mind, and that even if they often do not act in accordance with them, they think that these goals are the ones they actually pursue as philosophers. I am not going to dispute this. My concern, instead, is with other factors that do not seem to be intrinsically tied to the discipline, but rather reflect some basic needs and general trends in American society at large.

I limit myself to two of these that seem to have an increasing influence on what philosophers actually do, *qua* philosophers. The first is the need for job security; the second is the drive for professional success. Both are quite understandable. Consider the first. Philosophers are men and women who need to have a stable job situation in order to support themselves so they can do philosophy. There is nothing unique about the profession of philosophy in this regard. But the range of jobs philosophers can have and the availability of those jobs are quite different from those that apply to jobs in some other professions. Physicians, plumbers, and even lawyers, do not generally have to worry about employment after graduation. Most of them can find positions related in one way or another to what they studied or were trained for. In some professions, such as certain kinds of engineering, the employment situation might be tight at some times, but in general graduates in these fields do not have as much difficulty finding jobs as philosophers do.

Increasingly, trained philosophers are being placed outside the world of academic philosophy. Philosophers are hired by hospitals for example, to help healthcare professionals sort out and deal with some of the issues that surface in such contexts. They also find employment in Internet companies, law firms, and in business and the arts. But it is a well-established fact that the career choice of most trained philosophers is in the academy and that most philosophers who work as philosophers work in the academy. The use of philosophy in other contexts, what it is often referred to as "applied philosophy," is still underdeveloped. This situation contrasts with that of other professions, in which there are many equally desirable professional tracts. Besides, the demand for philosophers is certainly much less than for other professionals, even if they share similar difficulties with some other academic careers.

Here is one of the points that needs to be made: after spending many years of their lives preparing themselves professionally, philosophers find themselves in an increasingly difficult situation to find positions that will permit them to do what they are supposed, and want, to do. This means that more and more philosophers have to adapt themselves to the requirements of the marketplace to be able to stay as philosophers. Perhaps we can put the matter in this way: a philosophy job under most conditions seems to be a necessary condition of practicing the profession of philosophy, but the increasing scarcity of these jobs also increases the constraints on philosophers. One can support oneself by sweeping floors, waiting on tables, bar tending, or day trading, but to carry on as a philosopher under those conditions is very difficult. For one thing, there is the question of time. Philosophy requires considerable time. Philosophical texts are not often easy reading, philosophical issues are complex, and coming up with good answers to philosophical problems takes much intellectual effort. And for another, isolation from other philosophers is not conducive to philosophy, for the discipline thrives in the give-and-take of dialogue. Consultation with, and criticism by, others seem to have been of the essence from the beginning of the discipline. A job that does not allow one to have plenty of time to philosophize and the opportunity to exchange ideas with other philosophers provides no proper support for a philosopher.

In short, philosophers must meet the requirements of the marketplace to be able to get a philosophical position and practice what they were trained to do. Indeed, they are increasingly at the mercy of the marketplace when it comes to what they do. If the marketplace demands Gadamerians, that is what philosophers have to be in order to get a job; if it requires Fodorians, that is what they need to become; if it wants applied ethicists, they must give up any interest they have in metaphysics; and so on. In this, the philosophical marketplace is not different in general from the marketplace in industry or business, but there are some important specific differences involved. I shall turn to the requirements of the marketplace in philosophy shortly, but before I do it, let me consider the second overall purpose that drives philosophers to action: professional success.

Again, there does not seem to be anything peculiar to philosophers in this respect, insofar as a desire for success appears to be built into any activity in which humans engage. If I try to fix the drain in the kitchen sink, clearly I aim to be successful at it. And if my aim is to put out a fire, again I want to do it effectively; I do not want to fail. This is the natural state of things. One would have to be very sick to wish the opposite of what one is trying to accomplish, although I am told by psychologists that this is not only psychologically possible, but frequent. This is not the point, however; the point is that most philosophers, as most plumbers or physicians, would like to be successful at what they do. Here we have something that goes beyond the previously identified aim of employment security. Now we are dealing not just with being able to do whatever philosophers do, but also with being successful at it. But what is success in philosophy?

Some might respond that, in order to answer this question, I need to state after all what it is that philosophers do, in spite of the reluctance I expressed earlier to do so. But I still do not think this is necessary. Let me explain. Success can be measured in at least two ways. In one way, by the achievement of the aim that is pursued; and in another way, by certain socially accepted standards. Philosophical success in the first sense involves the achievement of whatever goal it is that philosophers aim to achieve. If this is what we have in mind, we must choose among the many aims philosophers appear to pursue *qua* philosophers, and this would lead precisely where I do not want to go. There are, however, other more tangible, and less contested, measures of success in the profession. Note that I am not arguing that these are the proper measures of success, but merely that these are the measures that function effectively today in the United States. My claim is sociological, not philosophical. Although there may be others, three of these stand out: money, fame, and power. Money usually involves a high paying position at a major research university or an elite college. Fame is measured by the number of other philosophers who are acquainted with, and discuss, one's work – never mind whether they are critical of it or not; this is often referred to in the profession as "visibility." And power translates into the degree to which one's opinion is taken seriously in the apportionment of jobs, grants, and publication venues. One could think of this third measure as authority.

This does not mean that there may not be other measures of success, or that to be successful in philosophy requires all, or even any, of these. Indeed, some of the greatest philosophers in history did not enjoy any of these measures during their lifetimes. Just consider Spinoza and Nietzsche, for example. Nonetheless, it is also true that many members of the profession in the United States today think of these three measures as criteria of success. One thing is to teach at an Ivy League institution, and another to do so at a community college; one thing is to have written an article that has been widely anthologized and cited, and another to be the author of an article no one refers to; and one thing is to be called upon to referee manuscripts for Oxford University Press and issue judgments on the value of projects for the National Endowment for the Humanities, and another not to be asked one's opinion about any professional matter.

Surely, it is clear that the three measures of success to which I have alluded correspond, *mutatis mutandis*, to the three greatest measures of success in American society today. So philosophers are not so different, after all, from the rest of America, for in general America thinks of success in terms of money, fame, and power. But now we need to ask about what the requirements of security and success impose on philosophers. In order to answer this question we need to turn to the American philosophical community and examine how it functions, that is, how it apportions jobs (security) and money, fame, and power (success).

II. The American Philosophical Community

Before I identify some of the factors at work in the American philosophical community that I believe function as obstacles to the participation of Latinos in the profession of philosophy and the involvement in the public life of the nation of those members of this group who have become philosophers, I should note that the published evidence to support my claims is very scant. Indeed, there are no studies on this topic. Plenty of data support the claim that members of certain racial and minority groups are underrepresented in philosophy.[3] And attention has been drawn to the very limited participation of philosophers in general, let alone minority philosophers in the public arena.[4] But no attempts have been made to establish the sociological factors behind these facts, although there are studies about the situation of particular minority groups in philosophy.[5] And attention to Latinos is very limited. This means that the points I make here are largely speculative and based on anecdotal evidence. Still, I have been a member of this profession for almost 40 years and I have actively participated in the administration of several professional philosophical associations, including the APA, so my observations are first hand and span a number of years. But serious research in this area remains to be done. This means that my analyses should be taken as tentative hypotheses rather than well-substantiated conclusions. I offer them because the task is pressing and we must begin somewhere. Also important to note is that what I say about the American philosophical community might also apply, *mutatis mutandis*, to other academic groups and disciplines but my concern here is exclusively with philosophy.

With these caveats and clarifications in mind, let me propose at least five factors concerning the functioning of the American philosophical community that stand in the way of the incorporation of Latinos to the philosophical profession and the public life of the nation:

1　It is a divided community.
2　Its divisions are often not in terms of philosophical points of view, but rather of a familial, genealogical sort.

---

[3]　Educational Testing Service, *Black, Hispanic, and White Doctoral Students: Before, During, and After Enrolling in Graduate School* (Princeton, NJ: Educational Testing Service, 1990), p. 2.
[4]　Jorge J. E. Gracia, "Hispanics, Philosophy, and the Curriculum," *Teaching Philosophy* 22, 3 (1999), 241–8.
[5]　E.g., Outlaw, *On Race and Philosophy*.

3   The families that constitute this community see as their goals to ensure the well-being of their members and to perpetuate their status (security and success).

4   There is a chronic state of rivalry, conflict, and hostility among some of these families.

5   The APA is largely organized in a federal rather than centralized way.

The first point is that, although the contemporary American philosophical community may appear *prima facie* to be a rather cohesive and unified group of scholars devoted, as the name of the discipline so eloquently proclaims, to the pursuit of wisdom, the reality is quite different. Indeed, this community is divided. It takes only attending one of the yearly conventions of the Eastern Division of the APA to confirm this judgment. These conventions, attended by roughly 20 percent of philosophers in the United States, have two programs. One is the official program of the association. This program is organized into more than 80 sessions with more than 250 participants. In addition to the official program, there is also the societies program. This program is organized by the many specialized philosophical groups that are currently operating in the country. The number of satellite sessions is around 100, and there are more than 300 speakers who participate in them. The philosophers who participate in the official program and in the societies program, moreover, do not always communicate or even try to communicate. The picture that the meetings of the Eastern Division of the APA presents, then, is anything but cohesive or unified.

Within this tower of Babel, two large groups stand out, the so-called analytic and Continental. If one looks closely at them, it becomes clear – and this is the second point that I wish to stress – that there is not much that can be found, in terms of philosophical position, approach, or even terminology, that unites each of them, separating it from the other. Consider the case of the analytic group. The strongest bond of the group at present is genetic. Present analysts were students of certain philosophers who in turn were students of certain other philosophers, and so on. In other words, present analysts have a common intellectual ancestry which goes back to certain key figures: the members of the Vienna Circle, Ludwig Wittgenstein, G. E. Moore, and Bertrand Russell.[6] But when it comes to philosophical views, or even method, the unity of the group breaks down rather quickly.

If analysts have little in common beyond genesis, Continental philosophers have even less, for this denomination includes widely different groups and

---

[6]   Max Black, *Philosophical Analysis: A Collection of Essays* (Englewood Cliffs, NJ: Prentice-Hall, 1963), p. v.

genetically different families. Marxists, Process Philosophers, Postmodernists, Hegelians, Phenomenologists, Neo-Kantians, Existentialists, Heideggerians, and some Thomists, Pragmatists, and Peircians, among others, fit into this group. I qualify the last three groups by "some" because they have members who identify with analysis, others with Continental philosophy, and still others argue for categories other than these.

Even if we take the category, Continental philosophy, strictly, omitting any of those who do not wish to be identified with it, the only thing these philosophers seem to share is their aversion to analytic philosophy. But this aversion cannot be explained in terms of something Continental philosophers have in common – not even a view of what is wrong with analysts, for their opposition to analysts is not always based on the same reasons. Some object to the analysts' emphasis on language; some to their anti-metaphysical bias; some, to their scientism; some, to their rejection of the use of metaphorical language in philosophy; some, to their use of symbolic logic; and so on. More than anything else, however, their opposition is political: Continental philosophers believe that analysts have monopolized power in the profession, relegating non-analysts to a marginal role, and they accuse analysts of philosophical intransigence and provincialism.[7] Still, within the particular subgroups that make up the overall Continental group, one can easily detect the same familial ties we saw in analysts. Often these subgroups share a common intellectual history that goes back to certain authors who function as intellectual ancestors of current members of the group.

This leads me to the third point mentioned, namely, that these "genealogically" tied groups function as families that identify their main goal with the preservation of the well-being of their members and the status of the families themselves, rather than the preservation of any particular point of view. This leads to competition which is not often for wisdom – to see who has more of it, who has better access to it, or who can get it faster – but rather for jobs (security) and money, fame, and power (success). The result is that often truth gets lost in the process. Power counts because it leads to money and fame. In concrete terms, what matters, for example, is to have many students and place them in positions of power, so they can preserve and extend the power of their intellectual mentors.

Obviously, the increase and preservation of power requires the annihilation of the power of others and thus generates a chronic state of rivalry, conflict, and hostility among the families, which is the fourth point to which I referred

---

[7]   Richard Bernstein, "Philosophical Rift: A Tale of Two Approaches," *New York Times* (Dec. 29, 1987), A-1 and A-15; and Mandt, "The Inevitability of Pluralism," in Cohen and Dascal (eds.), *The Institution of Philosophy*, pp. 77–101.

earlier. Power generates power and weakness generates weakness. So power is the key to security and success. With power, we can more easily block the publication of the work of those who disagree with us; we can more easily get our students placed at the right places; and we can more easily make possible the publication of materials that support our own philosophical families. For this system to work, there must also be a network of faithful associates; we must build IOUs; and we must block others and encourage allies. In short, we must build and maintain a philosophical machine where patronage rules.

In the United States, this is facilitated by the fact that the profession works through a system of referees, specialists who give opinions on the merits of proposals and manuscripts submitted to presses, journals, or foundations. Presses and foundations are run by non-specialists who need advice from specialists in order to make a decision. And journals are run by specialists who, however, often do not know much about the fields of a large number of the manuscripts they receive. Once these specialists are named to the boards that assist non-specialists or other specialists in different areas, they tend to perpetuate themselves, their students, the students of their friends and associates, and their allies and supporters. Moreover, they are in a position to recommend other referees for particular projects.

Books are generally not subjected to blind refereeing. This means that the referees know the author of the book they are refereeing, a fact that facilitates the elimination of rival scholars and points of view. A standard procedure in the profession is to block the publication of materials that do not make reference to the work of the referee; another is to eliminate texts critical of the referee's work. This is justified in moral terms. Most philosophers actually believe that it is their duty to block the publication of texts that do not refer to themselves or are critical of their point of view. If these works do not refer to their own work, they reason, it must be because the author is not well acquainted with the pertinent sources and, therefore, they judge the work to be immature. If the work is critical of their own views, it must be that the author is wrong, or confused.

The situation of articles is somewhat similar to that of books, except that in their case most often the identity of the author is not known to the referee. Most articles are supposed to be refereed blindly. All the same, editors of journals have much to say about the publication of articles. Of course, one must keep in mind that some of the most prestigious journals receive large numbers of articles of which they can publish only a small fraction. Under these conditions, when they must reject a high percentage of the manuscripts they receive, are they not entitled to use all the means they have at their disposal, including personal preferences, to reject some of them? Besides, do not editors of journals have the prerogative, and some would say the duty, to set the tone for the journal, to encourage a certain philosophical style, and even to promote a certain point of view?

The same applies to grants. Once a particular group gets hold of a grant mechanism, it is almost impossible to get it open to others. The genetic factor sets in and prevents members of other philosophical families from participating. There are extreme situations. In some subfields of philosophy, a single person practically dominates it. True, it is difficult to keep this machine oiled, and fortunately, some fields are sufficiently open to allow some non-genetically related persons to play a role, but breaking down machines takes time, and most of them work quite efficiently. Particularly unfortunate is that many "successful" philosophers tend to go on working well into their seventies and thus keep their machines in order for decades. Moreover, sometimes they are successful in passing them on to younger favorites, who ensure a still longer period of operation.

The fact that almost no members of the American philosophical community are consciously aware of this situation makes matters much worse. Most philosophers think of themselves as engaged in the pursuit of truth and often make explicit pronouncements to that effect. Indeed, even those who reject the possibility of finding truth, do not acknowledge that they are engaged in a search for security or success. I know of no one who has explicitly painted the familial picture of the profession I have painted. There have been accusations to this effect of one group against another (e.g., Continental philosophers against analytic ones) but even this is not frequent. It is common nowadays to find philosophers from different traditions who criticize the analytic/Continental divide, for example, and others who explicitly want to see themselves merely as philosophers. Yet, often in the practical affairs of the profession they continue to behave along familial lines, disparaging the work of those who belong to families other than their own and favoring that of those who belong to their own. Indeed, it is particularly paradoxical to find Continental philosophers who present themselves as pluralists and thus as tolerant and even accepting of every philosophical tradition, trying to block the activities of analysts. The sociological forces at work in the profession are very seldom acknowledged.

The fifth and last factor that I would like to note might be referred to as the Federal Model according to which the APA is organized. According to this decentralized model, the mission of the APA is to serve the membership through its support of the three divisions in which the association is divided. There is to be a Central Office, but the function of this office is merely the coordination of the activities initiated by the APA divisions (the Eastern,

Central, and Pacific) and the facilitation of these activities. Power is effectively vested on the divisions, not the Central Office. Accordingly, it is expected that initiatives should primarily arise from the divisions and any decision made at the Central Office needs to be ratified by the divisions before it is implemented. The divisions, echoing the view of their members, are primarily interested in putting up meetings at which papers can be read and listened to, a mechanism for hiring and placing philosophers, and a place where publishers of philosophy books can display their wares. This is what most members of the APA can agree on, this is what the APA has been doing for the past 100 years, it is what the charter says it is meant to do, and it is what it fundamentally should continue to do.

In this, the APA is quite different from other professional organizations which generally follow what might be called a Centralized Model. If this model were to be applied to the APA, then the association would lead rather than implement the wishes of the divisions and represent the membership through them. There would be a strong Central Office whose task would be not merely the organization of meetings where papers are presented, hiring takes place, and books are displayed, but more importantly still, to be on the watch for the role that the association can play in public life. This office and its leaders would be attuned to what is going on in society at large, and try to be perceptive of its needs, bringing those needs to the attention of the APA membership.

The advantages of the Federal Model are obvious. Let me mention just four. First, it gives the majority of the members of the association what they want, namely, a place to read papers, to hire new people, and to look at new books. Second, it makes the association more responsive to the majority of its members by being closer to them through the three divisions. Third, it prevents the creation of a costly and bloated bureaucracy in the Central Office. And fourth, it keeps the reins of power in the hands of philosophers rather than professional administrators, that is, in the hand of elected members of the profession who do not see themselves as bureaucrats but rather as practitioners of philosophy.

The disadvantages of this model are also obvious. Let me mention also four. First, the association tends to be conservative and resistant to change, which in turn prevents it from taking up the measures required to meet the challenges of a changing society. Second, it makes it more difficult to open the doors of the association to those who are not already entrenched in it. Third, it allows for the creation of regional fiefdoms whose leaders are not accountable to anyone. And fourth, it overrepresents some and underrepresents others insofar as there are great disparities in resources and membership in the divisions.

III. General Consequences and Effects on Latinos

In sum, the American philosophical community is not united or cohesive; philosophers are not always devoted to the search for wisdom, and as a group they can hardly be regarded as scholars engaged in careful, disinterested deliberation who always follow high principles. Moreover, this community is divided into families which are quite protective of their members, hostile to outsiders, and fight fiercely for their turf. Philosophers in the United States today find themselves immersed in a social environment controlled by groups that adhere to traditions with long lists of dos and don'ts. Moreover, the present organization of the APA tends to favor the preservation of the status quo and isolate the association from public life.

An indirect result of this state of affairs is the widespread use of typecasting. In the current climate, philosophers tend to be typecasted early in their careers in terms of families and traditions. No one is just a philosopher. One is an analyst or a Continentalist, an Aristotelian or a Peircean, a scholastic or a Kantian, and so on. Moreover, once someone is typecasted, nothing that the person does seems ever to be considered except in the context of the stereotype under which he or she has been classified. This means that once an analyst, always an analyst; once a Hegelian, always a Hegelian. Typecasting, of course, has very serious consequences. One of these is that it serves to put aside and marginalize. He is X, and X is not good, or not important, or not pertinent, or whatever, therefore I do not have to bother with him. Typecasting fits nicely within the family structure of contemporary American philosophy and contributes to emphasize some of the features I have been describing.

Another result of the organization of the American philosophical community in families is that it favors the development of dynasties and a certain philosophical aristocracy. As happens with all aristocratic systems, questions of blood purity – for philosophers, intellectual orthodoxy and pedigree – surface, and quarrels about degrees of purity and lineage become important. How faithful is X to Y? How much of a Ynian is X? Is he a student of Y or Z? Any philosopher knows how concerned philosophers are with questions such as these, and with the gossip that such questions tends to generate. Of course, aristocracy involves exclusion and censure. Those who do not have the same blood or who mix it indiscriminately, are rejected and condemned. He is not really a Ynian! He does not belong with us. The technique of dismissal, so prevalent in American philosophy today, is put to good use in this context, and this in turn engenders resentment, anger, and warfare.

Those philosophers who want security and success, whether Latinos or not, must pay the price families exact for them. What is this price? For one thing, it is essential that a philosopher belong to a family, and a powerful one at that. It will not do to belong to a family that has little control over the "benefices" that are given out in the profession. One needs to belong to the right family, one whose leaders have power and are well placed. A young philosopher has no power and needs a sponsor – yes, call it a godfather if you will. Some studies show that the single most important factor in the likelihood of getting a Nobel Prize in science is to have studied with someone who has gotten one, a fact which supports the view that intellectual descent is most important when it comes to a certain kind of success. Of course, one could argue that this just means that one is at the cutting edge of the field. But there is more to it than this. It also has to do with the control of resources required for scientific breakthroughs. Science is an expensive enterprise that requires an infrastructure, and those who control that infrastructure also control the possibility of breakthroughs. Philosophy is not an expensive field; we do not need much equipment to practice it. Nonetheless, we need time, libraries, jobs, and good colleagues, and these are controlled by certain groups of people who are regarded as having the proper authority.

Of course, there is a price to be paid for belonging to a powerful family. One must fit, and to fit involves a certain obedience or deference to the leaders of the family. One very common way in which a young philosopher advances is by attaching himself or herself to a powerful senior philosopher and talking about his or her work. Fame is one of the things that philosophers crave, so helping them to get it is one sure way of earning their gratitude. Besides, if you talk about my work, it is in my best interest to see that you get as large a forum as possible, for I will also profit from your success. There are many examples of young philosophers who have "made it" in this way.

Obedience and deference are not the only prices that need to be paid in order to belong to a powerful family. There is also loyalty, partisanship, adherence to the standards of the tradition, adoration of sacred cows, and so on. All these have consequences. For those who fit and do what is required, the main undesirable consequence is a certain lack of intellectual freedom, and the growth of a dogmatic attitude. But for those who do not fit exactly the required mold, or do not adhere to the standards and traditions accepted by particular philosophical families, the result is ostracism. With ostracism comes employment insecurity and lack of money, fame, and power. In some cases, it means the end of a philosophical career.

This situation affects everyone in the American philosophical community, not just Latinos. The requirements of job security and success and the situation of philosophy in the United States affect everyone who wants to pursue a career in philosophy. But the impact on Latinos is particularly important in the present context. Elsewhere, I have discussed various factors involved in how the situation of American philosophy affects Latinos.[8] I will not repeat them here. Let me just say that in this case the Northern Eurocentric (English, French, and German) bias of the philosophical families that dominate the philosophical profession in the United States today interferes with the integration of Latinos in the profession. Much of the same could be said about other groups. I cannot speak for every underrepresented minority group, but I suspect that most of them will find difficulty fitting within the parameters established within certain traditional philosophical families. Some minorities, for example, might find it difficult to fit within families that have religious affiliations. Indeed, philosophical questions arising from the experiences of these people might be regarded as out of order, or dismissed at the outset. Others might face the same ethnic bias that Latinos face because they also come from non-European areas of the world. And still others might find that the set of problems favored in the profession leave no room for the issues that concern them.[9]

Unfortunately, in spite of serious consequences for Latinos and other members of some minority groups, these matters have not been explicitly raised in the profession until very recently, and only seldom and in very particular contexts. African Americans have certainly complained publicly that racial issues and Black philosophy in general have been ghettoized in the profession, if not altogether excluded. After all, many Black philosophers have been banished to departments of African American Studies.[10] Latinos have been less vocal, although voices are beginning to be heard about the exclusion of Latino issues and Latino or Hispanic philosophy from the philosophical marketplace. But it is outside philosophy that such voices surface more frequently.[11] This is all very new and there is still much that needs to be done to make both Latinos and the philosophical community at large aware of the way in which sociological factors in this community affect Latinos in particular.

---

[8] Jorge J. E. Gracia, *Hispanic/Latino Identity: A Philosophical Perspective* (Oxford: Blackwell, 2000), pp. 159–88.

[9] Cf. Anita L. Allen, "Interracial Marriage: Folk Ethics in Contemporary Philosophy," in Naomi Zack (ed.), *Women of Color and Philosophy: A Critical Reader* (Oxford: Blackwell, 2000), p. 197.

[10] For the issue of race and philosophy, see: Outlaw, *On Race and Philosophy*; and Charles W. Mills, *The Racial Contract* (Ithaca, NY: Cornell University Press, 1997) and " 'But What Are You Really?' The Metaphysics of Race," in Charles W. Mills, *Blackness Visible: Essays on Philosophy and Race* (Ithaca, NY: Cornell University Press, 1998), pp. 41–66.

[11] Suzanne Oboler, "It Must Be a Fake! Racial Ideologies, Identities, and the Question of Rights," in Jorge J. E. Gracia and Pablo De Greiff (eds.), *Hispanics/Latinos in the United States: Ethnicity, Race, and Rights* (New York: Routledge, 2000), pp. 125–46.

Finally, we turn to the organization of the APA. The overall lesson in what I have said should be obvious. The relative stagnation that has characterized issues related to minorities for most of the last 30 years in philosophy seems to be a result in part of the fact that the APA has generally followed the Federal Model during those years. If we want to make the association more socially conscious, it appears that it has to move toward the Centralized Model. This Centralized Model favors minority and disadvantaged groups who have no voices in the organization, whereas the Federal Model favors those who are already well represented in it. However, every change comes at a price. For the Centralized Model does have some clear disadvantages. What to do, then? I do not see my task here as making a recommendation on what to do, but rather as pointing out some issues that the American philosophical community needs to address as it moves through the twenty-first century, a century in which American society will be changing drastically.

Aside from preventing Latinos who work in philosophy to enter and flourish in the philosophical profession, the ways in which the American philosophical community functions also interferes with the development of Latinos as public intellectuals. Philosophers qualify as public intellectuals when they engage with the issues that concern society in a form that is open to the members of society at large and who address those issues in a language that is intelligible to the general public. Philosophers such as Cornell West and Martha Nussbaum surely qualify. Being public intellectuals does not require that philosophers abandon their more technical and narrowly focused work; but it does require that they participate actively in publicly debated issues in broad forums and venues, such as newspapers, radio, and television.

The way the American philosophical community operates stands in the way of Latinos functioning as public intellectuals in at least three ways: first, because achieving security and success in philosophy in this community imposes on them requirements that prevent them from devoting the necessary time to and putting the required effort into addressing issues of interest to society at large. The need for a stable job (security) and the desire for money, fame, and power (success) require that these philosophers devote themselves fulltime to the narrow, competitive world of professional philosophy. This involves both strong efforts in the direction of networking and also subservience to what is approved by the philosophical families that hold the power in the profession.

This brings me to the second point, for although these families seldom share specific points of view, they do have Northern European (English, French, and German in particular) lineage and therefore work within certain parameters. Philosophers tend to talk about what their mentors talked about – the issues and questions – even if they disagree with their views. And philosophers also tend to favor a narrow, technical conception of philosophical achievement.

Naturally, this stands in the way of the discussion of topics that interest society at large, both because these are broad and because their public treatment requires a non-technical approach. In order to satisfy the requirements imposed by the American philosophical community, Latino philosophers must become Eurocentric and also give up on breadth and accessibility.

Finally, and this is the third point I wish to make, Latino philosophers who become public intellectuals pay a heavy price: they are often dubbed non-philosophers and their ideas are summarily dismissed. Why? Because they fail to meet the parochial standards applied by the different families that control the profession. This applies also to philosophers who are not Latinos or members of minority groups, but it is perhaps more common to members of minority groups. Some philosophers, such as Martha Nussbaum, have been able to preserve their philosophical profile in spite of their active involvement in public issues, but this has not been the case with others, such as Cornell West. Indeed, more than once I have heard "successful" members of our profession commiserate about the latter's public image.

IV. Economic Survival and Intellectual Flourishing

Let me finish this chapter with two thoughts. The first concerns the way in which the functioning of the American philosophical community affects Latinos who wish to become professional philosophers. The moral of the story I have told is that many of the sociological factors endemic in the philosophical community constitute barriers to the recruitment of Latinos in the profession and to their function as public intellectuals in American society. The division into familial groups, the struggle for security and success, and the weakness of the federal organization of the APA contribute to this.

Apart from this sociological conclusion about the effects of the way the American philosophical community affects Latinos in the profession, there is also a second, more general philosophical inference that can be drawn from the discussion: sociology does have a place in philosophy. Indeed, recent studies have shown that philosophical emphases and directions are often guided, as happens with scientific research, by factors that have nothing to do with philosophy as such. One such example is the development of indigenist studies within philosophy in Japan.[12] And something similar is happening in

---

[12] Matthew Chew, "Politics and Patterns of Developing Indigenous Knowledge under Western Disciplinary Compartmentalization: The Case of Philosophical Schools in Modern China and Japan," in Kusch (ed.), *The Sociology of Philosophical Knowledge*, pp. 125–54.

the United States with issues of race and ethnicity. Social factors are behind many recent developments in these areas. This means that we need to consider these social phenomena.

Some philosophers do not draw a distinction between sociology and philosophy, or a sociological history of philosophy and a philosophical one. I am not one of them. In my view philosophy and sociology are two different branches of learning which can be distinguished conceptually, even if in practice social and philosophical factors are often mixed.[13] But regardless of one's view on this matter, it should be clear that the philosophical profession is a social profession. So it is important for us to be aware of how the sociology of the profession affects the practice of philosophy, whether we believe that philosophy is a kind of sociology, as some do, or that it is not, as I do. And from the narrower perspective of Latinos, it is important that our social story be told, otherwise it will be very difficult to integrate Latinos into the philosophical profession to the degree warranted by our numbers in American society.

But what philosophical justification can be given for efforts to incorporate Latinos into philosophy and other areas in which they are underrepresented? This question has to do with affirmative action and is discussed in the next chapter.

[13] Jorge J. E. Gracia, "Sociological Accounts and the History of Philosophy," in Kusch (ed.), *The Sociology of Philosophical Knowledge*, pp. 193–211.

Affirmative Action: Meaning and Justification

In 1970, when I was about to graduate from the University of Toronto with a PhD, I put myself on the market for a position in philosophy. Affirmative action was already a reality in American society, but conditions were quite different. The United States had just gone through the stormy sixties, with the revolt of large numbers of young people against the status quo and the bitter protests against Vietnam. The Vietnam War was still being waged, but the late President Nixon was firmly in control and had an unquestionable mandate. Philosophy jobs had become scarce. The rapid expansion of graduate programs in philosophy in the sixties had already produced the glut of PhDs which has become endemic in the American philosophical market.

I interviewed with the State University at Buffalo and, after visiting the campus, the Department of Philosophy voted to recommend to the Dean that I be appointed as assistant professor. There was already some pressure in the University to hire minorities. The department at the time had an African American, a Japanese American, and a Korean American in a faculty of about 30, but no Latinos, so my appointment was presented as a minority one to the Dean, partly as a strategic move in order to ensure quick and favorable action.

A few days after the department chair, the late William Parry, had phoned me to give me the good news about the department vote, I got another phone call from him explaining that the University Affirmative Action Committee had problems with the appointment, for I did not look anything like a member of a minority group. The reasons given were that I did not come from a disadvantaged background and that, although I had at one time resided in the United States, I was at the time living in Canada. The question of citizenship did not come up, but I imagine it was hovering in the background. Bill asked me whether I considered myself Hispanic (the term Latino was not in vogue at the time) and then requested some ammunition he could use with the committee.

I did not hear back from Bill until he called me to say that the letter offering me the job was in the mail, although the Affirmative Action Committee had refused to classify me as a minority. He explained that the Dean had gone ahead all the same, and so that, as far as the University was concerned, I did not qualify as Hispanic. My question to him, then, was: So, what am I? If I am not Hispanic, what should I consider myself? I was miffed! Of course, Bill could not answer and he openly sympathized with my chagrin, but noted that one should not expect much from university committees. Bill was quite a cynic; he had been an academic for many years and had suffered under the McCarthy witch hunts of the fifties. Nothing surprised him when it came to academic politics.

A few years later, the Department of Philosophy at Buffalo was on the market to replace some of the faculty members we had lost through retirements. The Dean said that, considering university policy, the size and composition of our department, and the scarcity of resources at his disposal, he could only approve a minority appointment. In the pool of candidates who had applied for the job, there were one Latin American and one African. Neither one had permanent residency in this country nor was disadvantaged in any sense of the word. Moreover, like myself, they were foreign born and were not naturalized American citizens. Yet the Affirmative Action Committee had no reservations about approving an offer to either one of them.

What cogent reason could be given for the committee's decision with respect to these two cases and mine? The only one I can think of is that the criteria of qualification being used were different because the composition of the committee was different. But this is not very helpful.

The case of a young man who was a high school classmate of one of my daughters is also instructive. We were fond of this young man, for he was a mature, pleasant fellow, although he was not particularly bright, a fact reflected by his grades in high school. All of us were worried about his prospects for college. But he had the good fortune of having had a Mexican American great-grandmother. He had no other connection to the Latino community. His father's last name was English and so was his mother's last name. All his other great-grandparents were of English or German descent and he had never met his Mexican American great-grandmother – she had died long before he was born. Neither he, nor his family, had ever taken an interest in anything vaguely related to the Latino culture or community in this country or in any other. The only living connection he had to anything Latino was through his friendship with my daughter. Moreover, he was the son of a full professor in one of the science departments at the university, and his mother was well established in her own career. When it came to applying for college, however, this young man, on the advice of his parents, applied to one of the premier universities in the nation as a Hispanic minority and got in. Given his desultory record in high school and his mediocre scores in the SATs, it is clear the reason he was accepted was his status as Hispanic. I know from experience that academics can be hypocrites and can manipulate the system when they wish to do so, but this case gave me a shock, nonetheless.

Another contemporary of my daughter's was also applying to college at the time. She had gone to one of Buffalo's most expensive private schools. Her parents could well afford it, because her father was a physician with a substantial income. The high school record of this girl was weak, and her subsequent record in college confirmed her generally limited talents. Nevertheless, she was given a scholarship in a well-known university and kept it for the four years she attended it on the basis of her minority status as a Hispanic.

I am sure most Americans are acquainted with cases similar to the ones I have mentioned. Some of these cases are so outrageous that they get into the newspapers and popular media. A few years ago, I read in the *Buffalo News* that there was evidence that some applicants had been allowed to qualify as Hispanic minorities for positions in the Police Department on the basis of having taken Spanish in high school.[1] On the other hand, no Latinos other than Mexican Americans or mainland Puerto Ricans qualify as minorities for medical school applications.

These examples should illustrate the extraordinary confusion that prevails in the United States concerning affirmative action for Latinos. The confusion runs deep. It centers on the who, what, and why of affirmative action: the "who" concerns the identity of the group in question: Who qualifies as Latinos and who among us, if not all of us, should qualify for affirmative action? The "what" concerns the aims of affirmative action. What aims need to be pursued and in what way? Finally, the "why" concerns the rationale for affirmative action in the case of Latinos. Why do, or should, we need affirmative action for Latinos? What reasons can be adduced in favor of affirmative action for us?

The discussion in this chapter is divided into three parts. The first provides an answer in terms of the view defended in chapter 1, to the question: Who counts as Latino? The second to the question: What are the aims of affirmative action? The third to: Why should there be affirmative action for Latinos? I make three claims: First, although Latinos do not have a property or set of

---

[1] Luo Michel, "Group Claims Some Police Officers Posed as Hispanics in Order to Gain Employment," *Buffalo News* (January 20, 1998), B1 and B10.

properties that unite us at all times and places, and our unity rather resembles that of a family throughout history, Latinos are recognizable as a group and distinguishable from other groups at particular times and places and this is sufficient to implement affirmative action policies. Second, affirmative action aims to ensure equal opportunity to members of groups which have suffered discrimination on the basis of gender, race, or ethnicity, to provide reparation for past wrongs to members of these groups, and to promote the participation of these groups in the political and cultural life of the nation. Third, affirmative action for Latinos considered as a group is justified on the basis of participation in the life of the nation, rather than on the basis of equal opportunity or reparation.

I.   Who Counts as Latino?

I discuss the question of who counts as Latino and the difficulties involved in it in chapters 1 and 2 above, so I dwell on it only briefly here. The difficulty with determining who counts as Latino is that Latinos do not appear to share any properties in common. Linguistic, racial, religious, political, territorial, cultural, economic, educational, class, and genetic criteria fail to identify Latinos in all places and times because not all Latinos speak the same language, are of the same race, hold the same religious beliefs, belong to the same political party, live in the same territory, display the same cultural traits, enjoy the same economic status, have the same degree of education, share the same social class, or come from the same genetic line. It is not just that there is not a metaphysical essence to Latinos, but that there are not even epistemic criteria that can be used for all times and places to establish who is Latino. In response to this problem, some argue that there is no such a distinguishable group or that the group is an arbitrary collection without identity. Of course, if this is so, then to speak about affirmative action for Latinos is absurd.

Nevertheless, Latinos do form a discernible group of people united by a web of historical relations that also separates us from other groups in the way a family is separated from other families. At any particular time and place, there are familial relations that Latinos share and which both distinguish us from non-Latinos and are the source of properties that can be used to distinguish us from non-Latinos. Particular physical characteristics, cultural traits, language, and so on, can serve to distinguish Latinos in certain contexts, although they cannot function as criteria of distinction and identification everywhere and at all times. In a place where all and only Latinos speak Spanish, for example, the language can function as a sufficient criterion of Latino identification even if, in other places, it does not. Likewise, in a society or region where all and only Latinos have a certain skin color, or a certain religion, these properties can be used to pick out Latinos, even if elsewhere there are Latinos who do not share these properties. Latino identity does not entail a set of common properties that constitutes an essence, but this does not stand in the way of identification. We can determine who counts as Latino in context. We can tell a Latino from a non-Latino in most instances.

But there will be borderline cases and cases that overlap. Still, for our purposes, this is sufficient insofar as it makes affirmative action possible. Many of the problematic cases should be able to be resolved in most instances through negotiation, but it is not necessary that they all do. As mentioned in the first chapter, that some cases are difficult to determine, and some are even undecidable, does not entail that all cases are so, or invalidate all classifications. Society is not like geometry. Geometry is an abstraction, and that is why triangles can be so easily classified as such. If they are geometrical figures and have three angles, they are triangles, and if not, they are not. Everything in the domain of geometrical figures is either a triangle or it is not. But our world is not like that. Most of our concepts that apply to the world of experience have borders that are not rigid and members about which it is not clear whether they belong or not in a particular category. In some cases we can, with some careful analysis and consideration, come to an informed decision. In other cases, we might have to adopt an ad hoc rule. And in some cases we might simply conclude that the case cannot be decided.

In the case of Latinos in the United States in particular, there are added reasons that facilitate an answer to the question, Who counts as Latino? Two of these may be considered. First, we are treated as a homogeneous group by non-Latino Americans; and second, even though Latinos are not homogeneous, we are easily contrasted with European and African Americans because, in context, we do not often share many of the features more commonly attributed to these groups. Our identification in the United States is generally possible, although it is not always unproblematic.

II.   What Are the Aims of Affirmative Action?

The second area of confusion concerning affirmative action for Latinos concerns the aims of affirmative action considered in general. One or more of three aims are often identified: First, to ensure equal opportunity for those who, because of their gender, racial, or ethnic background in particular, have not had equal access to opportunities open to members of different gender, racial, or ethnic backgrounds; second, to make reparation for past wrongs which are the result of discrimination against groups on the basis of gender, race, or ethnicity;[2] and third, to promote the participation of underrepresented gender, race, and ethnic groups in the life of the nation.[3]

These three general aims also entail more specific ones. Here are several examples which are frequently mentioned: removal of structural obstacles in society to the development of the target groups, such as, for example, rules that exclude African Americans from certain jobs merely in virtue of the fact that they are African Americans; elimination of prejudices that in certain situations can give an unfair advantage to some members of society over others, such as, for example, the prejudice that Latinos are procrastinators (the *mañana* philosophy), which can eliminate them from consideration in jobs where performance by certain times is of the essence; special education and training of members of target groups who have been deprived of certain social advantages because of their status, so as to prepare them to compete effectively with other members of society, such as for example, special efforts to provide education for women in situations in which they have been deprived of education because of their gender; adoption of laws and regulations which ensure the equitable distribution of goods and services among all members of American society, such as for example, laws which prescribe equal treatment of women with respect to salaries; compensation for past wrongs which resulted in harm to the groups against which discrimination has been exercised, or which precluded these groups from having certain opportunities for advancement available to members of society who are not members of the groups in question, as for example, granting land and money to Native Americans to compensate them for past abuses; and appointment of members of underrepresented gender, racial, and ethnic groups to positions of leadership in the life of the nation.

Unfortunately, these aims are not always what the public at large, or even government bureaucrats, understands as aims of affirmative action. Affirmative action is frequently taken to involve the arbitrary imposition of artificial quotas, the unjustified preferential treatment of women and minorities, and the placement of unqualified women and minorities in positions for which qualified non-minority males are available.

---

[2]   More narrow, legal definitions of affirmative action, however, imply the exclusion of reparation. See J. Angelo Corlett, "Latino Identity and Affirmative Action," in Jorge J. E. Gracia and Pablo De Greiff (eds.), *Hispanics/Latinos in the United States: Ethnicity, Race, and Rights* (New York: Routledge, 2000), pp. 223–34.

[3]   I speak mainly of gender, race, and ethnic groups here, but some of what I say applies also to other groups in which age, handicaps, and similar factors, are involved.

III.   Why Should There Be Affirmative Action for Latinos?

To answer this question we need to go back to the three general aims of affirmative action mentioned earlier: equal opportunity, reparation for past wrongs, and participation in the life of the nation. The justification for these is usually made in two ways: in terms of justice or in terms of utility. I will not try to adjudicate between these, for to do so would require more space than I can give to this matter here. The first justification argues that justice requires affirmative action with respect to certain gender, racial, and ethnic groups. The second argues for the same based on utility. For equal opportunity and reparation the justification in terms of justice is based on the principle that no one should suffer discrimination and unfair treatment because of gender, race, or ethnicity, and those who do should be compensated for the harm that such discriminatory treatment causes them. The utilitarian justification is based on the principle that to maintain conditions of discrimination based on gender, race, or ethnicity and not to compensate those who have suffered it is counterproductive to the well-being of society as a whole and its members.

The justification on the basis of justice for the third general aim of affirmative action, participation in the life of the nation, is based on the principle that in a democratic nation every member of society should be given the opportunity to participate in the life of the nation and every reasonable effort should be made to facilitate and encourage such participation. The justification on the basis of utility is based on the principle that it is socially counterproductive, in utilitarian terms, to accept a situation in which not all members of society are given the opportunity and encouraged to participate in the life of the nation and, therefore, to neglect making every reasonable effort to facilitate and encourage such participation.

None of what has been said is unproblematic. For example, no solution has been offered to the conflicts that equal opportunity or reparation may create between groups and individuals or among groups themselves. After all, any diversion of resources from some individuals or groups to others, even when those groups have suffered discrimination, seems to violate the very principle on which the action is based.[4] Likewise, nothing has been said concerning the fact that compensation for past wrongs often goes to those who have not actually suffered the wrongs. Consider, for example, that reparation for slavery

---

[4]   For some of these difficulties, see: Thomas W. Pogge, "Group Rights and Ethnicity," *NOMOS* 39 (1997), 187–221; and Nathan Glazer, "Individual Rights against Group Rights," in Will Kymlicka (ed.), *The Rights of Minority Cultures* (Oxford: Oxford University Press, 1995), pp. 123–38.

today would have to go to persons who have never been slaves. Nor have I made an attempt to distinguish between conquered groups (e.g., Mexican Americans who lived in the southwest before the Mexican American War) and immigrant groups (e.g., Cubans who immigrated to the United States after the 1959 revolution), although the argument has been made that these groups deserve to be treated differently.[5] Indeed, this is a controversial distinction that has been challenged, but which I need not use in order to justify affirmative action in the terms that I propose here.

Naturally, there are moves one can make to deal with the problems I have mentioned in passing, as well as with others raised by the justification of affirmative action, but this is not the place to do it. Moreover, it is not necessary in this context because I am going to argue that affirmative action is not clearly justified for Latinos considered as a whole on the bases of equal opportunity or reparation. Let us, then, move to the particular question that pertains to us, namely: Is affirmative action, understood as the implementation of measures which aim at equal opportunity, reparation, and participation, justified in the case of Latinos?

A. Equal opportunity and reparation

The first part of the answer is that affirmative action for Latinos, considered as a whole and understood to aim at equal opportunity and reparation, is not justified. The reason is that, although some Latinos suffer or have suffered unequal treatment, and they are harmed or have been harmed by such treatment, not all or even a majority of us have, and for those who have it is very difficult to demonstrate that they have done so because they are Latinos. Perhaps a comparison with the situation of African Americans and women will help clarify this point.

Consider the case of African Americans first. One fundamental justification of affirmative action for them is reparation for past wrongs committed against the group. The salient fact in the history of African Americans is slavery. This social aberration is probably one of the most, if not the most, dehumanizing state that can be imposed on a group of people. The atrocities that African Americans had to endure as consequences of slavery have been eloquently recorded elsewhere, so I need not repeat them here. It is sufficient to note that they were deprived of their culture, language, religion, freedom, basic human rights, education, and dignity. Moreover, a strong case can be made that some

---

[5] See Will Kymlicka, *Multicultural Citizenship: A Liberal Theory of Minority Rights* (Oxford: Oxford University Press, 1995), pp. 11–26, although his terminology is slightly different from the one I have used. I refer to his view in chapter 6 as well.

effects of slavery extend to all African Americans to this day. There is, therefore, much in the way of reparation that is justified for African Americans. There is also the fact that African Americans are not always treated as equal to other members of American society even now. When certain social choices become available, it seems that, unless affirmative action is brought to bear, European Americans are still frequently favored over African Americans in many cases. This indicates that African Americans do not enjoy equal opportunity. Here is another reason why affirmative action is needed. Finally, and most important, the discrimination and abuse African Americans suffer and have suffered has been the result of their race. Being black is the fundamental reason for their mistreatment in American society.

The case for women also involves reparation and equal opportunity. It is a fact of human history that women have generally been relegated to a second-ary, subservient role. With few exceptions, power has been concentrated in masculine hands, and even in the few occasions when women have been able to grasp power away from males, they have enjoyed it for very short times, and it has seldom led to the permanent improvement of women's lot in society. To this day, in many countries women do not share in the rights of men, and in many cases have few rights of their own to speak of. Often, whatever power they have is only vicarious, because males have granted it to them. Indeed, many personal and social gains made by women have been the result of mas-culine needs or wants. Consider the fact that women like Cleopatra and Madame Pompadour derived their power from the weakness of males who needed or wanted them. Consider also the reason women in the United States joined the workforce during World War II: the need to fill spaces vacated by men. And why does a large proportion of married women work in the United States today? Surely one reason is that the salaries their husbands make are not enough to satisfy the needs of the home. In short, most women have suffered some form of discrimination and the adverse effects of discrimination, and they have suffered them because they are women. Therefore, this can be used to justify affirmative action in terms of equal opportunity and reparation for them.

In contrast with African Americans and women, the argument based on reparation does not seem to work for Latinos for three reasons: (1) not all, not even most, Latinos have suffered discrimination; (2) the degree of discrimina-tion and abuse some have suffered never reached the levels suffered by African Americans or women; and (3) it is difficult to prove that the reason some Latinos have suffered discrimination and abuse is because they are Latinos. We have not been subjected to the kind of abuse African Americans and women have been subjected to. Unlike African Americans, Latinos have never been slaves in the United States; we were not brought into this country as slaves to work for others and be subservient to their whims; we were not sold as commodities; and we were not deprived of our culture, language, religion, freedom, basic human rights, education, or dignity as a result.

And, unlike women, we have not as a whole played a secondary role in society. From the very beginning, there have been areas of the country in which we have preserved some of our customs and culture, and in which we have had considerable independence to be different. Not that there have not been difficulties, but some Latinos have enjoyed positions of leadership going back a while. And many of us have been able to keep our language and much of our cultural heritage. I do not know any African American who stills speaks the native tongue of his or her people.

It is hard to argue that this country owes Argentinian physicians, Colombian odontologists, and Chilean intellectual historians anything by way of reparation. What did the United States owe José Martí, the father of the Cuban nation? He spent quite a bit of time in this country and it was thanks to the hospitality he received here that he was able to work toward Cuban independence. And what does the United States owe me on the way of reparation? I came to this country as a political exile, with $5 in my pocket, and I had the opportunity of going to college and graduate school, and even of writing books such as this one. These are not isolated cases. It is just quite plain that many Latinos have not had the experiences that almost all Blacks, and many women, have had.

Under these conditions, reparation does not seem justified for Latinos across the board, unlike the case of Blacks and women, where a credible case might be made for it. There is nothing, or not much, that must be given back to Latinos *as a group* because it was taken away from us. And there is no harm to us *as a group* that cries out for repair. But is this conclusion so clear?

Indeed, it is not. One could very well point out, for example, that there have been serious wrongs committed against some Latinos in some places, such as Mexican Americans and Puerto Ricans, even if such wrongs have not been committed against all Latinos. And that, although some of these groups have not been slaves in the literal sense of the word, they have actually had to live in conditions of virtual slavery. Consider the case of Mexican Americans. The conquest of 45 percent of the Mexican territory by the United States during the last century, the subsequent annexation of the territory, and the imposition of American culture, political structure, and law on the inhabitants of the territory against their will is certainly a great wrong. Here are some people who, prior to the conquest, were living in the country of their choice, in their own lands, in the midst of their own culture, and under their own laws. Yet, as a result of American military conquest, they found themselves in a different country, under a different government and different laws, and they were forced to adapt to a different culture which was imposed on them. Moreover, in some cases their freedom of movement and livelihood were drastically reduced. In short, it makes sense to argue that this is a case in which restitution and reparation apply.

The case of Puerto Ricans is somewhat similar. After the United States won the Spanish–American War, Puerto Rico became an appendage to this country. This resulted in some changes that were certainly unwelcome by Puerto Ricans and that have adversely affected the population of the island. One of these was the imposition of English as official language. This was very damaging to Puerto Rican society and culture. It left Puerto Ricans in a linguistic limbo, prohibited from using the language they knew and unable to use the language imposed on them. The result is that some of them lost the language proficiency they had in Spanish without gaining the fluency in English that is required for integration into American society. The consequences of this are quite evident today among some Puerto Ricans: confinement to ghettoes, low school per-formance, under education, social alienation, and so on. So here, again, a case could be made for restitution and reparation.

All the same, the situation of Mexican Americans and of Puerto Ricans is not quite like that of African Americans. What the United States did to African Americans appears to be in a class of its own, and for this reason Latinos cannot have the same claims to reparation that African Americans have. Moreover, the situation of women appears idiosyncratic as well. But even if a case for affirmative action could be made on the basis of reparation for Mexican Amer-icans, Puerto Ricans, and some other Latino groups as it can be made for African Americans and women, it is questionable that it can be made for Latinos as a whole, for many Latinos, both individuals and groups, have not suffered what a large number of Mexican Americans and Puerto Ricans have suffered.

The argument for affirmative action based on equal opportunity, used for African Americans and women, does not seem to apply to Latinos as a whole either. For reasons similar to the ones given in the case of reparation, it does not appear that Latinos, considered as a group, are subjected to the same kind of discrimination to which African Americans and women are subjected, or that we are subjected to it because we are Latinos. One reason for this may be that many Latinos do not look very different from the many Americans of Mediterranean ancestry, for example. It is often difficult to tell Latinos apart from Italians, Greeks, or Israelis. And even those Latinos who are more easily identifiable, do not stand out as starkly as most African Americans and most women do. Naturally, this makes it more difficult for those who wish to dis-criminate against us to do so. Not even the greatest bigots go around asking for ethnic identification of persons who look like themselves. As a result,

Latinos as a whole encounter less discrimination than African Americans and women, and the discrimination to which we have been, and are, subjected is less pronounced or nefarious, even if some Latino individuals and groups have encountered strong discrimination.

To say this, however, does not mean that affirmative action for Latinos is not needed. As long as there are some acts of discrimination against Latinos, there is a need for rectifying the situation that leads to them. But there is another problem: it is difficult to demonstrate that those Latinos who have been, or are, subjected to discrimination have been, or are, so subjected because they are Latinos and not for some other reasons. For example, some Mexican Americans may experience discrimination because of their facial features, rather than because they are Latinos; some Cuban Americans may experience discrimination because of their skin color, rather than because they are Latinos; some recent arrivals from Central America may experience discrimination because they do not speak English well, and not because they are Latinos; some Dominican Americans may experience discrimination because they are poor, and not because they are Latinos; and there is always the issue of culture – particular matters of dress and behavior may elicit discrimination against some Latinos that would not affect other Latinos. Whereas African Americans generally suffer discrimination because of their race and women suffer discrimination because of their gender, it is not at all clear that those Latinos who suffer discrimination do so because they are Latinos.

In short, the case for affirmative action for Latinos, when this is understood as reparation and equal opportunity, is difficult to make across the board, even though some Latinos appear to have legitimate claims of this sort. Note that I am not saying that it cannot be made. It is possible that it could, and if so, then affirmative action on the basis of equal opportunity and reparation would be in order. My point is that the pertinent empirical evidence – and the argument would have to rest on empirical evidence surely – is conflicting when it comes to the entire group. The burden of proof is on those who wish to defend affirmative action for Latinos on these bases. Because I find the empirical evidence unclear, I argue for affirmative action for Latinos on other grounds: participation in the life of the nation.

B.   Participation in the life of the nation

The justification for affirmative action in terms of participation in the life of the nation also may in principle take two forms: one based on justice and one based on utility. Again, I will refrain from adjudicating between these at this time. The first is based on the principle that, in a democratic nation, justice requires that every member of society be given the opportunity to participate in the life of the nation and that every reasonable effort be made to facilitate and encourage such participation. If some members of society are not given such opportunities and no reasonable efforts are made to facilitate and encourage participation of certain gender, racial, and ethnic groups, the situation needs correction. The utilitarian justification runs along the same lines, except that it is based on the principle of utility: a nation in which all members of society are given the opportunity and encouraged to participate in the life of the nation achieves better results than one in which some members are not given the opportunity or encouraged to participate and not every reasonable effort is made to facilitate and encourage the participation of everyone.

In order for the argument based on participation to be clear we must answer at least three questions:

1   Who is to participate and be encouraged to participate?
2   What degree of participation is required?
3   With regards to what is the participation to take place?

In principle the answers to these questions would appear to be quite straight-forward: Everyone should participate and be encouraged to participate, as far as possible, and with respect to every aspect of the life of the nation. When one looks more carefully at this answer, however, it is clear that it is unsatisfactory. First, it is questionable whether "everyone" should extend to such persons as illegal immigrants, tourists, terrorist infiltrators, and so on. Second, the degree of participation must necessarily be limited by practical considerations. For example, in a very small democratic community, it is possible for all the citizens to get together and agree on a certain course of action, but in a large nation, political participation has to be vicarious, through some form of indirect representation. Finally, it makes no sense to say that everyone must participate in every aspect of the life of the nation. Not everyone should teach mathematics, work as a physician, or be a member of the legislature. Clearly the answers to these questions need considerable elaboration. For my purposes, I do not need to provide a full story about them; it suffices to show that, in at least some aspects of the life of the nation, participation by Latinos is desirable in terms of justice or utility, although the degree of participation will depend also on the aspect in question. In order to simplify matters I have chosen two areas where it seems that participation is important in the case of Latinos. The first is political participation, which is the easiest to justify; the second is cultural participation, and this presents more of a challenge.

I understand political participation to involve being engaged in the process whereby decisions that affect the life of the polity are arrived at. Being engaged implies that those who participate in the process are consulted either directly, by being asked what they think, or indirectly by having their representatives asked. In principle, the justification for political participation can be made both in terms of justice and utility.[6] In terms of justice because it is unfair to arrive at decisions and adopt laws which affect persons who have not been allowed to voice their opinions and have not been given the opportunity to do what they can within the democratic process to prevent such decisions from being taken and such laws from being adopted. The argument in terms of utility is, *mutatis mutandis*, similar.

With respect to cultural participation the situation is less clear. It appears that cultural participation entails at least the freedom to engage in cultural practices, such as religious observances, speaking the language of one's choice, listening and playing the music one likes, and so on. One can argue, however, that freedom here needs to be understood more strongly than as just being allowed to do certain things. Freedom needs to be understood as providing the means to allow for freedom to engage in cultural practices to take place. One thing is to be free to eat in the sense of being allowed to do it; another is to be free to eat in the sense that we are provided with the means to do it. Similarly, cultural participation does not mean just being allowed to engage in cultural practices and activities of one's choice, but also to be given the resources that make possible to do it.

This understanding of freedom to participate is obviously too strong, however, for it would entail, for example, that society would have to provide resources to different religious groups, groups with different musical preferences, and so on, and this is clearly unacceptable. A weaker version of this view argues that what is involved here is both the removal of obstacles that stand in the way of cultural practices and also an open, respectful, and accepting attitude toward the cultural practices of others. It is not enough not to stand in the way.

Even this modified position encounters a difficulty, namely that not all cultural practices are benign and, therefore, acceptable. Consider, for example, such practices as female circumcision, opposition to certain medical treatments known to be beneficial, and so on. Clearly there are limits to the cultural freedom that can be allowed – cultural practices which adversely affect others

---

[6] See, for example, Iris Marion Young, "Together in Difference: Transforming the Logic of Group Political Conflict," in Kymlicka (ed.), *The Rights of Minority Cultures*, pp. 155–76.

or the polity as a whole, should not enjoy the open, respectful, and accepting attitude about which we are speaking. Participation in the cultural life of the nation must be understood within these parameters.

The particular question that concerns us here is whether affirmative action, understood as measures to increase participation in the two areas mentioned, namely politics and culture, is justified for Latinos. Justification in this case requires two conditions to be satisfied: (1) Latinos are identifiable; and (2) Latinos do not participate at all, or participate insufficiently, in the political and cultural life of the nation.

Satisfying the first condition should not be a problem if we take seriously what was said earlier concerning who counts as Latino. Although Latinos are not homogeneous and have no common properties at all times and places, we can generally be identified in context, and certainly we are, with few exceptions, easily identifiable in contemporary American society. Satisfying the second condition involves showing that in fact Latinos participate less in the political and cultural life of the nation than our numbers would seem to warrant.

Someone might want to object that the justification of affirmative action in terms of participation in the life of the nation is not different from the justification based on equal opportunity. After all, can we not frame the former as affirmative action intended to ensure equal opportunity to participate in the life of the nation? My response is that if one construes participation in the life of the nation as a kind of opportunity, then obviously justification of affirmative action on the basis of the first is not different from that on the basis of the second. But I do not think participation in the political and cultural life of the nation can be construed as an opportunity. There is a difference between these two kinds of justification for affirmative action. Equal opportunity generally refers to the distribution of goods and services in society – such things as jobs, salaries, health services – and it is stretching things quite a bit to think of the participation in the political and cultural life of the nation as a good or service in this sense.

I cannot engage here is an overall justification of affirmative action based on the participation of Latinos in the political and cultural life of the nation, but statistics confirm that there are fewer Latinos in government and that fewer of us vote in elections than our numbers would seem to warrant. Moreover, it is evident that many cultural traits generally associated with Latinos today seem to be relegated to a secondary and marginal role. When we consider expressions of so-called high culture, such as art, literature, and philosophy, most instances associated with Latinos are ignored, dismissed, or squeezed out to make room for something else. Moreover, there is relatively little openness, respect, and acceptance of cultural traits associated with Latinos.

And, indeed, in some cases, as with language, there is open hostility in certain quarters.[7]

In chapters 4 and 8 of this book I discuss at some length the situation of Latinos in one area of American society, philosophy. This should suffice to illustrate the claim that Latinos do not participate fully in the life of the American nation.

IV.   Affirmative Action for Latinos

The answer to the question whether there should be affirmative action for Latinos is yes and no. Yes, to the extent that affirmative action makes sense for Latinos, because, although we are part of American society, nevertheless we constitute a distinguishable ethnic group which must be given the opportunity, and encouraged, to participate in the life of the nation, for reasons of justice or utility. No, to the extent that affirmative action is not always justified for Latinos. Only secondarily and in specific cases can a case be made for affirmative action based on equal opportunity and reparation. Efforts are required to promote the participation of Latinos in American life.

Now, let me go back to the anecdotal cases presented at the beginning of the chapter to illustrate how my view helps us deal with practical affirmative action decisions. Was the University Affirmative Action Committee right in rejecting me as a minority candidate? No, it was wrong insofar as I am identifiably Latino and Latinos were at the time underrepresented in the Department of Philosophy and are still underrepresented in philosophy in general.

---

[7]   One measure of the marginalization of Latinos is that even affirmative action measures, such as providing government funds for Latino art, have often been counterproductive to this extent: they have created a kind of cultural ghetto for Latinos who, as a result, have a place separate and distant from the place of "mainstream" culture. See John David Skrentny, *The Ironies of Affirmative Action: Politics, Culture, and Justice in America* (Chicago: University of Chicago Press, 1996). The ghettoification of art is clear in statements of Cuban-American artists. See for example, the interviews in Jorge J. E. Gracia, Lynette Bosch, and Isabel Alvarez Borland (eds.), *Identity, Memory, and Diaspora: Voices of Cuban-American Artists, Writers, and Philosophers* (Albany, NY: State University of New York Press, 2007) and the webpage for the 2006 NEH Summer Seminar, Negotiating Identities in Art, Literature, and Philosophy: Cuban Americans and American Culture (http:// philosophy.buffalo.edu/contrib/events/neh06.html); and Jorge J. E. Gracia's webpage on Cuban-American art (http://www.philosophy.buffalo.edu/capenchair/CAOC/ index.html).

Was the later committee right in accepting the Latin American candidate as a minority? Yes, for the same reason given in my case. Was the elite college which accepted as Latino the friend of my daughter with the Mexican American great-grandmother, right? No, for this young man could not, in any meaningful sense of the term, qualify as a member of the Latino community. Was the elite college that gave a scholarship to the daughter of our prominent Latino friend, because she was Latino, right? No, because the purpose of a scholarship is to make possible for someone disadvantaged to go to school, or to compensate someone for past harms based on discrimination. But as we saw earlier, neither justification applies to Latinos considered as a whole, nor did it apply to the daughter of our friend.

The question of affirmative action for Latinos is closely related to the question of whether they have linguistic rights. This controversial issue is discussed in the following chapter.

Linguistic Rights: Language and Children

The issues surrounding linguistic accommodation rights, also often referred to as linguistic or language minority rights or as recognition rights, are many and complex.[1] They include, among many others, those expressed by questions such as: Do ethnic groups have linguistic rights? What qualifies as a linguistic right, if there are any? Should the government fund programs in which the languages of ethnic groups are taught at the taxpayer's expense? Should the government require linguistic proficiency in any particular language as a requirement of citizenship? Should the government provide translations of its laws and other pertinent documents into languages other than that of the majority in the country for the sake of groups which have some other language as their native tongue? Do all minorities who speak languages other than the language generally used in a country have linguistic rights? Is there a threshold that these minorities have to reach in terms of numbers, or certain criteria they have to meet, in order to qualify for linguistic rights?

Some of these questions are parasitic on more basic ones, such as whether ethnic and racial groups have rights at all *qua* groups, or whether it is only their members that have rights *qua* individuals. That is, in the case of Latinos, for example, whether we have rights, *qua* Latinos, that are different and differently justified than the rights we have *qua* human beings or *qua* citizens of the United States. Similar questions could be posed in the case of countries,

---

[1] See, for example, Will Kymlicka, "Do We Need a Liberal Theory of Minority Rights?" *Constellations* 4, 1 (1997), 72–87; and Leonardo Zaibert and Elizabeth Millán-Zaibert, "Universalism, Particularism, and Group Rights: The Case of Hispanics," in Jorge J. E. Gracia and Pablo De Greiff (eds.), *Hispanics/Latinos in the United States: Ethnicity, Race, and Rights* (New York: Routledge, 2000), pp. 167–80.

such as Peru or Mexico, that have large ethnic minorities. The literature on these issues is vast and growing and the disagreements sharp. Indeed, even in cases in which agreement exists concerning certain aspects of the issues in question, practical questions come up related to matters of resources, priorities, and implementation.

The discussion of the issues that concern language rights in particular have been taken up in many different fields, such as education, law, politics, sociology, literature, and ethnic studies. And philosophers have not been far behind, for these questions, as well as many other related ones, pose interesting philosophical problems. As should be expected, however, the dimensions of the issues that concern philosophers have been more theoretical and generally formulated in the context of moral justification. Two camps are easily discernible: those who in some way argue for linguistic rights for minorities, and those who oppose them. At the forefront of those who favor rights are Will Kymlicka and Iris Young; on the other side are authors like Thomas Pogge.

In this chapter, I am concerned in particular with Pogge's argument in favor of the position called English-first in the context of the education of Latino children. Whatever language is considered regarding this issue is irrelevant. In other countries, such as Peru or Mexico, the position could be described as Spanish-first, for example. In order to understand better the parameters of the controversy, I begin with a brief discussion of the defense by Kymlicka and Young of linguistic rights for minority groups in general and Latinos in particular. What they and I say can be easily applied, *mutatis mutandis*, to the case of other ethnic groups in Peru, Mexico, Brazil, the United States, or other places; although my main interest here is with Latinos.

I.   Linguistic Rights for Latinos

According to Young, Latinos in particular have three sorts of claims of justice concerning language in the United States: recognition, equality, and public support for learning the majority language, that is, English.[2] Of these three, Young considers the first to be less important than the second, although still valid, and she does not evaluate the third in comparison with either the first or the second.

The claim of recognition concerns the acknowledgment that Spanish is one of the constituent languages of the United States. The reason, according to

[2]   Iris Marion Young, "Structure, Difference, and Hispanic/Latino Claims of Justice," in Gracia and De Greiff (eds.), *Hispanics/Latinos in the United States*, pp. 159–61. Young uses the terms 'Hispanics' and 'Latinos' interchangeably.

Young, is that Spanish is the language of some groups of people who were incorporated into the United States when this country expanded its boundaries and domination. When the United States integrated large segments of the southwest into the national territory, for example, the people living in those areas were native Spanish speakers. Spanish, then, should not be considered a foreign language brought here by immigrants, as German and Italian are, but rather one that belongs to some of its citizens from the very beginning and, therefore, to the country.

The second claim of justice concerns the fact that Latinos, by having Spanish as their native tongue, are at a disadvantage in American society. They are less able to participate in the life of the nation, are less likely to hold good jobs, and so on. The United States, then, should make up for these deficiencies by providing the social services that Latinos require in order that they not be penalized for being Spanish speakers and for not being as fluent in English as they are in Spanish. This should be looked at, according to Young, as a matter of compensation for past wrongs and inequities.

Third, if learning English is advantageous to Latinos, as it certainly is because this is the majority language and Latinos are expected to become fluent in it, the United States should make every effort to provide support for learning it. Free instruction and support needs to be provided so that every Latino can, without undue burden, learn English.

The argument that Kymlicka puts forth in favor of language rights is somewhat similar to one of the reasons to which Young refers. According to him, one needs to make a distinction between two kinds of linguistic groups.[3] Those who have been incorporated into the national territory as a result of conquest, colonization, or federation, and those groups who are the result of free and voluntary immigration. Linguistic rights apply in the first case, but not in the second. The reason is that incorporation in the first case was involuntarily, whereas in the second it was the result of a voluntary choice to come into the country. This means that in the first case these groups have the right to keep their language, whereas in the second this right does not apply. Whereas German and Chinese immigrants into the United States have no linguistic rights, those Mexican Americans who became part of the United States as a consequence of the incorporation of more than 40 percent of the Mexican territory into this country during the nineteenth century, do.

The consequences of both of these positions are very important for a variety of linguistic claims of justice by Latinos in particular. But the positions have found considerable resistance. Although Young's third claim is hardly

---

[3]   Will Kymlicka, *Multicultural Citizenship: A Liberal Theory of Minority Rights* (Oxford: Oxford University Press, 1995), ch. 2.

disputed, her first two claims are controversial in that arguments can be mounted along various lines against them. For example, a rather callous line of argumentation could point out that the burden of learning the main language of the place where one lives is on the residents, who need not be compensated for their lack of knowledge of the language. And one could also mount arguments against the idea that Spanish has a different status from other languages, such as German or Italian, because it was a language native to the areas where the United States expanded. After all, it is rather ironic to argue this way, when Spanish, as English, was not the native language of anyone in the Americas before the Spaniards arrived.

The way Kymlicka justifies linguistic rights for certain groups can also be attacked with a variety of arguments. For example, the distinction on which it is based could be undermined by arguing that it is disingenuous to claim that immigrants subject to political persecution immigrate voluntarily. Indeed, even those who come to the United States because of economic exigency, one could argue, do not have a choice: starving is not a realistic option. If this is so, the idea that only the conquered have linguistic rights collapses, and the case for Latino linguistic rights with it.

Whether Young and Kymlicka are right or not is not important for us here, however. I mention their views to show that linguistic rights are an important topic of discussion among philosophers today and that there is a variety of ways in which such rights are supported. Instead, I concentrate on a different, although related, issue that has also received considerable attention in recent years and has provoked strong disagreements and controversy. It concerns the language in which children in the United States should be educated. In the case of Latinos in particular, it is especially telling both because Latinos constitute the largest minority and ethnic group in the country and because there are large numbers of the group whose proficiency in English is quite limited and others whose proficiency is non-existent. The issue in the case of Latinos has to do with whether Latino children should be taught in English, Spanish, or both.

Generally speaking, there are at least five main positions that one may take with respect to this issue in the context of Latinos. They may be labeled: English-only, Spanish-only, English-first, Spanish-first, and English–Spanish equal. The first maintains that the language of instruction for all children living in the United States should be English only and, therefore, that Latino children should be taught only in English; the second argues that the language of instruction of Latino children should be Spanish only; the third, that English should be given priority over Spanish; the fourth, that Spanish should be given priority over English; and the last position proposes treating English and Spanish equally in the education of children.

It should be clear from the discussion that follows that, although I generally refer to the situation of Latinos, what I say about this ethnic group could very well be applied, *mutatis mutandis*, to other ethnic groups in the United States, and that it can be applied to ethnic groups in other countries as well. However, it should also be clear that the arguments used by Young and Kymlicka do not have the same results with respect to the education of children belonging to all ethnic groups. Kymlicka clearly holds that only ethnic groups that have been incorporated into the national territory as a result of national expansion (such as presumably Mexican Americans from the southwest of the United States or the Tarahumara in Mexico) have linguistic rights, and only children from those groups may claim the right to be educated in their native tongues. This means that, for Kymlicka, the choice between the five possibilities outlined earlier in a case such as that of Mexican Americans, for example, should be up to them, and the government should honor their choice.

Young's view is that in the case of Spanish, one of the reasons for linguistic rights is that Latinos were incorporated into the national territory of the United States as a result of territorial expansion, and this makes Spanish constitutive of the country, although Spanish speakers should be offered the means to learn the language of the majority at the government's expense. With respect to the education of children in particular, then, one would be entitled to surmise that she favors teaching children in Spanish, although efforts should be made to make them fluent also in English. In short, in terms of the possibilities outlined earlier, it appears that Young would rule out Spanish-only and English-only, and would favor a form of Spanish–English equal.

Clearly, then, in both cases we have a strong endorsement of the rights of some minority groups, particularly Latinos, to have their children taught in languages other than English. To this extent, their views contrast with the position for which Thomas Pogge argues and which is the main concern of this chapter.

II. Pogge's Argument for English-first

I take up Pogge's particular argument in favor of English-first for three reasons. First, it is one of the most clearly stated arguments that have been given for this position, and it reflects the political liberal view predominant in this country. Many other arguments found in the literature are confusing, they often contain much rhetoric and appeals to emotions that cloud the issue, and their supporters often adhere to marginal ideologies. Second, Pogge's argument appears on the surface to be compelling, both because it seems to be sound and because it makes sense. And third, Pogge's views tend to receive attention. I argue, however, that Pogge's argument fails for reasons I explain below.

Pogge presents his argument in the context of his criticism of what he takes to be Kymlicka's position concerning the language of instruction in school for children of linguistic minorities, but here I am not concerned with the details of Pogge's criticism or his interpretation of Kymlicka's argument. The argument Pogge presents to justify his position can be considered in isolation from these other matters without losing any of its intended force.[4]

The conclusion that Pogge wishes to defend is that "choosing English as the universal language of instruction is part of the most effective method for helping students develop fluency in English."[5] The foundation Pogge provides to support this conclusion is the principle that "the best education for each child is the education that is best for this child."[6] To which he adds: "The most important linguistic competence for children now growing up in the United States is the ability to communicate in English, and the language of instruction in public schools in the United States should therefore be chosen by reference to the goal of effectively helping pupils develop fluency in English."[7] Pogge is aware that this argument rests in part on empirical grounds that he does not explore for lack of proper expertise, so he weakens his claim noting that his aim is not to settle the matter altogether, but rather "merely to sketch what the debate leading up to such a settlement might look like."

The objections I present against Pogge's argument are intended to show that, in addition to the empirical factors that must be considered before a final settlement of this matter can take place, there are also other issues that Pogge neglects to take into account and which are essential to any discussion of this issue. By ignoring them, Pogge's claim is weakened considerably and his argument turns out to be both ineffective and misleading.

In order to facilitate the understanding of the issues, let me present Pogge's argument in the following schematic form:

P1 The best education for a child is the education that is best for the child.

P2 The education that is best for a child in the United States is one in which English is given priority.

C1 Therefore, the best education for a child in the United States is one in which English is given priority.

P3 To give priority to English is to make English the language of instruction.

C2 Therefore, the best education for a child in the United States is one in which English is the language of instruction.

[4] For Pogge's formulation, see Thomas W. Pogge, "Accommodation Rights for Hispanics in the United States," in Gracia and De Greiff (eds.), *Hispanics/Latinos in the United States*, pp. 181–200. The argument is given on pp. 192–7.

[5] Ibid., p. 194.

[6] Ibid., p. 193.

[7] Ibid., p. 194.

In what follows, I challenge the three premises (P1, P2, and P3) on which the final conclusion (C2) of this argument is based. Let me begin with the general principle expressed in P1.

A.   The best education for a child is the education that is best for the child (P1)

One way to justify P1 is to say that it is analytic, that is, trivially true, because the meaning of 'the education that is best for X' is included in, equivalent to, or entailed by the meaning of 'the best education for X.' Naturally, if one takes this view, one cannot question the truth of P1, although this does not mean that one has to accept its force in the case in which we are considering: One could argue that tautologies are empty and irrelevant to what happens in the real world. By making P1 analytically true, its force of application is lost.

A line of defense against this charge could argue that P1 is not analytic. This requires us, however, to understand 'the education that is best for X' in such a way that its meaning is not included in, equivalent to, or entailed by the meaning of 'the best education for X.' This can be done by claiming that in ordinary language 'the education that is best for X' and 'the best education for X' are elliptical, and once the ellipses are unpacked, it becomes clear that the meaning of the first is not included, entailed, or equivalent to, the meaning of the second. 'The best education for X' might be taken in an absolute sense to refer to general conditions of desirability, for example, whereas 'the education that is best for X' might be taken to refer to a relative and contextual situation and thus to particular conditions.

If this defense of P1 were adopted and the principle were not regarded as analytic, then in order for it to be made applicable to real situations in the world, it would have to be contextualized, and this contextualization would have to include a reference to the way in which its subject and predicate are to be interpreted and the criteria for their interpretation. For example, one could argue that 'the best education for X' makes sense only if a criterion of what is best is made explicit, and 'the education that is best for X' makes sense only if the circumstances surrounding that education are specified. This means that much more work needs to be done for P1 to be of any practical use. Consider some possible choices.

What principles or factors can be used to make the meaning of 'the best education for X' relevant to real live situations? Obviously, the answer is: Something that will make it materially relevant. But what could that be? Many things come to mind and have been used throughout the history of ethics for this purpose. For some philosophers, the source of this determination consists of the views held by certain people. In the case we are considering, this could turn out to be the natural parents of the child, the adopted parents of the child, the society of which the child is a part, the ethnic group to which the child belongs, the religious community in which the child was born, a group of elders in the society in which the child lives, an authoritative figure in that society, a judge, a court, an appointed jury, and so on. But one can also make the expression materially relevant by referring to a particular good, such as pleasure, virtue, wealth, knowledge, fame, power, physical prowess, beauty, fellowship with a divinity, social conformity, peace of mind, tranquility, control over one's mental and bodily functions, and so on, although these, when they are not determinate enough, would in turn need further specification. For example, a particular kind of pleasure could be picked, such as physical pleasure, and a particular kind of knowledge, such as empirical knowledge, could be indicated, although even these might require further specification.

In short, the expression 'the best education for a child' is simply too formal to make any practical difference in a real live situation and, therefore, needs to be supplemented if it is going to be of use. Moreover, depending on how one supplements it, the results could be very different. If what is best for a child is the development of physical prowess, then the kind of education the child should have would be very different from an education based on one whose aim were the development of peace of mind, say. Moreover, if it is a particular person or group of persons who determine what is best for a child, then again the results could be very different from those in which a different person or group of persons determines what is best for the child, as in fact we see illustrated in our experience every day. What is judged to be best in education for children of Evangelical Christians, Islamic fundamentalists, and humanists are quite different things.

But contextualization and the difficulties it poses do not apply only to the subject of P1. It applies also to the predicate ('the education that is best for X'), for it does not make sense to speak of the education that is best for a child in the abstract. The goal of a child's education must be related to a context, and that context plays a role in what makes it possible for the education to be legitimately judged to be good or bad. Consider a case in which a child's parents and the community in which the child lives speak a particular language different from the language of the larger community of the country. Under these conditions, it would seem necessary for the child's survival and proper functioning within its immediate community to be able to communicate in the language of that community. Indeed, the immediate community in which a child is raised largely determines the opportunities open to the child, and the rules of that community establish how the child may avail itself of those opportunities. Think of the Kurds in Iraq under Saddam Hussein, for example, who were deprived of certain rights and privileges from birth because of their ethnicity. So, clearly the proper language of education appears to be that of the immediate community in which the child finds itself, at least in part, and perhaps primarily. Not to take the particular situation in which a child finds itself into account makes no sense.

Let me sum up what I have argued so far by pointing out that the first premise (P1) on which the argument for English-first presented by Pogge rests is too formal to be of any practical use. If it is understood to be analytic, then its practical relevance is questionable. But even if it is not, much needs to be added to it to make it practically relevant. Moreover, many of the ways that can be used to make the principle expressed by P1 materially relevant conflict with each other. This means that no progress can be made toward the determination of what the best education for a child is until a clear understanding of the basis on which particular ways of making P1 relevant are chosen and their justification completed. In the meantime, P1 cannot be accepted as true and therefore used to justify the conclusion Pogge wishes to establish. Now let me turn to P2.

B.   The education that is best for a child in the United States is one in which English is given priority (P2)

Can we accept P2 without serious question? The first thing that needs to be said is that this premise does not pose the formal difficulties that plague the first. P2 is not formal in that it not only identifies what is best for a child in terms of linguistic education, but it also points to the place in which this is so: English should be given priority in the instruction of children in the United States. And, of course, this is taken to apply to all children regardless of their ethnic background, the identity of their parents, and so on, so there should be no difficulty applying it to Latinos. Having said this, however, there are serious questions that can be raised about P2. These questions are closely related to the way in which one goes about making more specific the principle expressed in P1. Whether in fact an education in which English is given priority is best for a child in the United States depends on at least two things: first, what is best for the child, and, second, who determines what is best for the child. Pogge fails to address adequately either of these.

With respect to the first, he speaks of the "self-interest" of the child and "the advantages" that a child who is proficient in English would have in the United States, but he does not identify such interests and advantages beyond a general reference to social, economic, and political ones and the future professional life of the child.[8] The generality of this claim makes it both inadequate and largely irrelevant when it comes to making concrete choices, for one can always question exactly what, in a particular situation, will satisfy the criteria. But perhaps more importantly, the claim is also highly disputable insofar as "interest" and "advantage" are not generally accepted as bases for the construction of a sound morality by most, indeed not even many, philosophers.

With respect to the second factor on which giving priority to English in the education of children in the United States depends, Pogge neglects to explore the question of who determines what is best for a child, even though this is essential for his argument to work. Consider the case in which the parents of a child determine what is best for the child. It is conceivable that the parents think that it is best for the child to be educated in such a way that a language other than English, say Spanish, is given priority for a variety of reasons. (Keep in mind that it is not those reasons that justify the judgment in this case, but the authority and legitimacy of the parents' choosing. Nor does the parents' authority entail that this matter concerns the interests of the parents, as Pogge seems to assume.) But is this the only possible answer? Obviously not. What is best for the child could be determined by a judge, society at large, or an institution, for example, as in fact has been argued by many. And in all these cases, what is best could differ, depending on the person or persons who determine it and the reasons they use to justify their choice.

I am not arguing that Pogge is wrong in proposing that what he considers to be the best interests of a child (whatever those may be) are in fact the best interests of the child. My point is rather that he assumes they are, whereas in fact this is a very contested issue that goes back to the beginning of philosophy, and which still is much debated and about which strong disagreements exist. Likewise, it makes no sense to speak about the best interests of a child, in a practical context such as education, without providing a proper justification of how those interests are determined and by whom. The fact that Pogge's argument does not acknowledge these matters constitutes a serious flaw in it.

In short, Pogge's attempt to establish the thesis that an education in which English is given priority is in fact the best education for children in the United States on the basis of the self interest of the children is ineffective, because those interests are disputable and the persons responsible for determining them remain unidentified. Besides, are we to assume that what qualifies as best for one child is also what qualifies as best for every child and in every situation? Perhaps so, if the circumstances under which children find themselves are

---

8   Ibid., pp. 181 and 194–6 in particular.

always the same, or at least very similar. But this is far from being the case in the United States. Many Latino children live in ghettoes in which the only means of effective communication, survival, and advancement is through Spanish, not English. Under those conditions it would be hard to argue that learning English is in their best interest and more important to them than learning Spanish.

In sum, the problem with the second premise (P2) of the argument presented by Pogge in favor of the English-first position concerning the education of children in the United States is that, although it is quite specific when compared with P1, it contains an assumption derived from P1 which is disputable. Now let me turn to P3, the third premise on which the final conclusion rests.

C. To give priority to English (English-first) is to make English the language of instruction (P3)

As it stands, without further clarification, the expressions 'English first' and 'to give priority to English' can mean a variety of things, insofar as 'first' and 'priority' are terms that have different meanings when used in different contexts.[9] Two of these meanings are particularly significant when considered in the context of the principle for which Pogge argues. In one, 'English first' and 'priority in English' are taken temporally, so that the principle in question means that English should be temporally the first language of instruction to which children are exposed: children's instruction should begin in English. But this does not entail, of course, that other languages might not be taught later, or even that some languages might not be taught simultaneously with English. Understood in this sense, the principle can be questioned, for some educators believe that in the case of children whose parents do not speak English, it is better for a child to become literate in the language of the parents first and then transfer that skill to English. The objection, then, is that there are empirical reasons why it is best for children to begin learning in the tongue of their parents and only later, when that language has been effectively established for oral communication, reading, and writing, should other languages be introduced in instruction.[10] These educators point out, for example, that becoming literate in a language is one of the most difficult things that humans accom-

---

[9] Cf. Aristotle, *The Complete Works of Aristotle*, ed. Jonathan Barnes, Vol. 1: *Metaphysics*, trans. W. D. Ross (Princeton, NJ: Princeton University Press, 1995), 1018b10–1019a15.

[10] Kymlicka, *Multicultural Citizenship*, p. 97.

plish, and it is much easier to do so in the language of one's parents, to which one has been exposed from birth, than in a language to which one has not had parental exposure. After all, it is from the parents that a child first learns linguistic sounds used for communication, and that knowledge is essential for the more difficult task of connecting script to meanings.

In another way, 'English-first' and 'priority in English' can be understood to refer to a goal, so that proficiency in English is favored over proficiency in some other language. And this is, indeed, the sense that Pogge seems to have in mind, as he puts it in one of the texts cited earlier. But, of course, if the meaning of the English-first principle is taken to refer to the primary goal of English proficiency, then the principle does not entail that children should be taught temporally first in English as already noted, that they should be taught exclusively in English or in English for a time, or even that they should not be taught exclusively in Spanish for a time. It only entails that measures should be taken to achieve effectively the primary goal of English proficiency. The means of achieving this goal can be determined on the basis of the children's circumstances and the empirical research that shows which is the best way to achieve it – a fact which Pogge recognizes. In this sense, it would be possible to argue that languages other than English (i.e., Spanish for Latinos) should be taught to some children and be taught to them temporally first if it contributes to making the children literate in one language so that this skill can be more easily transferred to English later. The only requirement is that whatever language is taught, it not be an obstacle to the achievement of English proficiency and, in fact, facilitate it. The principle of English-first, understood thus, has nothing to do with the time at, or means by, which English is taught. Nor does it concern whether children are taught languages other than English, provided this does not interfere with the achievement of English proficiency.

From all this, it is clear that neither of the two ways of understanding the English-first principle presented can determine when English should be taught to children, or the choice of the language of instruction that should be used to educate them at various periods of their training. The reason is that these practical matters depend on the results of empirical research with respect to the most effective ways of making children proficient in English, particularly those whose parents do not speak English. In neither case do we have a situation in which the principle by itself could be used to abolish programs of so-called bilingual education in which children are taught Spanish first and English later (temporally speaking), or are taught Spanish and English simultaneously, as long as the programs have as a primary end to have children become proficient in the use of English, and there is evidence that suggests they are effective in achieving such proficiency. Indeed, even if in some cases these programs may also have as a goal for the children to become proficient in Spanish, this would not signify, as long as they have as a primary goal to make children proficient in English. Of course, if the aim of the program were to have children become proficient in Spanish and not English, or to give Spanish proficiency priority over English proficiency, then the situation would be different. But these positions are different from the English-first view. I described them earlier as Spanish-only and Spanish-first respectively.

What is the practical significance of the English-first principle? None when it comes to the time of teaching English, or the teaching of children in Spanish or some language other than English. If I am right in this claim, why is it that this principle has been so intensely debated and disagreements are regarded as significant?

III.   A Worrisome Suspicion

I suspect the answer to this question is that there is more to this principle than meets the eye. This makes the principle misleading and worrisome. The English-first principle might be surreptitiously intended – although most likely some supporters of it are not conscious of it – to do more work than it is explicitly acknowledged by those who favor it. I suspect that behind its use there is a commitment to English-only supported by a misguided sense of American nationality in which the United States is identified necessarily as an English-speaking country and those who are not proficient in English are not quite, or truly, considered American citizens. This is a dangerous notion, for it means that a political construct, the nation, is transformed into a cultural one, in which language is one of its distinguishing features. Once this is done, it is inevitable that certain groups of people who do not share the "official" culture, that is the culture considered normative in the nation, become subject of discrimination and segregation. There is plenty of evidence that the push for a cultural or an ethnic conception of the American nation and American citizenship is alive and well.[11] And if those who favor it get their way, then there is little hope for the recognition of the oppression to which some minority ethnic groups have been, and would likely continue to be, subjected in the United States.

---

[11]   See: Suzanne Oboler, " 'It Must Be a Fake!' Racial Ideologies, Identities, and the Question of Rights," in Gracia and De Greiff, (eds.), *Hispanics/Latinos in the United States*, pp. 125–44; Kymlicka, *Multicultural Citizenship* and "Do We Need a Liberal Theory of Minority Rights?"; and Samuel P. Huntington, *Who Are We? The Challenges to America's National Identity* (New York: Simon and Schuster, 2004).

Hopefully, my suspicion is not well founded. But unless Pogge and other proponents of the English-first principle explain exactly what they mean by it and show how it can make any difference in the actual linguistic education of children, while distancing themselves from cultural and ethnic conceptions of the American nation, I cannot but entertain it. I should point out that Pogge does explicitly distance himself from the English-only position, but unfortunately much of what he says could be used to support an ethnic conception of the American nation.[12]

IV. Language Priority in the Education of Latino Children

I have shown that the three premises of the argument used by Pogge to establish the principle of English-first in the education of children in the United States are not specific enough. This renders them inadequate to support the conclusion of the argument. Moreover, I have pointed out that, even if one accepts that the principle of English-first establishes the goal for a proper education of children, including Latino children, in the United States, the principle makes little practical difference when it comes to the actual implementation of which language should be taught to children and when. Finally, I have suggested that perhaps the principle works as a cover for the more radical view of English-only, based on an understanding of English as the proper language of the United States, in turn supported by an ethnic conception of the American nation.

At the same time, let me make clear that I have provided no arguments against the English-first position or in favor of any substantial view as to the language of choice when it comes to the education of children in the United States, regardless of their ethnic background. Nor have I taken into account any empirical research regarding the linguistic education of children, although I have pointed out that many of the decisions that concern the issues I have discussed hinge on the results of that research. Finally, I have not substantiated the suggestion that the English-first position is intended to do more work than its proponents acknowledge. My concern has been exclusively with Pogge's argument in favor of the English-first view, particularly as it applies to the teaching of Latino children in Spanish. However, my criticism also applies if the structure of Pogge's argument were to be used to justify similar positions concerning dominant languages in other parts of the world, as well as the relation of English to minority languages other than Spanish in the education of children in the United States.

[17] Pogge, "Accommodation Rights for Hispanics in the United States," p. 196.

Latino/a Philosophy

Philosophy: Latino vs American

Ethnic groups develop as a result of both internal and external factors. In Parts I and II of this book I discussed some of the external social factors that affect Latinos, but the book would be incomplete without a discussion of some of the internal factors that play a role in the formation and development of Latino identities. One of the most explicit of these factors consists in what Latinos think about themselves and the world, particularly our philosophy.

I. Our Philosophy

The general rubric, "Latino philosophy," is related to several other categories, such as Hispanic, Iberian, Latin American, Ibero-American, Argentinian, and Mexican philosophy, among others. These correspond roughly to various ethnic, sub-ethnic, national, and regional divisions. In chapter 3, I proposed that the very notion of Latino comes under the broader notion of Hispanic, which includes such other categories as Spanish, Spanish American, Iberian, and Iberian and Latin American. Iberian philosophy usually refers to the thought produced in Spain and Portugal, and Latin American thought sometimes excludes thought produced in French or Dutch. For our purposes, concerned as we are with Latinos in Latin America and the United States, the important category is Latino philosophy, understood as including the philosophical work produced by Latinos both in Latin America and the United States. Latino philosophy in the United States has close ties to Latin America and does not have an extensive history. Moreover, most Latino thought in the United States has roots in Latin American philosophy. It is appropriate, then, that we pay particular attention to the work of Latin American philosophers.

II.   The Problem of Latino Philosophy

The notion of a Latin American philosophy has been a subject of heated con-troversy for most of the twentieth century and gives us a way of approaching Latino philosophy. The problem of Latino philosophy may be formulated in a question: Why ask what Latino philosophy is? The reasons why we ask ques-tions vary considerably. Questions have many purposes, and their purposes often reveal something about the kind of answers that those who ask them seek to provide. It makes sense for us to begin by asking for the purposes behind the question about what Latino philosophy is.

Four purposes are interesting for us to consider in this context: pedagogical, historiographical, validational and authenticating, and ideological. Concern-ing the pedagogical purpose: when I teach a course on Latino philosophy I need to decide which thinkers to discuss and which texts to assign to students. This entails that I need to know what Latino philosophy is, that is, what qualifies as Latino philosophy and what does not.

The second mentioned purpose is historiographical. Some of us are inter-ested in the history of Latino philosophy, and this again requires that we determine the object of investigation. Questions about authors and materials to be studied surface again.

The third purpose has to do with issues of validation and authenticity. It is quite clear that some of those who teach and study Latino philosophy are concerned with establishing its legitimacy, because they consider themselves to be Latinos, or because perhaps they think that it is a good thing for Latinos to have a philosophy of our own. This goes along with the fact that 'philosophy' is an honorific term, perhaps not as honorific as 'novelist' or 'artist,' but none-theless appreciated enough so that every culture and ethnic and national group would like to have one.

Finally, concerning the ideological purpose, some of those who ask and answer the question of what Latino philosophy is have as their primary aim to grind a certain ideological ax. They are concerned with it not for a love of knowledge in general, or even of knowledge about Latino philosophy in par-ticular, but rather because the study of Latino philosophy will help them reach some other aim, be that political, religious, or what have you.

Aristotle noted long ago that the purpose, that is, what he called *telos*, determines both what something is and its function. The *telos* of a human being for him, for example, is the acquisition of a certain kind of knowledge. This *telos* determines both what is distinctive of humans (rationality) among other similar beings (animals) and their function (to reason). If we take this idea seriously in the case we are considering – and it is particularly pertinent because the study of Latino philosophy is a purposeful human activity – then we should expect that there might be differences in what is considered Latino philosophy among those who study it, depending on the purposes they have in mind. Teachers will primarily have a pedagogical aim, and consider their object of study differently perhaps than historiographers. And something similar could be said about those who have an ideological aim or those who search for validation and authenticity. In the case of some other subjects, perhaps there might not be significant differences on the basis of various aims, because the object of study has fairly well-established boundaries and its goal is also agreed upon. When we are concerned with cancer, for example, matters appear easier, at least in principle, insofar as the overall aim of the study of cancer is to cure and eradicate the decease. Anything that contributes to this aim is fair game to the investigator.

But Latino philosophy poses difficulties, because the purpose in studying it is not so clear or uniform, and what qualifies as Latino philosophy is not well established. True, some authors and texts are clearly part of Latino philosophy in the broad sense I am using here and regarded as such by everyone. No one disputes that Antonio Caso, Risieri Frondizi, Leopoldo Zea, and Francisco Miró Quesada are Latino philosophers. Although there are disagreements as to the value and originality of their work, this work is uniformly accepted as philosophical and belonging in the canon of Latino philosophy when this includes Latin American philosophy. Hence, any course on Latino philosophy can, and perhaps should, include the study of these figures without apology, and the same goes for historiography. Even those motivated by ideology or validation consider them part of the canon, and either use them to support the case they want to make or consider them exceptions of one kind or another to whatever principles they wish to peddle. In short, the authors mentioned, and their work, are part of what is taken as Latino philosophy, whether we like it or not.

It is equally clear that many philosophers do not qualify as Latinos and their work is not part of the corpus of Latino philosophical texts. Aristotle, Aquinas, Descartes, and Habermas, for example, do not, and no one working on Latino philosophy would be taken seriously if he or she said that they were part of Latino philosophy, even though some Latino philosophers have been heavily influenced by their ideas. References to these authors in works or courses on Latino philosophy are acceptable, but their work is not studied as Latino. To understand Frondizi's views on the self, for example, references to Christian von Ehrenfels are essential, for Frondizi used this philosopher's ideas about value and *Gestalt* to develop his own views. But it is obvious that, whereas Frondizi is clearly a Latino philosopher, and part of the Latin American philosophical canon, von Ehrenfels is not.

The authors I have mentioned pose no problems for the pedagogue or historiographer of Latino philosophy. But problems surface when we consider texts and authors such as the *Popol Vuh*, Bartolomé de Las Casas, Sor Juana Inés de la Cruz, Francisco Romero, Frantz Fanon, José Gaos, Héctor Neri-Castañeda, Jorge Luis Borges, and Renzo Llorente.

The problem with the *Popol Vuh* (the book that contains the Maya myth of creation) is twofold. First, this is not a clearly philosophical text in the most widespread western understanding of the term. After all, there are many texts like this in the western tradition and they are never included in the philosophical canon. Consider, for example, the Egyptian *Book of the Dead* and the biblical books of Genesis and Job. Even the *Iliad* and the *Odyssey* are not generally included in courses on the history of philosophy except to illustrate the change historians of philosophy see between religious and literary texts and the work of the pre-Socratics. If this is so, then why should we include the *Popol Vuh* in the study of Latino philosophy? Perhaps for the sake of validation, to render philosophical legitimacy to the peoples of Latin America before the Iberians arrived? Or perhaps the issue is ideological, namely, that one wishes to change the way we generally think of philosophy in the West because one has some other idea in mind about the nature of philosophy and its role in the social context.

Bartolomé de Las Casas poses a different problem. He is a Spaniard who lived part of his life in Latin America and applied the scholastic philosophy developed in the Middle Ages and practiced during his time in the Iberian peninsula to the Latin American context, particularly to the question of the humanity and rights of conquered peoples. His place of origin and the philosophical framework that he used count against him being part of the Latino philosophical canon, but his concern with issues arising from the Latino context, his advocacy for the well-being of pre-Columbian peoples, and the influence he exerted in the way both Latinos and non-Latinos think about these issues support his inclusion in the canon. Besides, no one can doubt that Las Casas's scholastic mode of argumentation fits what is considered philosophical in the West, and the philosophical issues raised by the conquest cannot be raised without mentioning Las Casas or his work. His thought is clearly philosophical and inspired by the Latin American situation. Are there other reasons why we should include him in Latino philosophy? Should we include him for ideological reasons, because he mostly said the right things and defended oppressed pre-Columbian populations? Should we include him because otherwise Latino philosophy would not exist at the time, or would not make sense without reference to him? So what do we do with him and why?

The case of Sor Juana is difficult in a different way. She was prevented from writing philosophy in the way that was common at the time because she was a woman. So in a sense we do not have any work from her that can be classified as philosophical, strictly speaking. Yet, this prohibition did not prevent her from precisely making a case against it in rational and rhetorical terms. She also wrote poems that have ethical or moral relevance, although her style, as a humanist, was not what counts as strictly philosophical in the West. Keep in mind that Renaissance humanists have a hard time being included in the western philosophical curriculum or the philosophical research canon. When was the last time you saw a course in philosophy that discussed the work of Lorenzo Valla, or a history of philosophy that does not do more than mention his name as a humanist? So, on what basis should we include Sor Juana in a course on Latino philosophy, or include her as a figure to be studied in the historiography of Latino philosophy when similar authors in Europe are generally excluded from consideration in courses and studies of European philosophy? Because she is a woman and we want to validate women's philosophical capacity? Because there is a certain ideological ax that we want to grind? Because the history of Latino philosophy makes no sense without reference to her?

Francisco Romero fits well the criteria of western philosopher: his writing is in line with standard philosophical texts, he was influenced by well-established western philosophers, and the topics he discussed are common in the history of European philosophy. Yet, he was born in Spain, not Argentina. He was an immigrant to Argentina, just like I am in the United States. Is he part of Latino philosophy, then? In my case, my name appears on some lists of American philosophers, so there is no reason why he should be treated differently in Latin America. But again, matters are not clear, for some people might argue that I am not an American philosopher.

The case of Frantz Fanon is more complicated. He wrote in French and was born in Martinique. Does Latin America include this part of the world? Since the French created the term 'Latin America,' I am sure they would answer affirmatively, but few authors take this French part of the Americas into consideration when studying Latino philosophy, and no anthologies of Latino philosophy include the work of authors from this part of the Americas. There is, of course, a very serious bias against any author who is not Spanish speaking. Even Brazilian authors have problems of inclusion. Moreover, anything outside of the Iberian sphere of influence is almost automatically excluded. So, on what basis do we include Fanon: ideology, validation, an expanded version of Latin America?

José Gaos is also a difficult case. He came to Latin America as an older person, fleeing from political instability in Spain, but his impact on Mexico in particular was enormous. No history of Mexican philosophy makes sense without examining this impact, and perhaps no history of Latino philosophy does either. Moreover, he also appropriated much that could be considered as arising from the Mexican situation; one could argue that he philosophized from a Mexican context. But should we, then, include reference to José Ortega y Gasset (who also had an enormous influence on Latino philosophy) and Ginés de Sepúlveda (who had no influence but engaged Las Casas in a philosophical controversy arising in Latin America)? Can we consider Gaos in the same category as Caso or Frondizi?

Héctor Neri-Castañeda was born in Guatemala and emigrated to the United States when he was already trained in philosophy. But his entire career took place in this country and his thought has no discernible relation to anything Latino. Indeed, like Mario Bunge, he seems to have shunned anything dealing with Latin American thought, although he was very much in favor of promoting the interests of Latinos in the United States. Can we include him in a course on Latino philosophy as part of that philosophy? And if we do, do we do it merely because of ideology, legitimation, or pride?

Everyone agrees that Jorge Luis Borges had a fantastic intellect, his work is highly suggestive philosophically, and he is a great writer. But is his work part of Latino philosophy? The issue here is the nature of the work, not the Latino credentials of the author. Some have argued that Borges's work is part of Latino philosophy, and in order to include it they erase the distinction between philosophy and literature.[1] This proposal has a clear ideological and validation aim in the Latino context, although similar proposals about the inclusion of literary figures in philosophy have been made in other contexts as well.[2] Those who argue for this position hold that "academic philosophy" in Latin America has not been particularly original, interesting, or of high quality, whereas Latin American literature is at the top of the charts. Moreover, no one questions that much of this literature is very philosophical (as with Borges, for example). So, why not change the definition of philosophy to include at least some literature and then have great philosophy and philosophers in Latin America, the likes of Borges?

Finally, we come to Renzo Llorente. Here is a son of Cuban immigrants, trained in the United States, living in Spain, speaking with a Castillian accent,

---

[1] See: José Luis Gómez Martínez, "Posmodernidad, discurso antrópico y ensayística latinoamericana," *Dissens, Revista Internacional de Pensamiento Latinoamericano* 2 (1996), 45; and Pedro Lange Churrión and Eduardo Mendieta, "Philosophy and Literature: The Latin American Case," *Dissens, Revista Internacional de Pensamiento Latinoamericano* 2 (1996), 37–40.

[2] Ermanno Bencivenga, William Irwin, Jorge Gracia, and Deborah Knight explore this question in Jorge J. E. Gracia, Carolyn Korsmeyer, and Rodolphe Gasché (eds.), *Literary Philosophers: Borges, Calvino, Eco* (New York: Routledge, 2002).

and interested in Latin American philosophy. Is he a Latino philosopher? Is his work to be included in the canon of Latino philosophy? He tells me that he has never thought of including it in the canon of Latin American philosophy.

Clearly we have no problem including the likes of Caso and Frondizi, or excluding the likes of von Ehrenfels and Descartes, but when we get to Las Casas, Sor Juana, Borges, and some of the others mentioned, we do. So, what should we do? Who is to be included in Latino philosophy and what criteria are we going to use to determine inclusion? And how are we going to conceive Latino philosophy in order to do this? These are the pertinent questions that we need to answer. Some of these belong to Latino philosophical historiography, but some are larger questions about the nature of philosophy and how to conceive it.

III.   Historiographical Characterizations of Philosophy

Before I turn to the philosophical dimension of these questions, it should be useful to look at how historians of philosophy explain historiographical characterizations of philosophy. Six are pertinent: one emphasizes factors external to the philosophies or views in question, three emphasize internal factors, and two fall somewhere in between.

The external factor most generally emphasized is place. Historians often speak of certain philosophies in various ways because they have been developed in particular places. Thus they speak, for example, of French philosophy as the philosophy produced in France; and Spanish philosophy is the philosophy produced in Spain.

Although in certain historical contexts the talk of place makes sense, there are difficulties that surface in others. One of these is that a place does not seem to have anything intrinsic to do with the philosophy that occurs in it. The place where philosophers philosophize seems to be rather accidental to the views they hold. We can live in Japan or in Germany and be convinced Heideggerians, for example. For this reason, the unity that location yields seems inadequate to explain the unity of many particular philosophies. Moreover, there is the question of significance. Where are we to find it? To say that French philosophy is such merely because it has taken place in French territory is of little interest as far as the nature of that philosophy is concerned. Finally, territorial boundaries are largely arbitrary, the result of historical accidents, and frequently change. So why should they be taken as providing the unity that justifies particular philosophies? Adding time helps, but it does not resolve the issue completely.

Internal factors seem more promising for the justification of the unity of the sort of philosophies mentioned in that they involve features that characterize the philosophies themselves, and so they seem to be intrinsic to them, that is, part of the conditions of their identity. These internal factors consist of certain topics, methods, and assumptions shared by the views that make up a particular philosophy. According to this position, medieval philosophy, for example, can be characterized by certain topics that other philosophies do not share, and the same goes for the method used in it and the assumptions under which medieval philosophers worked. Indeed, it is difficult to dispute that medieval philosophers were particularly concerned with certain problems such as the existence of God, the reality of universals, and individuation. Moreover, it is also clear that, at least after the twelfth century, they had very clear methodological views that they implemented in their philosophizing, many of which are revealed by the structure of the texts they left us. Finally, did not medieval philosophers work under the general assumption that God exists and has revealed himself to humans in sacred scriptures, even though most of them tried to provide rational grounds for this belief?

But not all the cases of particular philosophies are similar to that of medieval philosophy. The case of French philosophy, for example, is one in point. Can we identify a set of problems, methods, and assumptions that characterize all philosophy that we call French? If this difficulty were not serious enough, there is still a more worrisome one: Many of the philosophies whose unity we wish to explain are not dead, that is, they are still under construction. French philosophy is a good example, because in the last 50 years we have seen how much it has changed. Indeed, one could argue that there is not much in common in terms of problems, method, or assumptions between Descartes and Derrida. And the future may hold even more drastic changes. There is also the fact that even in periods of the history of philosophy that display remarkable unity of topics, method, and assumptions, there have always been philosophers who have not fitted into the model. Philosophy is one of those fields in which the challenges to the status quo seem essential to it, so it is hard to argue that there are always a set of commonalities that extend to everyone who is supposed to be covered by a general epithet.

This brings me to the last set of factors mentioned earlier that are used for the justification of the unity of such philosophies as French philosophy: language and style. I described these as falling between those that are intrinsic and those that are not. The reason for this characterization is that some philosophers consider them essential or intrinsic to particular philosophies, whereas others do not. The language or style in which a view is expressed is essential to the view, according to some authors, but others disagree, thinking on the contrary that a view can be expressed in a variety of ways and languages and yet be the same view. For the first, German is essential to the philosophy expressed in Kant's *Critique of Pure Reason*, for the second it is not.

Regardless of the position one takes with respect to this particular issue, historians often speak of certain philosophies as being characterized by their expression in a particular language, or by the style that is used in the texts that express it. French philosophy is philosophy written in French and German philosophy is philosophy written in German. Moreover, scholastic philosophy is philosophy that follows the scholastic style, and analytic philosophy is the philosophy that follows the analytic style, or so the argument goes.

The problem with this view is that neither language nor style functions as a necessary condition of many of these historiographical designations. Some German philosophy is written and carried out in German, but much of it is written in Latin. Indeed, there is even some current German philosophy that is written in English. And the case with style is even more compelling, for it is difficult to find a common style to all the particular philosophies that are identified by historians.

In short, the mentioned ways of distinguishing various particular philosophies are not always effective, even though in certain circumstances they can be. That is, they are useful labels that historians employ for certain determinate purposes, but these labels cannot be justified always in the same ways and in every context.

IV.   Latino Conceptions of Latino Philosophy

Latinos themselves, whether residing in the United States or in Latin America, have been concerned with Latino philosophy, although the labels under discussion differ, the two most common being 'Latino philosophy' in the United States and 'Latin American philosophy' in Latin America. I ignore these differences in the discussion for reasons given earlier.[3]

Two topics are pertinent for our discussion here. One is framed in terms of a question: Is there a Latino philosophy? Another concerns itself with distinguishing what is frequently called academic and non-academic philosophy,

---

[3]   The literature on this topic is quite extensive. Jorge J. E. Gracia and Iván Jaksić have collected the main texts in *Filosofía e identidad cultural en América Latina* (revised and expanded edition in preparation). For sources in English, see the third part of Jorge J. E. Gracia and Elizabeth Millán-Zaibert (eds.), *Latin American Philosophy for the 21st Century* (Buffalo, NY: Prometheus Books, 2004), and Jorge J. E. Gracia, "Identity and Latin American Philosophy," in Susana Nuccetelli (ed.), *Blackwell Companion to Latin American Philosophy* (Oxford: Blackwell, forthcoming).

although other terms are also used, such as western and non-western, European and autochthonous, genuine and imported, authentic and inauthentic, and so on. Both topics involve an understanding of philosophy in general and of Latino philosophy in particular. Elsewhere I have discussed in some detail the three most common approaches to the first topic and their understanding of philosophy: the universalist, culturalist, and critical. Here I present an abbreviated version of that discussion.[4]

The universalist views philosophy as a universal discipline and not different from science. Philosophy, like mathematics or physics, has an object that it studies and a method it employs in doing so. But neither the effectiveness of the method nor the truth value of the conclusions it reaches depend on particular circumstances or perspectives. Either material objects are composed of matter and form or they are not, and so Aristotelian hylomorphism is either true or false. The question of whether there is Latino philosophy, then, depends on whether Latinos have been able to produce the kind of universal discipline that one expects when one has science as a model. Its problems are common to all humans, its method is also common, and its conclusions are supposed to be true, regardless of particular circumstances. Just as water is composed of a certain proportion of hydrogen and oxygen, so there are certain conditions that determine the identity of an artifact over time. Most universalists see Latino philosophy as largely a failure in this respect.

The culturalist thinks, on the contrary, that truth is always perspectival, contingent on a point of view and that the method to acquire it is always dependent on a cultural context. Philosophy is a historical, non-scientific enterprise concerned with the elaboration of a general point of view from a certain personal or cultural perspective. But is there a Latino philosophy? Why not, culturalists ask? If Latinos have engaged in developing views from their perspective as individuals or as Latinos, and using whatever means they have found appropriate to do so, there cannot but be a Latino philosophy.

Finally, the critical approach considers philosophy a result of social conditions and closely related to those conditions. Some conditions are conducive to the production of philosophy, or what is sometimes called, authentic philosophy, whereas others are not. So, is there a Latino philosophy? For most critics the conditions operative in the area preclude the development of philosophy, because all the philosophy developed by Latinos is inauthentic and therefore not true philosophy. The dependence of Latin America on ideas imported from elsewhere, or its situation as dominated, prevents it from being authentic; its philosophy is borrowed and subservient.

---

[4] See ch. 5 of Jorge J. E. Gracia, *Hispanic/Latino Identity: A Philosophical Perspective* (Oxford: Blackwell, 2000).

The second topic that has dominated discussions of Latino philosophy by Latinos is concerned with the kind of philosophy that is practiced by Latinos. One is the philosophy developed in the academy, similar to what the scholastics developed in schools. It is a result of school activities and developed for academic purposes, the solution to puzzles of interest primarily to academics. The other is the philosophy developed outside the academy, and this responds to the needs and conditions under which it is developed. Its mode of expression is not academic, so it is frequently literary or polemical, and its concerns are not scholarly but real problems and issues confronted by Latinos. Often culturalists and critical philosophers accuse universalists of being academic philosophers, and therefore of not being authentic or responsive to the practical and social needs of Latinos. Universalists respond by accusing culturalists and critical philosophers of not doing philosophy at all, but rather of developing the kind of personal or cultural narrative that has no scientific or universal value.

It should be obvious that these positions beg the question insofar as they begin with pre-established conceptions of philosophy that de-legitimize others. The issue, then, does not have to do with Latino philosophy as such, but with the nature of philosophy. It should also be clear that the answer given to the questions we have asked is not descriptive but rather prescriptive: we are normatively told what is or is not Latino philosophy, and therefore how we should think about, and deal with, it in the classroom and as historiographers.

So far little headway has been made when it comes to answering the question we have raised in a way that does not beg the question or even is useful for understanding the issues involved. Here I propose a model to answer the question. The model is the conception of Latino philosophy as an ethnic philosophy. This should serve to see how it is different and similar to other philosophies, including scientific or universalist philosophy, and it should help us decide what to include in courses on Latino philosophy and in its historiography.

V. Latino Philosophy as Ethnic Philosophy

An ethnic philosophy is the philosophy of an ethnos, so we must begin by adopting a conception of ethnos, and the one I propose is the Familial-Historical View presented in chapter 1. According to this conception, the main feature of an ethnic group is that it is like a large family in which no members necessarily have to share a common feature in order to belong to it, but nonetheless develop relations owing to historical conditions that in turn produce properties common to at least some members of the group which serve to unite them and to distinguish them in context from members of other groups. That there is no necessarily identifiable feature, or set of features, common to all members of an ethnic group throughout the history of the group accounts for the lack of agreement among members of ethnic groups, and among those who study them, concerning any particular conditions, or even kinds of conditions, that are necessary and sufficient for ethnicity.

An important consequence of this understanding of ethnicity is that there are seldom strict boundaries between ethne. Some people clearly belong, and some clearly do not belong, but there are others whose membership is not clear. This is not a corollary of the Familial-Historical View, but rather something quite evident in our experience. My view merely accommodates it. Consider the case of Latinos in the United States. I clearly belong because I was born in Cuba, have unique historical relations to other Cubans and some other Latinos, share in a diverse Latino culture some of whose features are common to some other Latinos, and so on. Clearly, my sons-in-law are not Latinos. One has English ancestry and his contact with Latino cultures is only secondhand, through marriage. And something similar can be said about the other. But what are we to say about the children they have with my daughters? Are they Latinos? The case is not clear. In short, ethnic boundaries are not always strict, and I say "not always" because there are some ethne in which they seem to be, while in others they are not.

When we apply this notion of ethnicity to philosophy, we get the view that an ethnic philosophy is the philosophy of an ethnos, and insofar as it is so, and members of ethne do not necessarily share features in common, the philosophy of a particular ethnos will not require any properties in common with other philosophies outside the ethnos or even within the ethnos everywhere it is located and throughout its history. This, I claim, is the best way of understanding the unity of Latino philosophy.

Historians of philosophy have worked very hard trying to find something common to the philosophy produced by Latinos, particularly Latin Americans, but they have failed miserably. I count myself among those who have tried, but reality has defeated us. It is indisputable that there are common elements between various philosophers, or even some philosophical movements, in Latin America. There is much that is common among scholastic authors or among positivists, for example. But it is not possible to find anything common throughout the history of Latino philosophy even if we consider only those authors that everyone agrees are part of it: no themes, no topics, no method, no language, and so on. Still we can explain the unity of Latino philosophy if we understand it as an ethnic philosophy. Latino philosophy is one insofar as all its parts are related in various ways that have helped develop particular properties in context, and which separate it from the philosophy of France or Britain. The unity of this philosophy, just like that of the Latino ethnos, has to do with contextual historical relations, and these also help to distinguish it from other philosophies in context.

What determines membership in an ethnos consists of both the internal and external factors that shape it in a unique way in a particular context. And so it is with the philosophy of an ethnos: Latino philosophy is the philosophy the Latino ethnos has developed in the circumstances in which the members of the ethnos have found themselves throughout history. It makes no sense to impose non-ethnic criteria on an ethnic philosophy. We cannot apply universalist criteria to a philosophy developed by a particular ethnos. Nor does it make sense to apply to Latino philosophy ethnic criteria developed by other ethne. We cannot apply to it criteria that were developed in Indian, French, or British philosophy, and then say that, because it does not fit those criteria it is not philosophy or not good philosophy. What Latino philosophy is, when it is understood ethnically, can be asked only in the context of the Latino ethnos.

As with an ethnos, membership qualifications are negotiated and depend on a variety of factors, some external and some internal. They have to do with what actually happens historically. One of those factors is what the members of the ethnos itself think, although this is neither a necessary nor a sufficient condition of inclusion or exclusion.

The advantage of this view is that it explains the historical continuity of Latino philosophy. It also explains that it may include texts that are not included in the history of philosophy of other ethne, or in scientific, universal philosophy. And it also explains how it is different, and why, from other philosophies. Moreover, it also serves to solve some of the problems concerning inclusion and exclusion raised at the beginning of this chapter, or at least raise questions regarding it that are interesting. What do we do with the *Popol Vuh*, Las Casas, Sor Juana, Romero, Fanon, Gaos, Neri-Castañeda, Borges, and Llorente? Are they part of Latino philosophy?

What do we do with the *Popol Vuh* and similar pre-Columbian texts? Susana Nuccetelli and Gary Seay include these texts in their recent anthology of Latin American philosophy, but they speak of them as "thought" rather than philosophy.[5] And Elizabeth Millán-Zaibert and I come right out and say that they are not philosophy strictly speaking; indeed, we do not include them in our anthology of Latin American philosophy cited earlier. On the other hand, Miguel León-Portilla, among others, has argued that they are to be considered part of Latin American philosophy.[6] Who is right?

---

[5]   Susana Nuccetelli and Gary Seay (eds.), *Latin American Philosophy: An Introduction with Readings* (Prentice-Hall: Upper Saddle River, 2004).

[6]   Miguel León-Portilla, *Time and Reality in the Thought of the Maya*, 2nd ed. (Norman, OK: University of Oklahoma Press, 1988). See also Laureano Robles (ed.), *Filosofía iberoamericana en la época del Encuentro* (Madrid: Editorial Trotta: Consejo Superior de Investigaciones Científicas, 1992).

If we were to adopt a strict understanding of philosophy as we have it (as exemplified in college curricula, journals, and other similar venues) in the West, they could not qualify. We do not include Genesis or the Egyptian *Book of the Dead* among the sources that are discussed in courses on western philosophy, so why should we include the *Popol Vuh*? On what bases can we justify their inclusion in a course or in an investigation into Latino philosophy? Legitimacy? Ideology? Authenticity? Pedagogy? Historiography?

However, if we adopt an ethnic conception of Latino philosophy, the issue becomes different and more complex, for then it turns on how these texts are related to the ethnos and what counts as philosophy for the ethnos. If there is such an ethnos as Latino, as I have argued, we can ask whether these texts are part of what counts as philosophy in the context of this ethnos. This means that whether they are to be accepted or not as Latino philosophy is not measured by some exclusively external standard of rationality, topical relevance, or methodology. Membership in an ethnos is contextual and historical, and what counts as something belonging to the ethnos, such as its philosophy, is not determined exclusively from the outside; it is negotiated between the outside and the inside, and it is determined for particular times and places, just as ethnic identity is. Although one can speculate that in the realm of possibility there might be ethne that are determined exclusively by internal factors – what the members of the ethne think – and others might be determined exclusively by external factors – causes other than the thinking of the ethne – in most ethne the factors that determine it are both internal and external. And this is very much the case of Latino philosophy.

Is the *Popol Vuh* to be included in Latino philosophy? The issue now shifts to whether pre-Columbians can be considered part of the Latino ethnos and why. Moreover, the question for us has also to do with how the Latino ethnos functions, is regarded by others, and regards itself. Tomorrow is another day, of course, and things might change. But this is just as it should be, for ethne are fluid historical phenomena.

Still, you probably want me to tell you what I think about the *Popol Vuh*: Does it belong or not to Latino philosophy? I do not want to answer the question, because I do not find it philosophically interesting. The interesting issue has to do rather with the kind of question we should ask in order to determine whether the *Popol Vuh* is part of Latino philosophy or not. And this, I claim, is different from the question that historiographers and Latinos have asked so far. Once the right kind of question is asked, I contend, we can proceed to examine possible answers, most of which will have to be dealt with in disciplines other than philosophy, such as history and sociology. But the issues that the question I propose raises are very different from what Latinos and historiographers of Latino philosophy have been asking thus far.

Let me add three more comments before I move to the next section, where I compare Latino philosophy with "scientific" philosophy. First, an ethnic philosophy, just as an ethnos, has no strict boundaries for all times and places. What counts as Latino philosophy considered ethnically may vary a great deal throughout the history of the ethnos. Second, an ethnic philosophy depends on the existence of the ethnos. If Latinos do not constitute an ethnos, then the whole notion of a Latino philosophy falls apart. Third, what is included in Latino philosophy, considered ethnically, can be much more, or much less, than if it is conceived differently.

When we adopt an ethnic understanding of Latino philosophy, we also encounter questions about its relationship to other philosophies, particularly "scientific, universal" philosophy, and American philosophy. I take up these questions in what remains of this chapter.

VI.　Latino Philosophy and "Scientific" Philosophy

The first question that we need to ask is whether "scientific" philosophy is itself ethnic. Science is heavily influenced by its context and the culture and environment in which it occurs, but science attempts to divest itself from those trappings and achieve a status that goes beyond such contexts. I think it is clear that it often succeeds. The claim "Taking an aspirin pill everyday generally helps prevent heart attacks in males" has been shown to be true.

However, the issue concerned with the independence of science from culture is not undisputed.[7] Some philosophers think that science can never entirely divest itself from its context, whereas others believe it can. We cannot settle this issue here, but we should be able to agree that most scientists regard science as striving to make claims that are not bound by context or perspective (the terminology varies from author to author), and science succeeds in doing so to some extent. This means that science can never be considered ethnic, as least in its purpose, and that what counts as science cannot be tied necessarily to an ethnos. In this, science is very different from ethnic philosophy, such as I have presented in the case of Latino philosophy.

So, we may ask, are British, European, French, Iberian, Roman, Greek, and western philosophies ethnic (I deal with American philosophy separately)? Clearly, most philosophers in these groups have thought of themselves as non-ethnic. Indeed, many of them have considered themselves to be scientists of a sort. But there has always been a group of philosophers, some even considered

---

[7]　See, for example, the discussion in Martin Kusch (ed.), *The Sociology of Philosophical Knowledge* (Dordrecht, Netherlands: Kluwer, 2000).

to be anti-philosophers by others, who have argued that some, or all, of these philosophies are the sort of thing I have claimed to be ethnic. Others think that, although these philosophies might have included ethnic elements at some point, their aim has always been scientific, and this aim sufficiently justifies their universal status. Why? Because the standards for inclusion as good philosophy have to do with methods and standards of truth that are not ethnically bound.

Obviously, we are not going to settle this issue here, nor do we need to in order to make the point I want to make. The point is that we can conceive Latino philosophy in at least two ways. We can think of it in ethnic terms, as the expression of a particular group of people who have been related in various ways in a historical context and who have developed a view about the world, including philosophy, that is informed by the circumstances in which they have found themselves. If we do this, we can then proceed to ask about which texts and figures fit that model, and the standards of inclusion are probably going to be different from those adopted in a non-ethnic model of Latino philosophy. In the non-ethnic model, the standards that count are those that philosophers all over the world have been trying to develop independently of ethnic contexts. So, only what meets those standards produced by Latinos, whether in the United States or in Latin America, qualifies as philosophy, and the labels 'Latino' or 'Latin American' merely refer to provenance.

The same Latino author or text may or may not count as part of Latino philosophy considered ethnically and as part of scientific, universal philosophy. We might want to say that the *Popul Vuh* counts as part of Latino philosophy considered ethnically, but that it does not count as part of scientific, universal philosophy. The cases of Romero and Frondizi are different for they count as part of both. And could there be someone who counts as part of scientific, universal philosophy in Latin America and not as part of Latino philosophy considered ethnically? There is no reason why not, although it would depend on the criteria of inclusion in Latino philosophy developed by the Latino ethnos. At present there would not be anyone, for the criteria of inclusion in Latino philosophy conceived ethnically includes those who work in scientific, universal philosophy.

One corollary of my position is the need to keep a broad conception of philosophy within which there are many varieties of the discipline. In the sixties and seventies, it was common for practitioners of British ordinary language philosophy to go around departments of philosophy saying that other people in the departments who did not practice their kind of philosophy were not philosophers and that their work did not count as philosophy. This dismissive attitude has never been absent in the United States, and it is frequently found among Latinos, both analytic and Continental, to name just two widespread philosophical traditions.

What can one gain from this attitude, except a sense of power in disenfranchising others? Would it not be more fruitful to try to understand what the other is doing that he or she calls philosophy? This is what I have tried to do here. My aim has been to show that there is a way of understanding philosophy in ethnic terms, apart from its understanding as, say, a universal science. Moreover, understanding philosophy ethnically explains why in certain parts of the world, philosophy is more broadly conceived than in other parts, and includes literature and religious treatises. Indeed, what counts as philosophy, understood ethnically, is very much a matter of context. To open the door to the understanding of philosophy in this way does not in any way undermine doing philosophy in some other way, for example, as a universal science, if that is indeed possible, which brings me to a last point.

We should be aware that many of the philosophies that have been peddled as scientific are anything but that. Recall that the very notion of science has changed much in the history of the West, let alone in the history of the world. What the scholastics conceived as science is quite different from what the moderns conceived as science. For the scholastics science consisted in the development of a deductive system in which conclusions followed necessarily from premises which were self-evident or based on self-evident premises, whereas for authors such as Francis Bacon and John Stuart Mill, science was a primarily inductive enterprise. So here again, to talk about a scientific philosophy must be qualified and contextualized, for what it may mean can be very different, depending on what one understands by science.

If scientific philosophy is philosophy that imitates science as this is practiced in the West today, I do not know that there are any current scientific philosophers. Just read the most "scientific" of them and you will find many holes, unsupported statements, unwarranted speculation, unempirical claims, and unquestioned assumptions, let alone undefined terms and shoddy methodology. Not too long ago, one of my daughters, who teaches medicine at a fancy university, told me that she was doing some research on the relation between race and medicine. I suggested that she look at some philosophical literature on the subject, and she did. But she found it completely useless, full of hot air, unsupported claims, and ideological assumptions. I was not surprised. Philosophy is not science and it has never been science, when science is conceived in the terms in which it is carried out in science departments of universities today. Those philosophers who claim that what they are doing is scientific, as the members of the Vienna Circle did, are often ignorant of science and blind to the enterprise in which they are engaged. They think what they do is science because they have numbered propositions in their papers and they talk about x, y, P, and Q. But there is more to science than that.

Of course, one can be in favor of clarity and rigor. One can be concerned with the same kinds of problems that Plato and Aristotle were concerned with. One can even understand that to do certain conceptual analyses logic is necessary, a point that Abelard made several centuries ago, repeating, without knowing it, a claim implied in much of what Aristotle and some other ancient philosophers did. And one can strive, as scientists do, to make claims whose truth does not depend on particular perspectives or cultures. But none of this entails that only philosophy that is so is philosophy, for even the greatest practitioners of clarity and rigor often fall short of the standards they would like to meet. Indeed, many of them are not even trying to be clear and rigorous in practice. And something similar can be said about their method and aims. It makes better sense to say that some of them practice philosophy with certain standards in mind, or that they belong to a philosophical tradition in which clarity and rigor are part of the *modus operandi*, although most philosophers who engage in self-criticism know that the validity of such standards is a matter of debate among philosophers and no general agreement about what they are has been achieved, even among those who claim to have and follow them. There are philosophers that follow other standards, and there are philosophers whose standards are set by their ethnic context, and this should not disqualify them from being labeled philosophers, even if they cannot be labeled "scientific" philosophers.

VII.   Universalism, Culturalism, and Critical Philosophy Revisited

How is the proposal I have presented concerning Latino philosophy different from the universalist, culturalist, and critical views defended by some Latino philosophers mentioned earlier? It accepts the view, contrary to what many hard culturalists argue, that there is a legitimate conception of philosophy that is not bound by context or perspective in aim or method, but this has to be qualified in two ways: First, the aim does not necessarily translate into a reality; indeed, it becomes very difficult to find philosophy that is completely neutral to context and perspective, even if its method is codified in non-contextual or perspectival terms. Second, this does not entail that philosophy is scientific in any sense of science that is current today, although this does not mean that it is not a rigorous enterprise that aims for universal validity.

The view presented differs from the culturalist view in that it makes room for a universalist philosophy, and from the universalist view in that it locates the universalist aspect of philosophy in its aim and method, rather than on a certain achievement of that aim even when the method is implemented. It also differs from the culturalist view in that the culturalist view is not an ethnic view. For the culturalist, what is important is the cultural perspective from which the philosophy is developed, and the originality that is supposed to result from that. But in ethnic philosophy what is important is the identity of an ethnos and what is considered philosophy for that ethnos. This means that ethnic philosophy is not bound by any single set of criteria, for ethne are changing realities whose parameters are historically contingent. And something similar applies to the critical position. Questions of authenticity, domination, and so on, do not enter into the picture at all unless they are relevant for a particular ethnic philosophy.

Having said this, it should be clear that the overall aim of my answer to the question, What is Latino philosophy?, has been to open a window to a dimension of reality that we otherwise would miss. And, of course, the reason for opening this window is that we need to decide what to study and what to teach when we study and teach Latino philosophy. We also need to answer the question Latinos have posed about the existence of our philosophy. Finally, there is also a deeper philosophical aim, namely the opening of a window to a different set of questions and ways of posing the problems of the nature of Latino philosophy in particular and of philosophy in general. Rather than sitting in judgment about what philosophy is or is not from a particular conception of the discipline, I have suggested a way of initiating a discussion that should be more profitable insofar as it engages a set of issues that otherwise would be ignored. If, as Aristotle said, curiosity is characteristic of humans, then we should welcome openings of this sort, rather than positions that preclude further discussion.

Is the distinction between ethnic and non-ethnic philosophy useful when thinking about Latino philosophy? I think so. If we adopt the ethnic model we are able to see things that we would not see otherwise, and vice versa, with the non-ethnic model. As historians of philosophy and as philosophers interested in Latino philosophy and the philosophically interesting historiographical issues raised by it, we can profit from both models, and it is fruitless to insist that we adopt one to the exclusion of the other.

It makes sense to use the notion of an ethnic philosophy to think about Latino philosophy, because Latino philosophy is precisely the philosophy of the Latino ethnos understood as the overall group to which all Latinos belong whether living in the United States or Latin America, or as a part of that ethnos. However, for Latinos living in the United States, their philosophy is part of the philosophy carried out in the United States, so we should explore that relationship. Let me turn, then, to the notion of American philosophy.

VIII.   American Philosophy

We can ask the same question we asked about Latino philosophy concerning American philosophy. Even to raise the question might appear extraordinary, for surely there appears to be a clearly American philosophy, and a great one indeed it is! Think of James, Dewey, Peirce, Santayana, and Royce, not to mention some recent arrivals in the scene such as Quine, Rorty, and Davidson. But is the answer so clear? For those who have kept up with what has been going on in the Society for the Advancement of American Philosophy (henceforth SAAP) for the past few years, this question is not new. We need only go back to John Stuhr's spirited response to the presidential address by Charlene Haddock Seigfried in 1998.[8] Stuhr presents this question as originally one of the two strategies one can pursue when trying to answer another question: Is American philosophy worth advancing? This strategy, which he characterizes as "characteristic of contemporary academic philosophy" when pursued in isolation from the second strategy, does not represent "philosophy in America at its best." American philosophy at its best should echo "classical American philosophy" in its aim to "develop strategies that will contribute to the advance of intelligence and shared meanings in real lives." When it does, American philosophy is worth advancing, but when it does not, then it is not.

Although I am very sympathetic to the practical aim that Stuhr identifies for American philosophy, I am puzzled by his dismissal of the theoretical question concerning the nature of American philosophy. After all, he does use the term 'American philosophy,' and it seems rather odd to hold that attempting to develop a clear understanding of what a term one uses means is somehow counterproductive. More puzzling still is the claim that one should not ask for such clarification unless one is involved in a practical project such as the one Stuhr points to. I am also puzzled by his reference to academic philosophy. Does he mean to exclude himself from this? If I am not mistaken, Stuhr pursues philosophy in the Academy and the articles that are read in SAAP meetings and are published in the *Transactions of the Charles S. Peirce Society*, where his essay appeared, are nothing if not academic. Of course, Stuhr might have something different in mind from what is usually meant by 'academic,' but then I think we are entitled to ask him what that is.

Here I am not going to dispute any of these points, or assail the view that Stuhr has articulated. Rather, I am going to pursue the very question he deems

[8]   John J. Stuhr, "Sidetracking American Philosophy," *Transactions of the Charles S. Peirce Society* 34, 4 (1998), 841–60.

to be both academic and counterproductive. I hope to show that there is nothing wrong with the question, although there are some things wrong with the assumptions many make when asking it, and it is these assumptions that produce answers that are clearly wrong, or at least puzzling. Indeed, I believe it is probable that Stuhr's objections against the question are the result precisely of such assumptions. My ultimate goal is to see how Latino philosophy is related to American philosophy.

Although recent publications indicate the existence of disagreements as to the proper way of understanding American philosophy, most authors writing about it in the United States agree that this is a historically justified label.[9] If we travel a few hundred miles to the South and cross the Río Grande, however, the answer to the question has never been taken for granted, and in fact the issue raised by the question has been a topic of discussion since the nineteenth century and of heated debate since the 1940s.[10] In Latin America, what is meant by 'American philosophy,' or more properly in Spanish, *una filosofía americana*, is something quite different.

It is not necessary to recount the many debates around this issue here, nor do I want to dispute the views of those who would respond to the question I have raised with an emphatic "yes." Rather, I want to point to an aspect of this matter that can have some philosophical interest, in addition to whatever purely historical interest it may have for the understanding of Latino philosophy. I present it as a claim with two bases: first, the term 'American philosophy' has more than one meaning and, therefore, can produce ambiguities when it appears in a question such as the one we have raised. Second, even when the different and pertinent meanings of the term are distinguished, we still can raise a question as to whether it makes sense to speak of an American philosophy in the senses identified, for in order to be able to do so we would have to explain how that meaning is justified by a historical fact, namely the unity of the kind of American philosophy in question.

My task here is threefold: first, I identify three senses of 'American philosophy' that are pertinent for our discussion; second, I point out that the most

---

[9] Apart from the above-mentioned article by Stuhr, see also: Charlene Haddock Seigfried, "Advancing American Philosophy," *Transactions of the Charles S. Peirce Society* 34, 4 (1998), 807–39; Leonard Harris, "Prolegomenon to a Tradition: What is American Philosophy?" in Leonard Harris, Scott L. Pratt, and Anne S. Waters (eds.), *American Philosophies: An Anthology* (Oxford: Blackwell, 2002), pp. 5–6; and Scott L. Pratt, *Native Pragmatism: Rethinking the Roots of American Philosophy* (Bloomington, IN: Indiana University Press, 2002).

[10] See the various texts presented in Gracia and Jaksić (eds.), *Filosofía e identidad cultural en América Latina*.

common ways in which these meanings are justified do not make historiographical sense; and, third, I argue for a way of justifying at least two, if not
all three, of these senses of 'American philosophy.' And all of this is done, let
us not forget, to help us establish the relation between Latino and American
philosophy.

A.   Three senses of 'American philosophy'

When a good number of philosophers hear the term 'American philosophy,'
they think of it as the philosophy produced in the United States. This is one
of the standard ways in which the term is used and understood. American
philosophy in this sense is the philosophy produced by Americans when these
are in turn understood as United States citizens. Indeed, this sense of the term
has spread widely. In Europe, this is how the term is commonly used today,
and even in Latin America, this use of the term has made inroads. The roots
of this usage can be traced back in part to the use of the term 'America' to refer
to the United States.

But this is not the only meaning attached to the expression 'American philosophy.'[11] In Latin America there are two other meanings that are also present.
One goes back to the fact that the term 'America' was attached to what in the
United States is now commonly known as 'the Americas,' that is North,
Central, and South America and the Caribbean islands. Corresponding to this
broad concept of America, there is a concept of American philosophy, in which
the term refers to the philosophy produced anywhere in the Americas. This
meaning of the term is very widespread in Latin America, although it is slowly
losing ground to the narrower one mentioned earlier.[12]

In addition, some Latin American authors have from time to time spoken
of America as what José Martí called "our America," and by this they mean
what is often referred to as Latin America in the United States. That is, they
think of America primarily as Latin America, and when they speak of the part
of the Americas that are not this, they qualify their expressions, saying something like "North America" or "Anglo America," for example. Corresponding
to this, we have a sense of American philosophy as the philosophy of Latin

---

[11]   I assume that it makes no difference whether one uses the English term 'American
philosophy' or the Spanish term *'filosofía americana.'*

[12]   Examples of this use are everywhere, but see, for example, the abstracts of several
of the presentations made in the section entitled "En torno a la filosofía americana"
of the Third Inter-American Congress of Philosophy, in *El Tercer Congreso
Interamericano de Filosofía* (La Habana: Publicaciones de la Sociedad Cubana de
Filosofía, 1950), pp. 49–64.

America, or the philosophy of America which is not produced in Anglo America (that is, the United States and Canada).[13]

In short, we have at least three different senses of 'American philosophy': the philosophy produced in the United States, the philosophy produced in the whole of the Americas, and the philosophy produced in Latin America.

A side point that perhaps would be interesting to explore, but to which I refer only briefly, concerns the reasons why all three of these senses of the term 'America,' and the corresponding expression 'American philosophy,' have developed. Clearly, the senses of 'America' are primary, and it is only secondarily that philosophy has been brought into the picture. So we may ask: What factors have played a role in developing the primary meanings of 'America'?

It seems clear that these have to do, at least to a great extent, with power, wealth, and ideology. The assignation of the name 'America' to the United States certainly appears to have to do in some ways with the power and wealth of the United States. This kind of phenomenon is not new, and can apply to nations as well as languages. For example, the term 'Spanish' has come to be associated with the language of the Castilians most likely because Castilians became the dominant people in the Iberian peninsula. The term *Hispania* was first adopted by the Romans to refer to the entire Iberian peninsula, but the derivative term 'Spanish' did not maintain its peninsular breadth, at least when it came to languages. Likewise, the power and wealth of the United States has been influential in the adoption of 'America' as a name for this country.

The case with the use of 'America' for Latin America, of course, cannot be made along the same lines. Here the rationale is perhaps a matter of ideology, for it could be the result of a reaction against the widespread use of the term to refer to the United States. Those who favor this use are very much aware of the power and wealth of the United States, and they want to put limits to it.

Let me now go back to the particular issue that is pertinent to us. And let me begin by raising a question that has to do with the justifications that are commonly used for the conception of American philosophy along the three lines indicated. First, I consider these justifications in general, as they would apply to historiographical characterizations of philosophy in order to see whether they make sense. I am concerned with characterizations such as French philosophy and Italian philosophy, as well as medieval philosophy and Eastern philosophy, because it seems that these have much in common when it comes to their historiographical legitimacy, but I am not concerned with characterizations such as Hegelian philosophy or good philosophy. The last two involve either authorial or value concerns that complicate matters in different ways.

---

[13]   Ibid.

B. Unity of American philosophy

I adopt a general, and hopefully not too controversial, understanding of a philosophy as a view of the world or any of its parts that seeks to be accurate, consistent, comprehensive, and supported by sound evidence. Because philosophical views are developed through human activity, we can also speak of philosophy as the very activity whereby we develop such views. And because we communicate through texts and express philosophical views in texts, we can also speak of philosophy as texts. Finally, we also speak of a philosophy as a set of procedures, skills, or even habits related to the development of views of the sort mentioned.[14] For our purposes, however, and in order to simplify matters, I adopt the first understanding, according to which a philosophy is fundamentally a view that meets the specified conditions. This makes sense to the extent that all other understandings of philosophy seem to be derived from it, or to have it as its goal. The goal of the activity of philosophizing and of the procedures to be followed in philosophizing is philosophical views. And the function of the texts we often call philosophy is precisely to communicate philosophical views.

We need not consider the case of American philosophy understood as Latin American philosophy because I have already presented a way of understanding Latin American philosophy as part of the larger category of Latino philosophy, and our concern is precisely with the relation of Latino philosophy to American philosophy understood in some other way. Let's consider, then, the case of American philosophy when this is understood as the philosophy produced in the United States.

I am not an expert in this field, but let me suggest nonetheless that it would seem very difficult to find in one or more of the factors mentioned earlier, the conditions that justify the unity of American philosophy conceived in this sense. This claim is supported by those experts in the history of American philosophy who have discussed the identity of American philosophy. Compare the styles and philosophical assumptions of Quine and Royce, for example. Territory does not seem to help, for there have been "American philosophers" who have worked in Mexico and Europe. Even the language is not a determining factor both because there are many non-American philosophers who

---

[14] I have developed these views at greater length in Jorge J. E. Gracia, *Metaphysics and Its Task: The Categorial Foundation of Knowledge* (Albany, NY: State University of New York Press, 1999). See also the volume of critical essays and my responses in Robert Delfino (ed.), *What Are We to Understand Gracia to Mean? Realist Challenges to Metaphysical Neutralism* (New York: Rodopi, 2006).

express themselves in English and there are American philosophers who express themselves in Spanish. There are not many of the latter yet, but I think we are going to see an increase in their number as time goes on and the Latino population of the United States increases.

Second, consider American philosophy understood as the philosophy of the Americas. This case should be easy to deal with, for if its two major components, Latin American or Latino philosophy on one hand and United States (and Canadian) philosophy on the other, do not have anything that explains their respective unities, then the unity of the two components put together would most likely remain unexplained.

In short, the criteria commonly used to account for the unity of American philosophy understood in the ways mentioned here do not appear to work. So, we may ask: Does this mean that we must abandon the idea of American philosophy altogether, or that, as Stuhr suggests, we should abandon the question about its nature? The answer is yes when it refers to American philosophy as United States philosophy. But this does not mean that we must abandon the attempt to account for the unity of the philosophy of such authors as Quine and Royce. And what label should we use and how should we understand that philosophy?

The label I propose is one parallel to Latino philosophy, namely, Anglo philosophy. This, like Latino philosophy, would be very general, and include reference within it to communities who live outside the United States, and communities that live within the United States. To Latinos in the United States and in Latin America would correspond Anglos in the United States, England, and Australia, for example. And to Latino philosophy and Latin American philosophy would correspond Anglo philosophy in the United States, England, and Australia. The unity of this philosophy is to be found in the historical, relational, and familial view I have proposed earlier to account for Latino philosophy, corresponding to the Anglo ethnos.

The reason none of the justifications of American philosophy that are usually proposed work is that they are based on the wrong conception of the kind of unity that such a philosophy can have. And I believe that it is likely that this assumption is also behind Stuhr's judgment about American philosophy. These justifications cash out the unity of American philosophy in terms of necessary and sufficient conditions or, as others put it, in essentialist terms. The idea is that American philosophy, in any of the ways in which we have understood it, is justified because anything that qualifies as part of it shares in certain features that are necessary, sufficient, or both to make it part of American philosophy. Some authors identify these features with a particular location, others with the people who produced the philosophy, still others think in terms of a certain style, some refer to assumptions, and so on.

Consider the long-established view that American philosophy is to be identified with pragmatism.[15] This is understood to involve a certain style of doing philosophy, a concern for certain particular topics, and the use of certain strategies to deal with them. Much is made of the attention paid to experience, social practices, practical application, and a conception of truth in terms of "what works." Indeed, the effort to identify this core of characteristics has recently received a boost from Latino/Hispanic philosophers who have tried to explore the relations between Latino/Latin American/Hispanic philosophy and American philosophy, and have seen in pragmatism a bridge of sorts between them.[16]

But how the various elements of this core can be put together is rather controversial, for when one looks carefully at pragmatists, one discovers a rather bewildering variety of emphases, approaches, and views. For someone like Charles Sanders Peirce, pragmatism seems to be primarily a matter of meaning. William James, by contrast, emphasizes more a subjective and personal aspect. And John Dewey appears to be more concerned with the community, whence his interest in education. How can all these be lumped together? Perhaps under very general labels that can then be interpreted differently in more particular terms when we speak of individual authors and their thought. But do we need to do this? Do we need to understand pragmatism as a kind of Procrustean bed on which all American philosophers are to be stretched? Where are the particular properties – the views, the specific methods – that justify the label?

Mind you, I am not arguing against using the label 'pragmatism.' I am not even arguing against understanding it in a very general way to refer to a rough core of properties, some of which are shared by certain philosophers or their philosophies. I am merely questioning whether the label means that there is a set of necessary and sufficient conditions that apply to every pragmatist or to his or her philosophy. And I am even more skeptical when the label is used to describe all American philosophy.

Surely not every figure whose views are discussed in books on the history of American philosophy is a pragmatist, even when this is taken very generally. We do not have to go hunting for counterexamples in histories of philosophy;

---

[15] See Elizabeth Flower and Murray G. Murphy, *A History of Philosophy in America* (New York: Capricorn Books, 1977).

[16] See Gregory Pappas, "The Latino Character of American Pragmatism," *Transactions of the Charles S. Peirce Society* 34 (1998), 93–112, and José Medina, "Pragmatism and Ethnicity: Critique, Reconstruction, and the New Hispanic," *Metaphilosophy* 35 (2004), 115–46 (reprinted in R. Shusterman (ed.), *The Range of Pragmatism and the Limits of Philosophy* (Oxford: Blackwell, 2004), pp. 112–43).

we have ready examples at hand. Am I not an American philosopher? Have I not been educated in the United States, write philosophy in English, and work in an American university? Am I not considered to be an American philosopher? Yet, I am certainly not a pragmatist. The number of philosophers who fit the category of being American philosophers and not being pragmatists is very large. Indeed, it includes many phenomenologists, existentialists, Marxists, Thomists, and so on.

I think it would be much better to realize that pragmatism is not a historically accurate description of all American philosophy. And, as I have argued, it is much better to understand American philosophy as Anglo philosophy, when this is conceived, as I have done with Latino philosophy, in historical, relational, and familial terms, as an ethnic philosophy. Anglo philosophy is best conceived as a set of views about the world that are historically related in ways that make it possible to distinguish them from other views and to group them together. It is not necessary that they all have the same assumptions, and so on. It is sufficient that whatever belongs to Anglo philosophy be related to other views that also qualify as Anglo philosophy in ways that separate them from still other views.

Earlier I used this theory to explain the unity characteristic of Latino philosophy, and I believe the same strategy can be used to explain the unity of Anglo philosophy in principle. In order to justifiably conclude that this is the case in fact, however, we need to do more, namely, to examine whether Anglo philosophy understood in the way I suggest displays even this kind of unity.

So, what philosophy is SAAP devoted to studying? It could either be (1) the part of Anglo philosophy that is produced in the United States, or (2) all philosophy that takes place in the United States. Can we understand the unity of (1) or (2) in familial, historical, and relational terms? Only specialists in this area can answer this question. I am in no position to do it with any sense of security and certainty. But even from the perspective of a non-specialist, it looks like one could make a case that (1) can be understood in this way, justifying the putting together of such philosophers as Edwards, Jefferson, Quine, Santayana, Weiss, Farber, Owens, Rorty, Beardsley, and Lonergan. If it is understood as (2), however, the familial historical connection becomes more of a problem, because even Latino philosophy in the United States would have to be included.

Naturally, the conclusions one reaches concerning the understanding of American philosophy as the philosophy of the United States will determine to some extent what we make of American philosophy in the other sense, namely, as the philosophy of the Americas, or Latino and Anglo philosophy combined. If it turns out that there is no way of explaining the unity of Latino and Anglo philosophies considered separately, it would appear to make little sense to try to account for their unity when they are considered together. Of course, logically it would still be possible that there be some unity to American philosophy considered as the product of everything produced in the Americas, but this is unlikely if there is no unity to each of its two major components. If there is some unity to each of its two major components, however, as I have argued, the question remains as to whether there is some unity to this overall notion of American philosophy. For this, I think the evidence is limited. It is a fact that some Anglo philosophers have had an impact on Latino philosophy, although this influence can never be compared with the influence that some European philosophers have had on it. Consider, for example, the impact that authors such as Max Scheler, Nicolai Hartmann, and José Ortega y Gasset had on Latino philosophy. A substantial number of the philosophical writings produced in Latin America in the first three-quarters of the twentieth century make reference to these authors, the problems they posed, and the positions they adopted. By contrast, one finds only occasional references to Anglo philosophy; one has to look hard to find them.

Moreover, whatever influence there has been, it has been a one-way street, for references to Latino philosophy by Anglo philosophers are practically non-existent. There is the occasional scholar of the history of philosophy who pays some attention to Latino philosophy, but none of the major philosophers seems to have taken notice of Latino philosophy, let alone to consider its merits seriously.

All this supports the view that the notion of an American philosophy as the philosophy of the Americas makes no sense historically, for the philosophies produced in Latin America and Anglo America do not share many relations that would justify giving them one label. Indeed, what we find is an effort, quite frequent among some Latino philosophers, to distance themselves from anything that has to do with Anglo philosophy. The characterizations made of Anglo philosophy by these authors are quite unflattering and the moral they often try to draw is that Latino philosophy should keep as far away from Anglo philosophy as possible. Still, one could argue that this very antagonistic attitude points to a certain relation between Latino philosophy and Anglo philosophy which could be used to distinguish the philosophy of the Americas from the philosophy of other places in the world. Moreover, although no one can predict what the future will bring, greater communication between the North and the South, and the increase of Latino philosophers in the United States might pave the way for more exchanges between Latino and Anglo philosophy, and thus perhaps for the formation of the kind of familial-historical relations that would justify the historiographical conception of an American philosophy understood broadly to include both Latino and Anglo philosophy. Indeed, the fact that I am currently discussing the nature of

American philosophy in more senses than the one usually understood by Anglo philosophers points in this direction.

IX.   Latino and American Philosophy

Because Latino philosophy can be understood broadly to include the work of both Latino philosophers working in Latin America and in the United States, and the work of most Latino philosophers in the United States has roots in Latin American philosophy, I devoted this chapter largely to the discussion of Latin American philosophy. After raising the problem of how to conceive Latino philosophy, I defended the thesis that it is best understood as an ethnic philosophy, that is, the philosophy of the Latino ethnos. This conception needs to be contrasted to the notion of a "universal scientific" philosophy, although the latter notion has problems of its own. The view I proposed can be distinguished from culturalist (based on culture), universalist (based on universal claims), and critical (based on social conditions) views. Next I pointed out that, although 'American philosophy' may be used to mean exactly Latin American philosophy, it is sometimes used to mean the philosophy of the Anglo ethnos, and still at other times the combination of both Latino and Anglo philosophy. In addition I claimed that, today, Latino and Anglo philosophy do not form part of the same ethnic philosophy, although the future may change this state of affairs. However, if a scientific notion of philosophy is used, then there is little difference between what might be considered Latino and Anglo philosophy. This issue leads directly to the question of the canon and how Latino philosophy fits into both the American and world canons of philosophy. This is the topic of the next chapter.

Canon: Place and Future

Philosophers have not often been attracted by questions concerning the philosophical canon, how it is formed, and how it functions. In recent years, however, with a growing awareness of works by female and minority philosophers, some of these questions have received more attention in the United States.[1] Also developing, although still limited if compared with other philosophical topics, is an interest in philosophical historiography, which in turn has led to the discussion of the canon of the discipline.[2]

It used to be assumed that the canon of philosophy reflected not only what has been more influential but also what is best in the history of philosophy. What survived did so because it has permanent value for humanity, and because it has made a real contribution in the human struggle for excellence and truth. But these assumptions have come under fire, particularly in the second half of the twentieth century, and the voices of the excluded have endeavored to show that truth, perennial value, historical impact, and originality have not always been the determining factors in what has come to be regarded as the western philosophical canon.[3] The controversy has taken many turns. Some have to do with a general approach to canon formation and the

---

[1] See, for example, Mara Miller, "Canons and the Challenge of Gender," *Monist* 76, 4 (1993). This issue of the journal is entirely devoted to canons.

[2] See, for example, Jorge J. E. Gracia, *Philosophy and Its History: Issues in Philosophical Historiography* (Albany, NY: State University of New York Press, 1992), and Martin Kusch (ed.), *The Sociology of Philosophical Knowledge* (Dordrecht, Netherlands: Kluwer, 2000).

[3] See: Richard Schacht, "On Philosophy's Canon," and Merold Westphal, "The Canon as Flexible, Normative Fact," both in *Monist* 76, 4 (1993).

factors that influence it; others are more focused on the exclusion of particular groups of philosophers and texts from the canon.

This leads naturally to the question of the place of Latino philosophy in the philosophical canon used in the United States. Is Latino philosophy part of that canon, and if not, why not? I address these questions in this chapter. I begin by saying something about philosophical canons in general and how they are established, and because Latin American philosophy is part of Latino philosophy, and Latino philosophy does not have much history if understood as excluding Latin American philosophy, I refer primarily to Latin American philosophers.

I argue that Latino philosophy is excluded from the canons of both western philosophy and world philosophy as these are understood in the United States, and I propose reasons that explain this exclusion. In particular, I argue that various theories that purport to account for canon formation and the exclusion of Latino philosophers from the western canon fail to do justice to the situation because they ignore the role of tradition in this process.

I. Philosophical Canons

A philosophical canon consists in a group of philosophers and their writings that are the subject of repeated study and discussion both philosophically and historically.[4] It is important not to confuse a canon with a history of philosophy. A history of philosophy will presumably include anyone who is a philosopher and any text that is philosophical. This means that it is rather extensive. Historians will quibble here and there on whether to include an author or a text in a historical account of the philosophy of a period, for example, but most of them will try to be comprehensive and as inclusive as possible, although often they will use criteria to exclude authors and texts that other historians would like to include.

A philosophical canon is much narrower than the history of philosophy of a period or area. A canon does not include every author and text that has made a philosophical contribution in the period or area in question. Canons introduce parameters of inclusion that eliminate from consideration much that is part of history. Philosophically, the authors and texts which make up the canonical list are regarded as having produced something that has value beyond the immediate boundaries of their existence. Historically, their value is

---

[4] This has led some to argue that it concerns the classics (Westphal, "The Canon as Flexible, Normative Fact"), but this seems too broad a notion.

conceived often to be the impact these authors and texts have had. The history of philosophy is the source for all these authors and texts and includes many of the questions they explored and the texts they produced.

There are specific canons and general canons. Examples of the first are the philosophical canon specific to the Latin Middle Ages and the canon of western twentieth-century articles in the analytic philosophical tradition. Examples of more general canons are the canon of western philosophy or of world philosophy. To find philosophical canons one need only look at histories of philosophy, reference works in philosophy, anthologies of philosophical texts, and perhaps most important, the philosophy curriculum. Naturally there will be some differences here and there, but in general one finds considerable agreement on the list of texts and authors that are treated in histories, anthologized, and taught in the United States. Let me turn now to the specific claim about Latino philosophy.

II.   The Place of Latino Philosophy in the Canon

When one looks at canons, it is difficult not to notice that some authors and texts, and sometimes even entire philosophical traditions and schools, are excluded from various canons. Latino philosophy is a good example of a philosophy systematically excluded from both the western and world philosophical canons as these are conceived in the United States. This claim about Latino philosophy may be easily documented by looking at histories of philosophy, reference works, anthologies, philosophical societies, evaluating tools of philosophy as a field of learning, educational programs such as National Endowment for the Humanities Institutes and Seminars, PhD dissertations in philosophy and common areas of specialization in the discipline, and the college curriculum (in the United States philosophy is mostly taught at the college level).

Let me begin backwards, with the college curriculum. Is Latino philosophy part of the philosophy college curriculum in the United States? The answer is no, and the facts are quite clear. I have provided the relevant data elsewhere, so I will not repeat them here, but let me just mention that the number of college courses in Latino philosophy is extremely small, and none of them is required for majors.[5]

The number of PhD dissertations written on Latino philosophy in graduate philosophy programs is practically non-existent, and the number of specialists

---

[5]   For statistics, see Jorge J. E. Gracia, "Hispanics, Philosophy, and the Curriculum," *Teaching Philosophy* 22, 3, (1999), 241–8.

follows suit. Indeed, because the few persons interested in this field cannot find jobs teaching Latino philosophy, they usually write dissertations in other fields and keep their interest in this area on the side. A brief look at the APA's *Jobs for Philosophers* shows the lack of interest in the field in the profession. In the past few years, there have not been more than half a dozen advertised jobs whose primary area of concentration was Latino philosophy, and similarly few in which Latino philosophy was mentioned as an acknowledged area of competence.

At present, there are no graduate training programs in Latino philosophy. Indeed, there are only a handful of faculty capable of directing PhD dissertations in the field, and there are no PhD programs that have Latino philosophy as an area of strength or concentration. Suffice it to say that until the summer of 2005, the National Endowment for the Humanities (NEH) had never offered a summer Institute on Latino philosophy. Whether this was because no proposals had been made, or because the ones made had not been adequate, it is a telling tale about the situation of Latino philosophy in the United States. And yet, when the first Institute was offered in 2005, there were more than 80 applicants for only 25 available spaces; the Institute drew the largest number of applicants of any NEH Summer program that year.[6]

The evaluating tools of philosophical sub-fields and program rankings generally ignore Latino philosophy. For example, perhaps the most popular and commonly used tool of the field and program evaluation today, the *Philosophical Gourmet Report*, does not list Latino philosophy as a field.[7]

Another area to consider is philosophical societies, because they give an indication of particular interest within the profession. There are societies now for many individual philosophers and also for general periods of the history of philosophy and sub-areas of philosophical study. In the sixties a group of philosophers founded the Society for Iberian and Latin American Thought (SILAT). The society has been active ever since, but although it usually organizes programs at the meetings of the APA, attendance is low and it has been difficult to keep the society alive. The list of members does not go over a few dozens. Moreover, the APA itself did not have a committee for Latinos until the early 1990s, even though the Committee for Blacks in Philosophy dates back to the sixties.

With respect to anthologies of philosophical texts, we should consider two kinds: first, anthologies of philosophical texts by Latinos, and second, anthologies of philosophical texts in general. The number of anthologies (in English)

---

[6] For the 2005 NEH Institute, see the webpage (http://philosophy.buffalo.edu/contrib/events/neh06.html).

[7] See the webpage (http://www.philosophicalgourmet.com/overall.htm).

of Latino philosophy put together by philosophers is very limited. Risieri Frondizi and I compiled the first such anthology in the 1970s, concentrating on Latin American philosophy, but we could not find a publisher for it in the United States.[8] It was not until late in the 1980s that I found a publisher for a much revised version of it.[9] This was the only anthology available until a few years ago when three other anthologies appeared. One was an enlarged version of the earlier anthology, including the work of some Latino philosophers in the United States, another was a new one edited by Susana Nuccetelli and Gary Seay, and a third was a very specific anthology on current issues published by Eduardo Mendieta.[10] With respect to the presence of Latino philosophy in anthologies of philosophical texts in general, there are only a couple of the many hundreds published in the past 50 years that include anything from Latinos. Latino philosophy tends to be excluded from both specific and general anthologies.[11]

The past 15 years have seen the publication of a large number of reference works in philosophy. Dictionaries, encyclopedias, and other tools of philosophical research have become common, and most major presses have published versions of these. Some deal with world philosophy, whereas others concern western philosophy in particular, but very few include substantial articles on Latino philosophy. The very large encyclopedias do include some articles, particularly overall views of Latino philosophy in general, but they seldom include significant articles on periods or philosophers from Latin America. In some cases they do not include any articles on Latino philosophy and in others the editors include sections on authors who are not philosophers or are philosophers who work at the fringes of philosophy and are interested in marginal fields and approaches that have an exotic take on Latino philos-

---

[8] A Spanish version of it was published in Mexico in 1975, and reprinted in 1981, as Risieri Frondizi and Jorge J. E. Gracia (eds.), *El hombre y los valores en la filosofía latinoamericana del siglo XX* (Mexico City: Fondo de Cultura Económica, 1975, 1981).

[9] Jorge J. E. Gracia (ed.), *Latin American Philosophy in the Twentieth Century: Man, Values and the Search for Philosophical Identity* (Buffalo, NY: Prometheus Books, 1986).

[10] Jorge J. E. Gracia and Elizabeth Millán-Zaibert (eds.), *Latin American Philosophy for the 21st Century: The Human Condition, Values, and the Search for Identity* (Buffalo, NY: Prometheus Books, 2004); Susana Nuccetelli and Gary Seay (eds.), *Latin American Philosophy: An Introduction with Readings* (Upper Saddle River, NJ: Prentice-Hall, 2004); and Eduardo Mendieta (ed.), *Latin American Philosophy: Currents, Issues, Debates* (Bloomington, IN: Indiana University Press, 2003).

[11] See Jorge J. E. Gracia, *Hispanic/Latino Identity: A Philosophical Perspective* (Oxford: Blackwell, 2000), ch. 7; and "Hispanics, Philosophy, and the Curriculum."

ophy. An exception to this is the effort mounted by the *Stanford Encyclopedia of Philosophy*, an online source that might eventually establish itself as the single most important reference source for philosophy. The editor recently appointed a committee in charge of devising a substantial list of articles on Latin American and Iberian philosophy.[12]

Two kinds of histories are important for us to consider in this context: histories of Latino philosophy and general histories of philosophy or of western philosophy. There are no histories of Latino philosophy in English, and only a couple in Spanish. The histories of philosophy in Latin America often include sections on Latin American philosophy, but no history of philosophy written outside Latin America ever includes sections on Latino or Latin American philosophy.

From all this it is quite clear that Latino philosophy is not generally part of the western philosophical canon as understood in the United States. Now let me turn to some suggestions as to the causes for such an absence.

III.   Reasons for the Exclusion of Latino Philosophy from the Canon

One can easily think of many reasons why Latino philosophy has been excluded from the canons of western and world philosophy which are concordant with the traditional view of how the philosophical canon was formed and the criteria that determined it. Some of these have been actually proposed by historiographers. Rather than presenting a history of these positions, I approach the matter by first listing three ineffective views. Then I turn to three views that are more effective. Finally, I present what I consider to be an important, but neglected, reason behind this phenomenon, and its implications for Latino philosophy.

A.   Ineffective reasons

The view that could be regarded as most radical argues that Latino philosophy is not part of these canons because, simply put, it is not original. There is nothing in it that can have a claim to novelty. Latino philosophers have been content with repeating what other philosophers from other parts of the world, and particularly from Europe and the United States, have said and have said better. Their ideas are derivative and lack even the quality of making significant advances beyond their sources. Latino philosophers have been satisfied with

---

[12]   The committee is composed of Otávio Bueno, Manuel Vargas, and Gracia.

translating other philosophers and even that has not been very well done at times. Many reasons are adduced for this lack of originality but this is not pertinent for our purposes. The important point for us is that, according to those who subscribe to this view, this lack of originality justifies the neglect of Latino philosophy. Ironically, the view that Latino philosophy lacks originality and value has been supported by many Latino philosophers themselves, including some of the best known and important ones.[13]

Any serious student of Latino philosophy will realize that this judgment is unwarranted. If we accept that originality in philosophy can be measured in at least two ways – by the novelty of the problems posed and by the novelty of the ideas used to deal with those problems – there is plenty we can find in Latino philosophy to justify a positive judgment. Consider two authors, Bartolomé de Las Casas and Carlos Mariátegui. Both of these authors thought within well-established western philosophical traditions, but both used those traditions to deal with new philosophical challenges and they modified those traditions in order to meet those challenges. The challenge faced by Las Casas was the conception of the status of Indians and the treatment they deserved.[14] The question was new for Europe at the time and raised an issue that has acquired greater importance as time has passed. What are the duties of conquerors with respect to conquered peoples, and what are the rights of conquered peoples? Las Casas's answers to these questions were developed in terms of the Aristotelian framework within which he was educated, but the conclusions he reached were quite different from those of his more orthodox Aristotelian opponents, who equated Indians with what Aristotle considered Barbarians, and to whom he accorded no rights.

The case of Mariátegui is similar. The challenge he faced concerned the socio-economic situation of the Andean region and its original inhabitants.[15]

---

[13]   For a classic statement see: Augusto Salazar Bondy, *Sentido y problema del pensamiento hispano-americano*, with English trans. by Donald L. Schmidt (Kansas City, KN: University of Kansas Center for Latin American Studies, 1969). For a more recent view, see: Eduardo Rabossi, "History and Philosophy in the Latin American Setting: Some Disturbing Comments," in Arleen Salles and Elizabeth Millán-Zaibert (eds.), *The Role of History in Latin American Philosophy: Contemporary Perspectives* (Albany, NY: State University of New York Press, 2005), pp. 57–73.

[14]   Bartolomé de Las Casas, *In Defense of the Indians: The Defense of the Most Reverend Lord, Don Fray Bartolomé de las Casas, of the Order of Preachers, Late Bishop of Chiapa, Against the Persecutors and Slanderers of the Peoples of the New World Discovered Across the Seas*, trans. Stafford Poole (DeKalb, IL: Northern Illinois University Press, 1992).

[15]   Carlos Mariátegui, *Seven Interpretative Essays on Peruvian Reality*, trans. Marjory Urquidi (Austin, TX: University of Texas Press, 1971).

How should the relation between original cultures and imported ideologies be worked out in order to better the lot of the native population? The philosophical tradition from which he worked was Marxism, but Mariátegui modified it in substantial ways to adapt it to the situation of the Andean populations. Instead of expounding the orthodoxy worked out in Europe, he tried to adapt the principles that inspired Marx to a different situation and had no qualms about abandoning some of its linchpins.[16]

A second reason that appears to have some prima facie validity for the exclusion of Latino philosophy from the western and world canons of philosophy as conceived in the United States is that it is primarily of local interest. It does not have the claim to universality that is essential to any philosophy that can be included in the general philosophical canon. It is a local philosophy, interested only in local issues and problems and adopting strategies and methodologies that are only appropriate at the local level.[17] Latino philosophy has only an exotic interest; it is idiosyncratic; and it has little in common with western and world philosophy. Again, anyone familiar with the history of philosophy in Latin America can attest to the fact that there is little exoticism in it. Indeed, if anything, Latin American philosophy has been too concerned with the issues and problems it inherited from European philosophy, and it is European philosophy that its critics take to be the model of scientific rigor and universality. So it makes little sense to argue that it is its lack of attention to universal themes and problems that can serve to exclude Latino philosophy from the world canon of philosophy, and particularly of western philosophy. Practically any important philosopher in Latin America has been concerned with topics of universal concern. Consider the large literature in the first half of the twentieth century in Latin America on the objectivity and subjectivity of value.[18] Or think about the beginning of the second half of the century, in which authors such as Francisco Romero and Risieri Frondizi sought to determine what is essential to humanity and the human self?[19] And what do we

---

[16] See Ofelia Schutte, *Cultural Identity and Social Liberation in Latin American Thought* (Albany, NY: State University of New York Press, 1993).

[17] Leopoldo Zea is sometimes cited as being responsible for this local, culturalist view of philosophy in Latin America. For his view, see: "The Actual Function of Philosophy in Latin America," in Gracia and Millán-Zaibert (eds.), *Latin American Philosophy*, pp. 357–68, and "Identity: A Latin American Philosophical Problem," in Gracia and Millán-Zaibert (eds.), *Latin American Philosophy*, pp. 369–78; previously published in *The Philosophical Forum* 20, 1–2 (1988–9), 33–42.

[18] See Gracia and Millán-Zaibert (eds.), *Latin American Philosophy*, pp. 161–219.

[19] See Francisco Romero, *Theory of Man*, trans. William Cooper (Berkeley, CA: University of California Press, 1964); and Risieri Frondizi, *The Nature of the Self* (Carbondale, IL: Southern Illinois University Press, 1971).

make of the more recent developments in the philosophy of liberation that have found echoes in other parts of the world? There is indeed no basis for any kind of criticism of this sort. Still publishers and researchers from the United States tend to think of Latino philosophy as exotic and expect in it an essence that is idiosyncratic and particular rather than universal and of general application. Indeed, in the late seventies, when Frondizi and I were looking for a publisher for our anthology of Latin American philosophical texts, the many rejections we received generally pointed out that we had not included texts that showed anything idiosyncratic and peculiar to Latin American philosophy. Yet, the texts we included were from the most prominent Latin American philosophers at the time.

The third reason that might appear to explain the exclusion of Latino philosophy from the canons of western and world philosophy is that it has had no historical impact of any significance outside of Latin America, and even in Latin America to some extent. Latino philosophy has always been isolated and marginal.

Thus stated, this claim has no validity, although perhaps if presented more modestly there is some substance to it. The claim as presented has no validity in that Latino philosophy has been influential, although its influence has been in areas in which philosophy usually has very little influence, namely the social and political fabric of society. Unlike most western philosophy, which has often distanced itself from the social and political fray to concentrate on metaphysics, epistemology, logic, and the philosophy of science, Latino philosophy has frequently been involved in social and political issues. Its beginning marks this important dimension of it, when it served Las Casas to defend the rights of the original inhabitants of the Americas. And there were consequences, for Las Casas's tireless argumentation and defense were instrumental in bringing about changes in the laws used by Spain to govern the conquered inhabitants of the Americas.[20] Philosophy also was instrumental in the fight for independence from Spain during the late eighteenth and early nineteenth centuries. The liberators found in philosophy the ideological instruments to articulate their ideas of freedom and liberation, and later the development of laws to govern the liberated colonies.[21] And in the nineteenth century, the philosophy known as positivism became the standard bearer for the development of the newly liberated countries. Positivism was not a marginal, ivory tower ideology, but a veritable set of ideas used to work out the organization of societies and the development of programs that ranged from politics to education. In

[20] Las Casas, *In Defense of the Indians.*
[21] See Gracia and Millán-Zaibert (eds.), *Latin American Philosophy,* pp. 61–75 and 233–56.

countries such as Mexico and Brazil, for example, versions of positivism were regarded as national ideologies and went so far as to inform the mottos around which the new nations rallied.[22] All of this makes clear that Latino philosophy cannot be considered an armchair philosophy without historical influence. Its influence in Latin America has been very substantial and extends throughout the region and its history.

Still one may argue that this is not enough to include this philosophy in the world philosophical canon or even the western philosophy canon. The argument is that, although Latino philosophy may have had historical impact in Latin America, it has had no impact outside Latin America, and particularly in what is generally considered mainstream European philosophy. But even modified in this way the claim is false. Let me cite two examples, one early and one recent. The early example is the work of Antonio Rubio, whose *Logica mexicana* was printed and reprinted in Europe in the seventeenth century, and in fact became a textbook in many European universities. The second, more recent, example, is the philosophy of liberation, which has had a substantial impact on philosophical thinking in Africa, India, and other parts of the third world. Yes, the impact illustrated by the second example is not on mainstream European philosophy, but it certainly shows that this philosophy is having considerable influence on the philosophical development in the world outside Latin America. So, it makes no sense to argue that Latino philosophy is, or should be, excluded from the canon because it has had no historical influence outside Latin America.

In short, none of the three reasons proposed appears to justify the exclusion of Latino philosophy from the canons of philosophy in the West and the world, as conceived in the United States, or survives close scrutiny, although certainly all three may be contributing factors to such an exclusion. What is missing, then? Let me turn to other reasons that fare better than the ones proposed thus far.

B. More effective reasons

In the last chapter of my *Hispanic/Latino Identity*, where I discuss the situation of Hispanics within the American philosophical community, I suggest two reasons why Hispanic philosophy in general is marginalized in the United States. One of these is the perception that Hispanic philosophy is foreign, a product of a foreign people and a foreign way of thinking. The other is that Hispanic philosophy is not seen as part of mainstream Western European

---

[22] See Leopoldo Zea, *Positivism in Mexico* (Austin, TX: University of Texas Press, 1974).

philosophy, whether in its analytic or Continental strains. Since these two are considered to be the proper roots of United States philosophy, Hispanic philosophy in all its modalities (Iberian or Latin American) is left out, something for others to do. Because I explored these reasons in some detail in the above-mentioned book, I dispense with them here, although I still believe in their merit. Instead, I suggest three other factors that I think play roles in the neglect of Latino philosophy in the United States.

The first of these is that Latino philosophy is not perceived as exotic enough, unlike, say, the philosophy from India. Paradoxically, although Latino philosophy is regarded as somehow foreign and not part of the proper western tradition, it turns out that much of what Latino philosophers write and say looks and sounds very much like what many philosophers of the western mainstream say and write. So, in effect, there is no exotic appeal to Latino philosophy as there is in the philosophy of India or of similarly culturally remote (from a western perspective) areas of the world.

A second factor that contributes to the neglect of Latino philosophy is that Latin America as a whole lacks political and economic clout in the world. Power and wealth surely attract attention; the weak and poor get only neglect, and this extends to their history and their thought. Humans are guided by interests that gravitate toward those they fear or admire; they want to know them better either to protect themselves or to emulate them. But Latin America is the source of neither fear nor admiration, so it is generally ignored, and this extends to philosophy.

A third important factor has been the composition of the United States population. People tend to be interested in themselves (witness the endless number of studies by Italian philosophers on Italian philosophy, French philosophers on French philosophy, and so on – nationalism is a powerful incentive to scholarship and it is encouraged and supported by states), and until recently the percentage of Latinos in the United States was small. Numbers explain in part the attention that has been paid to Black and African philosophy, for example. Blacks themselves began a search for their historical and intellectual roots in order to counteract the perception that they had none, and the rest of the country followed to a certain extent because of the impressive size of the Black population and its increasing political clout. Latinos, of course, have been at a disadvantage in numbers until recently, but this situation is changing. Eventually, Mexican Americans, Cuban Americans, and other Latinos will want to discover their intellectual heritage and this will bring them to Latino philosophy, and the rest of the country will follow because of the numbers of Latinos and our growing importance in society. But this is not yet a reality.

There may be other factors that influence the precarious situation of Latino philosophy in the United States today, but I think the ones mentioned are enough to set us thinking about this issue. Let me propose now what I think is an important but neglected external factor: the role of tradition in the formation of any philosophical canon. I turn to this view and its implications for Latino philosophy in the sections that follow.

IV. Philosophical Canons and Philosophical Traditions

Tradition plays an important role in the establishment of philosophical canons. A philosophical canon is a list of philosophical authors and works, and such a list must be made by people, but not just anybody; the list is compiled by persons who have a say, that is, persons with authority. Only the opinion of some persons counts. And who determines whose opinion counts? Certainly other persons who themselves have established authority in the field. Consider art. Who determines the importance of artists and whether their work is canonical? Some will answer that it is the value of the work, but who determines the value of the work? The world is littered with works of artists who have not "made it," that is, who have not become part of the canon. Only certain artists are included in museums and art histories. And who determines who they are? Surely museum curators, art historians, and other people who are part of the artistic establishment.[23] The curator of the Metropolitan Museum of Art has much to say about the works that the museum acquires, and having a work in the Metropolitan goes a long way toward the establishment of the artist as canonical, because other museums will imitate the Metropolitan, and there will be exhibitions of the works of the artist in question and so on.

The case with philosophical canons is similar. There is an authoritative establishment, a group of persons who choose the discourse that is important and the authors to be included in dictionaries, reference works, and histories of philosophy. These persons establish the canon, although they do not do it by fiat; they have reasons, and those reasons have generally to do with what has gone on before, with credentials, and with continuity. So and so's opinion becomes important because he was a student of so and so, or worked with so and so. There are also judgments that have been made in the past and these are taken into account. This is in a sense like what happens with the American Constitution and its interpretation; there is a body of judicial opinion that cannot be disregarded. An art critic cannot begin by saying that art which has made it into the canon has to be taken out from it. A judge presented with a

[23] For a defense of the institutional theory of art, see George Dickie, *Art and the Aesthetic: An Institutional Analysis* (Ithaca, NY: Cornell University Press, 1974). The art canon is discussed by several authors in the issue of the *Monist* cited earlier.

difficult case cannot begin by ignoring past legal precedent, because a legal decision does not make sense unless it is taken in the context of that past, of previous opinions. The same goes for philosophy. It makes no sense to say that Aristotle must be eliminated from the canon. Philosophers often complain about the views of canonical philosophers. Who has not complained about Descartes? He seems to be a favorite whipping boy in philosophy. But can anyone be taken seriously who argues that Descartes should be taken off the canon of western philosophy?

Philosophical canons are the result of communities of philosophers and historians of philosophy who over time have come up with lists of philosophers and texts they regard as worthy of study and discussion, although the reasons they give may vary from author to author and the list may not be exactly the same in all cases. One could argue that it is merely the present community of philosophers and historians of philosophy that is involved in this process and claim that it is ultimately their views that are responsible for the canon. But this is a mistake, in that the community is extended over time and, although their opinions might differ, there is a continuity of practices. These practices constitute the tradition which is the source of the canon. Contrary to what many believe, a tradition is not a set of beliefs passed on, because seldom in a tradition do we have the same beliefs throughout.[24] Indeed, even when the linguistic formulas passed down in the tradition are the same, their gloss and interpretation depend on persons and their circumstances. More important than the actual set of beliefs are the community of people in question and their practices, for it is that community and those practices that lend authority to certain persons within the community and justify their choices.

Naturally, when considering persons with authority, one must also take into account the all important element of descent. Pedigree is essential in authority. We come back to the point that so and so has authority because he was a student of so and so. And the opinion of so and so is important precisely because he was a student of so and so, who in turn was a student of so and so, and so on.

We have, then, a familial structure based not on genetic descent but on intellectual descent, on intellectual pedigree, which is in turn based on practices that have been developed, passed down, and modified within the familial context. Yes, we are still families and tribes, and there are exclusions and feuds. Humanity is fundamentally composed of communities, and philosophy is not

---

[24] For arguments in support of this conception of tradition, see Jorge J. E. Gracia, *Old Wine in New Skins: The Role of Tradition in Communication, Knowledge, and Group Identity*, The 67th Aquinas Lecture (Milwaukee, WI: Marquette University Press, 2003).

different from other human endeavors. This explains why cultural, political, and ethnic considerations play a role in human projects, including academic ones. The philosophical canon is established within families tied by practices, that is, traditions. This explains inclusions and exclusions and it shows how difficult it is to break into a canon when one is not part of the tradition that ties the family in which authority rests.

V. Philosophical Canons in the United States

In the United States at present there are two major philosophical traditions, analytic and Continental. The analytic tradition goes back to the beginning of the twentieth century and the work of G. E. Moore and Bertrand Russell in England and the members of the Vienna Circle and Ludwig Wittgenstein on the Continent. It is called analytic because of its emphasis on the method of analysis, the breaking down of complex entities, usually conceived linguistically, into more simple ones as a means of understanding and solving philosophical problems. The Continental tradition goes back to the work of nineteenth- and twentieth-century phenomenologists and neo-Kantians. Its name originates in that its beginnings, in contrast with those of the analytic tradition, are primarily centered in Continental Europe and look back to authors who worked in Continental Europe. Neither of these major traditions has a set of doctrines that all its members hold; their members are mostly tied by certain practices and a genealogical intellectual chain.

These two traditions control most of the profession of philosophy in the United States: the jobs in universities, the publication venues, and the grants. But there are also other, less powerful traditions. For example, there is Marxism, much diminished in presence and visibility after the demise of the Soviet Union, but still operative in certain circles. Thomism continues to be promoted by the Roman Catholic Church and the institutions it controls. There is also what is known as American philosophy, which consists mostly of philosophers interested in the thought of American philosophers of various stripes, ranging from pragmatists to process philosophers. Some of these traditions ally themselves, or even fit, within the Continental tradition, and some are divided, as happens with Thomism, which has analytic and Continental branches, depending on the philosophers and approach favored.

These traditions have canons of authors and texts that have been worked out over fairly long periods of development, and the practitioners in the United States generally trace their intellectual ancestry to these authors and texts. Some of the practitioners are first and second generation students of the authors in question. For example, some of the members of the Vienna Circle settled in the United States, and they trained students who, in turn, trained other students, and so on. The same can be said about the Continental tradition, in which the authors in question are European or American students of those European authors. An important factor is that analytic authors generally work in English and read primarily English texts. Continental authors read primarily German and French authors and texts. Most analysts do not know well languages other than English, and for their purposes it is English that is the important language because it is English authors or German authors translated into English that originated the tradition. Continentalists know German and French but seldom do they know any other language; for them the important languages are these two because the authors that originated the tradition were German or French.

Under these conditions it becomes difficult for members of the mainstream philosophical traditions in the United States even to notice philosophers and texts that are not already part of the canon as they conceive it and particularly those that are not closely related to the philosophical community and traditions that establish the canon. First, there is the problem of language. Second, there is the already crowded canon of authors and texts and the pressure within the traditions to re-examine the canon and include authors and texts that have so far been excluded but are well placed within the tradition. And third, there is the lack of representatives in the power establishment of the traditions that have the authority to initiate changes, and would even consider marginalized members of the traditions. All this helps to understand why Latino philosophy is not part of the canon as understood in the United States, but there are also additional internal factors that merit attention and I explore these in the next section.

VI.   Latino Philosophy and the Western Philosophical Tradition

One of the important factors in understanding the exclusion of Latino philosophy from the world philosophical canon and the western philosophical canon is that Latin America does not have a philosophical tradition of its own. Latino philosophy is part of the overall western philosophical tradition and breaks down into the same traditions into which this overall tradition breaks down in the United States. Latino philosophy extends for close to 500 years. It began in 1550, when the first books of philosophy were published in Mexico, but its trajectory has mirrored the trajectory of European philosophy. It began with scholasticism and continued with Enlightenment thought, positivism, and the various currents that flourished in Europe in the nineteenth and twentieth centuries.

The second factor is that Latino philosophy is part of Hispanic philosophy, and the European leader of Hispanic philosophy is considered to be Spain, which is generally excluded from the western canon of philosophy for a variety of reasons, including the language barrier. Latino philosophy has had a close relationship to the philosophy in the Iberian peninsula. This begins with Counter Reformation scholasticism and the towering Spanish figures of Francisco de Vitoria and Francisco Suárez, among others, and continued following developments in the peninsula. Two interesting examples are the influence of Carl Christian Friedrich Krause, who had an impact in the peninsula and as a consequence became also important in Latin America. The other example is the influence of José Ortega y Gasset in Latin America, for not only did he introduce German philosophy into Latin America, but his philosophy had an extraordinary impact that is evident to this day.

The first factor is detrimental to the recognition of Latino philosophy in the western canon because the criteria of inclusion used are those of the western tradition. If Latin America were not part of this tradition and had its own tradition, the canon for which it would be considered would be the world philosophical canon, and the criteria of inclusion in it would be criteria proper to the tradition to which it belonged. Consider what happens with Chinese and Japanese philosophy. There is much in those two traditions that would not be included in the philosophical canon if the criteria used to judge them were the same used in the western tradition. But because Chinese and Japanese philosophy are not part of the western tradition, the criteria used to determine their inclusion or exclusion are the ones developed within the traditions of China and Japan. The West simply adopts what other traditions deem acceptable when it comes to the world philosophical canon. The case of Latino philosophy is different, because no matter what Latinos think may be worthwhile, it is the judgment of authorities in the western philosophical community that counts when it comes to canonical decisions. And because we are speaking of the canon as conceived in the United States, it is authority figures in this country that determine the inclusion or exclusion of Latino philosophy in the canon.

The second factor is detrimental because very few Spanish philosophers make it to the western philosophical canon. Only a few authors from the sixteenth century – Suárez and Vitoria perhaps – and Ortega y Gasset in the twentieth century, are ever mentioned. Portugal, of course, has no one who is part of the canon. And it is through Spain and Portugal that Latino philosophy is viewed. The result is that Latino philosophy is ignored. Here one could mention the issue of colonialism, of which postmodernists are so fond. For Spain and Portugal have always treated Latin America as a former colony, and its inhabitants as second-class; their thought has always been regarded as second best in the peninsula. Latin America has no agents to promote it in the right circles, and who control inclusion in the canon.

VII.   Incorporating Latino Philosophy into the Philosophical Canon

There are at least 10 initiatives that could help to incorporate Latino philosophy into the philosophical canon in the United States.[25] First among these is the publication of translations of works that would pave the way for the composition of anthologies that could in turn be used in the classroom. Translations are desperately needed, for there is practically nothing available and, as we know, Americans are monolingual – they only know English and they expect the rest of the world to learn, and talk and write to them in, it. Anything that is not English might as well not exist as far as the majority of Americans is concerned.

Second, reference works devoted to Latino philosophy need to be prepared. Even simple things like an up-to-date *Directory of Latino Philosophers* would be enormously useful.[26] A dictionary of Latino philosophy is badly needed. Part of the reason that so few general reference works in philosophy contain information about Latino philosophy is that it is impossible for non-Spanish speakers to find this information in English.

Third, a history of Latino philosophy is badly needed, but it has to be a history written by a philosopher and focused on philosophical problems for reasons I discuss in a different context in the next chapter. We do not need a literary history of Latino philosophy, or a political one. And certainly I hope we can avoid ideological ones. We need something along the lines of what Julius Weinberg did so well years ago for medieval philosophy:[27] a short, well-

---

[25]   See also the recommendations of the APA Committee for Hispanics in Philosophy's 2000 "Report on the Status of Hispanics in Philosophy." Posted on APA webpage (http://www.apaonline.org/apa/).

[26]   I made an attempt in this direction several years ago, but it was extraordinarily difficult because of the lack of cooperation by Latin American philosophers and, therefore, I have not attempted to keep it up-to-date. See Jorge J. E. Gracia (ed.), *Directory of Latin American Philosophers* (Buffalo, NY: Council on International Studies and Programs, 1988). Subsequently, José Luis Gómez-Martínez established a pertinent website at (http://www.ensayistas.org).

[27]   Julius R. Weinberg, *A Short History of Medieval Philosophy* (Princeton, NJ: Princeton University Press, 1964).

written account of the main problems and positions developed within the period and organized chronologically.[28]

Fourth, courses on Latino philosophy need to be developed. Latino philosophy should be a standard field of study at the college level, but in order to bring this about, we need the *imprimatur* of the APA. So we need to lobby the old boys' club that rules the association to put Latin American philosophy on the professional map. Needless to say that in courses in which Latino issues are discussed – ethnicity, rights, identity, affirmative action, and the like – we need to have students read materials from Latino philosophers. And we need to use similar materials in course topics where Latino philosophers have pronounced themselves with distinction, such as philosophical anthropology, values, human rights, national and ethnic identities, paraconsistent logic, and so on.

Fifth, the *APA Newsletter for Latinos* needs to be continued and supported. This is an extraordinary tool that could be enormously helpful to those who are looking for direction to develop courses on Latino philosophy and to become aware of recent publications and activities.

Sixth, at some point a journal should be founded. This is essential to promote the field. But the journal has to be a quality historical and philosophical journal. Literary, sociological, political, and ideological analyses should have no place in it. If they do, the journal will probably do more harm than good.

Seventh, monograph series should be encouraged. Unfortunately, this is not easy. I developed such a series several years ago for the State University of New York Press, but the number of philosophical manuscripts I have received for it has been small.

Eighth, Latinos should be encouraged to take a lead in the profession in the preparation of general reference works. In doing so they can have the opportunity to include in them Latin American philosophers and topics.

Ninth, training philosophers is essential. But considering the lack of interest and non-existent jobs for specialists in Latino philosophy, we should train people in two fields   one is the field that will get them a job, such as German Romanticism or sixteenth-century scholasticism, and the other nineteenth-century Latin American philosophy or colonial scholastic philosophy in Peru. In this way, we can get the person a job and at the same time we will have someone who will look for opportunities to insert Latino philosophy into the curriculum.

---

[28]   The book by Susana Nuccetelli, *Latin American Thought: Philosophical Problems and Arguments* (Boulder, CO: Westview Press, 2002), is a first step toward this goal, but it falls short of the Weinberg effort in the historical dimension.

Finally, we must keep SILAT going. One way to do this is to combine topics that have to do with Latin American philosophy and also other issues that confront Latinos in the United States today. One such issue has to do with identity, for this is very much in the air in this country and is an area where Latin American philosophers have written much. Another could be rights, of individual persons and groups. Again, this is current in this country, but it has also been explored in Latin America.

In short, we must not wait until manna falls from heaven. We need to move in practical ways to change the situation of Latino philosophy in the United States. I have suggested some measures as a way to get us started thinking along these lines, but surely there are many other things that could be done. Now let me turn to what I see as some possible pitfalls in the struggle to give Latino philosophy the place it deserves in the philosophical canon and college curriculum.

The first is the development of a ghetto for Latino philosophy. In many ways this is what has happened to some non-western philosophies, Chinese and Indian, for example, for these are part of the curriculum but they are segregated within it. It is practically unheard of that texts from Chinese and Indian philosophy are discussed in general courses in philosophy, such as metaphysics, epistemology, ethics, aesthetics, and so on. Even in introductory courses, these philosophies are ignored, and the textbooks for these courses seldom, if ever, include texts from these traditions. The same could happen to Latino philosophy.

The second danger is that teaching Latino philosophy becomes exclusively the province of certain groups within the profession, for this would ensure that Latino philosophy would remain at the margins. Whom do I have in mind? Five groups in particular: Those who see philosophy as not distinct from literature; those who are interested in so-called global studies; those interested only in political and social issues; those who view philosophy as a narrowly analytic discipline; and finally those interested only in issues of concern to Latinos. All these constitute separate groups in the profession. They also have somewhat narrow points of view and interests, and seldom engage in conversation with other philosophical traditions. In spite of good intentions, they tend to have tunnel vision, leaving out of the field much of what, to this day, has constituted it. For example, analysts leave out the philosophy of liberation and philosophers of liberation ignore analytic philosophy, and those who see no boundaries between philosophy and literature want to incorporate into philosophy all that we generally associate with Latino literature.

Clearly, if Latino philosophy becomes dominated by any of these groups, it will not be able to establish itself as anything more than a curiosity. But do not misunderstand me. I am not arguing for alienating these groups, or excluding them. Indeed, their points of view have as much right to be heard as any other point of view in philosophy. I am arguing, rather, against the effective takeover of a field which is varied and pluralistic by minorities (or even majorities) who, for a variety of reasons, will first impose boundaries that will exclude from the field much that needs to be included in it. Latino philosophy is not the same as Latin American literature, the philosophy of liberation, social and political philosophy, post-colonial studies, or analytic philosophy. This is quite evident to anyone who has bothered to read some of its history, and therefore the study of Latino philosophy should not amount to the study of any one of these alone.

Third, the extreme nationalism (or ethnicism or regionalism) of some Latinos tends to make them forget that Latino philosophy has been closely tied to Iberian philosophy throughout much of its history. Latin American colonial thought makes little sense if studied outside the context of sixteenth and seventeenth century Spanish scholasticism. And the development of twentieth-century Latino philosophy is historically unintelligible without reference to the *transterrados* (émigrés from the Spanish Civil War). There are some reasons for studying Latino philosophy on its own, separately from Iberian thought, but there are also many reasons for studying it in conjunction with Iberian thought. It makes no historical sense to forget historical facts for ideological cartels, particularly when these cartels are founded on uncritical nationalisms (or ethnicisms or regionalisms). In philosophy, perhaps more than anything else, the notion of a Hispanic, rather than just a Latino, community makes much sense, as I have argued elsewhere.[29]

VIII. Latin America, Globalization, and the Future of Latino Philosophy

The part of the world known as Latin America, that motley collection of countries located south of the Río Grande, has been, since 1492, regarded as a backwater place, subordinated to the interests of other places in the globe. During the more than 300 years of Spanish and Portuguese domination, it was a colony, and like all colonies, subservient to the whims and needs of colonial powers. Political independence in the nineteenth century did not essentially change the situation, although new economic masters took the place of colonial ones. The United States, England, and France, in particular, displaced Spain and Portugal as centers of hegemony for the region.

---

[29] I have presented an extended argument for this thesis in Gracia, *Hispanic/Latino Identity*.

The subordination of Latin America has permeated every aspect and dimension of the lives of Latin Americans. Economically, it has meant unchecked exploitation; politically, it has resulted in manipulation and interference; and ethnically it has been the source of cultural imperialism. Economic exploitation has taken many forms, including the unchecked exportation of natural resources. Political manipulation and interference has ranged from the imposition of political structures alien to the region, and even the creation of countries for the benefit of foreign powers, to the repeated invasion of sovereign states. Cultural imperialism has involved the imposition of foreign values, products, and ideas and the suppression of local ones.

The subordination of Latin America in philosophy in particular is as evident as in those other dimensions mentioned, and has been repeatedly noted by Latinos themselves.[30] During the colonial period, Spain and Portugal often set the agenda of what was to be discussed and how. Because of the pervasive influence of scholasticism in the Iberian peninsula, the language of philosophy in Latin America continued to be Latin well after it had been abandoned in the rest of Europe. And Spain in particular exercised considerable control on the books and educational materials that were allowed to circulate in Latin America.[31] Ground-breaking treatises of modern philosophy were often forbidden and, therefore, difficult to get. Moreover, the Iberian powers tightly controlled the educational institutions in the colonies, the curriculum, and pedagogy, through a system of regulations. Finally, the overwhelming power of the Iberian Roman Catholic Church, which saw itself as the defender of Catholic theology as formulated by thirteenth-century scholastics and sanctioned by the Council of Trent, made sure that the topics of discussion of concern to scholastics remained areas of continued attention.[32] Thus, we find a concern with such issues as the problems of universals and individuation to which substantial effort had been devoted on the part of medieval scholastics. Thirteenth- and fourteenth-century figures, long regarded as out of fashion in Europe at the time, were still being discussed with great interest in Latin America. Instead of Descartes and Newton, who had captured the fancy of

---

[30] See Salazar Bondy, *Sentido y problema del pensamiento hispano-americano.*

[31] See Vicente G. Quesada, *La vida intelectual de la América española durante los siglos XVI, XVII y XVIII*, cap. 1 (Buenos Aires: Arnoldo Moen y Hermano, 1910), but also Ismael Quiles, "La libertad de investigación en la época colonial," *Estudios* (1940), 511–24; and Guillermo Furlong, *Bibliotecas argentinas durante la dominación hispánica* (Buenos Aires: Editorial Huarpes, 1944).

[32] See Jorge J. E. Gracia, "El escolasticismo ibérico: Puente entre la antigüedad clásica y el pensamiento colonial iberoamericano," in Gracia, *Filosofía hispánica: Concepto, origen y foco historiográfico* (Pamplona: Universiad de Navarra, 1998), pp. 45–81.

Europeans, Latino intellectuals were encouraged to study and discuss Thomas Aquinas, John Duns Scotus, and Francisco Suárez, to mention just three of the most prominent ones. (Suárez flourished at the end of the sixteenth century, but his thought is rooted in medieval scholasticism.) Whole schools of Thomists, Scotists, and Suarecians thrived south of the Río Grande well into the eighteenth century, when only relatively few scholars, primarily working in seminaries and ecclesiastical circles, paid any attention to them in Europe.

In the twentieth century, the situation did not change substantially. Even a cursory look at the history of Latino philosophy in the first quarter of the century shows how dependant Latino intellectuals and philosophers were on outside influences. José Ortega y Gasset's well-known visit to Buenos Aires in 1916 was, indeed, a major turning point for Latin American thought at the time. He became an instant success, and the ideas he introduced created a focus of philosophical attention for the next fifty years.[33] But even before Ortega, the influence of French and English authors dominated the philosophical landscape in Latin America.[34] This phenomenon received a particularly significant push in the thirties, with the immigration of thousands of intellectuals fleeing the Spanish Civil War.[35]

In the context of this history, one has to wonder if the process of globalization that is taking place everywhere today is going to make any difference for Latin America in general and Latino philosophy in particular. Will Latin America continue to be a subordinated, backward place, where world powers and leaders can play their usual economic and political games, or will globalization give some room to Latin America and help it free itself from these forces of oppression? In the case of philosophy in particular, how will globalization change the pattern of subordination that has characterized it for the past 500 years? And will the influence of Latinos in the United States affect the situation? To be sure, only history will answer these questions, but nonetheless we can point to some elements that will play roles in the outcome.

A. Globalization

As the etymology of the word suggests, globalization has to do with a process which involves the whole globe. To globalize means to make global, or to affect

---

[33] See José Luis Gómez-Martínez, *Pensamiento de la liberación: Proyección de Ortega en América* (Mexico City: Ediciones EGE, 1995).

[34] See Jorge J. E. Gracia, "Introduction: Latin American Philosophy Today," *Philosophical Forum* 20, 1–2 (1988–9), 4–32.

[35] For a study of this group, see José Luis Abellán, *Filosofía española en América (1936–1966)* (Madrid: Ediciones Guadarrama, 1967).

the globe. Of course, the globe has been around for a long time, so it cannot be the end product of globalization or the object under construction through the process of globalization. This process must involve something else, and here two possibilities suggest themselves: some aspect of human experience and the human impact on the non-human dimensions of the globe.

In many ways, globalization has been present since the first appearance of humans on the globe. The moment we walked on the Earth we began "to populate" it, as religious scriptures usually refer to it, and this involved growing in numbers, migrating, coming into contact with other humans, altering our surroundings in ways which are not different from many other processes that have taken place in human history, and developing a consciousness of a growing world.

The process of globalization has had its ups and downs. There have been some periods of human history in which attempts at globalization have been more effective than at others. Recall Alexander the Great's campaign to conquer all the world known to him. This man wanted to bring under his power, and probably Greek culture, all of humanity as he knew it. Another quite success-ful effort, as far as it went, was the Roman experiment. Surely this process, unleashed by the military power of Rome, has to be considered an attempt at globalization, even if its results were limited and restricted primarily to the Mediterranean basin.

The most successful process of globalization before our century, however, happened during the age of European world exploration in the fifteenth and sixteenth centuries. The encounters with America and Equatorial and South-ern Africa, as well as the East, the colonization of many of these territories, and the attempt to bring peoples from all over the world under a few political and cultural umbrellas, were without a doubt, processes of globalization.

Still, in all these cases, the process of globalization encountered serious limitations. Some of these were conceptual. People did not quite think of all the Earth as one and of all human inhabitants of the Earth as members of the same family. Tribalism, among many other factors, stood on the way of true and effective globalization. In addition, technology was rudimentary, so that the globe still turned out to be too large to make it possible for events in one part of it to affect other parts quickly and effectively. When it took three months to go from Madrid to Havana, the lives of the people who lived in these places were only occasionally, affected by what happened in the other place. It took three months to know in Madrid that Havana had suffered a devastating hurricane, and it took an additional three months for Havana to learn the response of the Spanish King. The encounters between Europe and the Americas made the globe smaller, but technology was still such that people in different parts were allowed considerable independence and anonymity.

Today matters are quite different owing to the extraordinary technological advances of the nineteenth century and particularly the twentieth century. First came the industrial revolution and the development of the steam engine. This made possible both more efficient and quicker shipping and the development of the railroads. In the twentieth century, the revolution in transportation was even more drastic, with the invention of the automobile and the airplane. Then came the explosion in the means of communication: the telephone, the radio, and television. Finally, we have computers and the Internet. These technological advances make possible for an increasing number of people to know what is happening everywhere at all times. And this in turn has made it possible to influence people distantly located from each other. Isolation is becoming a thing of the past. Indeed, the old view that the fluttering of butterfly wings in one place changes automatically the course of human history is finally becoming true. A sneeze in Hong Kong makes someone catch the flu in Toronto. The world is becoming a *barrio*, because we now know what is happening everywhere at all times, or at least we can find out. Gossip has gone global.

Globalization appears to have two sides to it, a negative and a positive. On the negative side, much could be said. Let me mention first, homogenization. Increased globalization appears to lead to increased homogenization. Cultural variety is threatened and promises to give way to a uniform culture throughout the globe. Variety and diversity are being replaced by sameness. Wal-Mart, Coca Cola, and other cultural products of the industrialized world, and particularly the current dominant economic power, that is the United States, are quickly replacing local cultural products.

The negative dimensions of homogenization may be gathered under three headings: epistemology, metaphysics, and aesthetics. With respect to the first, homogenization would seem to lead to a diminished number of epistemic possibilities. If culture becomes homogeneous and uniform, it would appear that humans would have less cognizance of different possibilities. With respect to metaphysics, homogeneity would seem to discourage flexibility and change, and to encourage rigidity and lack of creativity, which in turn can undermine adaptability to new challenges. Finally, aesthetically, a homogenous world lacks the variety required for enjoyment. A world in which everyone eats the same foods, dresses with the same clothes, and reads the same books, would be boring.

Homogenization is not the only undesirable consequence of globalization. Globalization also seems to promote dominance and abuse of the many by the few. If regionally the control of technology can lead to domination, and this in turn can easily degenerate into the abuse of power and ideological control, there is no reason to think that things will be different in the larger world. As in the past, so likewise in the future, whoever controls the technology will control the world.

One clear effect of globalization is that the advanced and rich will have increasing advantages over the backward and poor. Economic influence, political power, and cultural impact will go one way. Coca Cola will become the drink of the world, if it is not already, and Wal-Mart will become the shop of the world. Naturally, these developments stifle local initiatives. The small shop may disappear, and the local drink could go the way of dinosaurs.

This situation is exacerbated in cases where there are tightly connected groups which have access to technology and can use it to impose their views, tastes, and power on others. This is nothing new. We all know how totalitarian regimes of the right and left have been able to use technology, from weapons to the media, to control populations. And we also know how international corporations are increasingly determining the economic fate of peoples all over the world. Motivated by the insatiable greed of stockholders, corporations are propelled into mergers and consolidations in order to increase profits, becoming economic mammoths with enormous power.

But there is another side to this story. There is also a positive side to globalization, for this process can improve the standard of living for parts of the human family deprived of the material goods enjoyed in developed countries. Moreover, the very ease with which knowledge can be disseminated and technology can be made available to many, seems certainly to have advantages. Still, these advantages do not undermine the negative consequences of globalization we have pointed out. The positive dimensions of globalization do not eliminate its very serious negative effects. Nor is it clear that the positive and negative consequences of globalization, taken together, will yield a positive rather than a negative tally. A positive view of globalization requires more than this.

One thing that could be said in favor of globalization is that it can work against the abuses of local power, for it diminishes the power of nations and accordingly of oppressive national regimes. For oppressed segments of the population in particular nations, such as women and ethnic minorities, globalization could be a way of eliminating or diminishing the oppression in which they live. Genocide, abuse, and discrimination cannot be kept secret in the global village. And once the existence of these is known, it is difficult for nations to ignore them. Consider how easy it was a few years ago for the superpowers to do as they willed when it came to segments of their own populations or of entire nations that were under their influence. Think of the Soviet Union and the invasion of Czechoslovakia, or the situation of the Jews within that same country. In this hemisphere, we can easily think of unwarranted United States interference in the internal affairs of Latin American nations. Likewise, the knowledge of how the United States treats some of its very citizens who belong to races and ethne other than the one, or ones, that are considered mainstream, creates embarrassment for the country and forces it to act in order to remedy injustices. There is also the concern for the influence that events in one place may have on events in other places. Chernobyl is not a local problem today. Globalization promotes the drift toward a world society in which nations lose some of their sovereignty to make way for the requirements of living together.

Knowledge is power, and knowledge of abuses may generate action. Likewise, knowledge of greener pastures elsewhere motivates those who have this knowledge and makes it possible for them to oppose and resist those who prevent them from living as they think they should. This surely is a healthy consequence of globalization. The curtailment of nationalism is seen by many as a bad result of globalization, but in fact it can be one of the best means to stop local and regional oppression. And there is still another side to this phenomenon. Technology has the capacity to empower the underdog. A shortwave radio has kept many who live under totalitarian and repressive regimes abreast of the truth. Imagine what the Internet can do! Ironically, technology can make it more difficult to control and manipulate information.

In short, establishing the value of globalization is not an easy matter. Globalization appears to be a mixed blessing, like most other things, in spite of the simplistic views that see it as either wholly good or wholly evil.

B.   Globalization and Latino philosophy

The process of globalization will probably have the same consequences on Latino philosophy as it is having in other areas of Latino experience. On the one hand, it could facilitate rather than hinder the hegemony of those philosophical groups that have power and dominate the use of technology. Today, it is possible to be completely up-to-date in Latin America about what is happening in Europe or the United States. If you emulate the analytic group in the United States, it is possible to have, almost upon publication, and sometimes even before publication, the latest thoughts of the leaders of this group. The Internet has made possible for someone in Argentina or Mexico to be in direct touch with someone in New York University, Rutgers, or Princeton. And the same goes for Europe, although Europeans are still behind in the use of technology. Still, soon they will catch up, and then Latino philosophers, who chronically feel left out, might be content to enter in a constant process of catching-up which will never be completed. For many of these, foreign philosophers are production machines whose philosophical dribble never seems to be interrupted or come to an end. Will Latinos be able to enter into dialogue with them? This is unlikely, because either they belong to different families or they belong to the same families but they are regarded as poor relations.

But there is another side to the story, of course. The picture of philosophy elsewhere might make Latino philosophers change their attitude, and see that they can do as well as philosophers from the hegemonic world. After all, what is the difference between them? At bottom the most important one is attitude. Will it happen? It is hard to tell. Globalization can go either way, and it depends very much on Latinos themselves and what they do with what they get.

One last point: it is in the nature of power to increase. It is like capital. Power calls for more power, and the powerful naturally want to become more powerful. This means that hegemonic philosophy cannot ultimately be blamed for what it attempts to do. Power cannot deny its nature. It makes no sense for Latinos to complain about their philosophical subordination. If they want to be significant players in the philosophical field, they need to resist the inroads of hegemonic philosophical families. But does this mean that they must themselves establish families and dynasties? Perhaps there is no other way. If this is so, it is indeed a very sad comment on the practice of philosophy today.

IX.   Latino Philosophy and the Canon

Latino philosophy is not part of the western or world philosophical canons as these are conceived in the United States. Moreover, after examining various reasons that could explain such an exclusion, I suggested that one important factor generally neglected is the role of tradition in the development of any philosophical canon. Finally, I pointed out that the fact that Latino philosophy is part of the western philosophical tradition works against its inclusion in the canon of that tradition and of world philosophy in general, as these are conceived in the United States. Traditions are based on communities and authority and Latino philosophers are not closely tied to the community that sets these canons in the United States and lacks champions in the authoritative philosophical establishment of the country. Then I suggested 10 measures that could help improve the standing of Latino philosophy in the American canon. Finally, I examined how the process of globalization can both benefit and harm the status of Latino philosophy in the world. In the next chapter I discuss the place of, and approach to, Latino philosophy in the Latino philosophical community.

History: Role and Approach

In the last chapter I pointed out that one of the reasons Latino philosophy is not valued in the United States and the world is the poor view that Latinos themselves have of Latino philosophy. In this chapter I explore some of the reasons why they have such a view and suggest some remedies. My main thesis is that it has to do in part with the way the history of Latino philosophy in particular, and the history of philosophy in general, are studied. For reasons I explained earlier, I focus on Latin American philosophy.

I.   The View of Latino Philosophy in Latin America

In Latin America, the prevailing situation of philosophy is similar to that in the United States and Europe, except for the fact that it is worse. The reason it is worse is that there are fewer resources to be shared. Under these conditions, loyalty to the philosophical family to which one belongs becomes even more important than in the United States or Europe. With fewer goods to go around, fewer jobs, places to publish, money for research, and so on, it is crucial to keep out those who do not belong to one's group and to promote those who do.

As in the United States, the larger division among Latin American philosophers is between analysts and Continentalists, but within these there are all sorts of subdivisions, some of which are homegrown, as is the case with philosophers of liberation. Apart from having separate associations, journals, research institutes, and venues for their publications and thought, each of these groups often depends on a leader, or small group of leaders. In Latin America, these tend to behave as *caudillos*. Their egos are large and their function is fundamentally to keep the group united. Most of them accomplish this task by controlling resources, positions, and publishing venues. In exchange for protection and patronage, they often require unconditional allegiance and loyalty to themselves. Some exploit their positions for personal goals and exercise unquestioned intellectual control. They are dictators in the small, and more often than not, they promote a cult to themselves and their ideas.

These petty tyrants are aware of their insignificance in mainstream western philosophy, so much of their effort is geared toward receiving recognition outside of Latin America. Traveling in the United States and Europe is an essential component of this strategy. Having their works translated into one of the languages widely read, such as English or German, is another. Still another is trying to connect themselves with well-known philosophers in Europe and the United States. They do the last by inviting these philosophers to Latin America, where their egos are stroked carefully, by arranging meetings in which their work is discussed, by writing about them, by offering to translate their works, and so on. These strategies are pursued with enormous zeal and determination. But more important still, Latin American philosophers flatter these philosophers by becoming their followers. In doing this, of course, they contribute quite effectively to keep Latino philosophy in the place where it has always been: subordinated to the interests of philosophers from elsewhere. This result is particularly paradoxical in philosophical groups that promote their efforts as a way to break the hegemony of European and American philosophy.

It is not an exaggeration to say that the history of Latino philosophy does not have a presence in general histories of western philosophy as already noted in chapter 8. An even superficial perusal of those histories, including some produced in Latin America itself, reveals that the history of Latino philosophy is not taken seriously. Latino philosophy is considered marginal to the history of western thought, a development of concern only to a few specialists who have particular interests in Latino cultures.[1] Moreover, when mentioned, Latino thought is often characterized as something idiosyncratic, and even exotic. Historiographers of the philosophical mainstream, then, do not feel the need to make reference to Latino philosophy.

This fact is well known to Latino philosophers, and many reasons and explanations of it have been proposed. The well-known Peruvian historian,

---

[1]   None of the well-known histories of western philosophy say much, if anything about Latin American philosophy. See, for example, the histories by Frederick Copleston, W. T. Jones, and Wilhelm Windelband. For other pertinent references, see Eduardo Mendieta, "Is There Latin American Philosophy?" *Philosophy Today* 43, Supp., 50–2 (1999), 50–3.

Augusto Salazar Bondy, claimed that it is in part the Latin American complex of inferiority with respect to Europe and the United States that has contributed to the alienation of Latin American philosophy from the mainstream of western philosophy.[2] And philosophy-of-liberation historians do not tire of reminding Latin Americans of their intellectually servile attitude, in part imposed by a system of ideological domination of first-world countries that emphasizes the marginal intellectual situation of Latin America.[3]

Moreover, the view we saw in the last chapter, according to which Latino philosophy generally lacks originality, is a commonplace. It is expressed by Latin American philosophers of very different persuasions, and with some reason, when presented as a description of a good portion of Latino philosophy. Latino philosophy has not, as a whole, moved beyond the repetition of philosophical views and positions developed elsewhere, primarily in Europe, but more recently in the United States as well. We find many philosophers who go beyond repetition, appropriating the problems that prompted the views they borrow, but it is not commonplace that we find attempts to give solutions to problems that go beyond what others have already suggested, let alone come up with new solutions to them. Most often one finds only attempts to adapt the views of Europeans and North Americans to the cultural, political, and economic conditions in Latin America.[4] There is, of course, authenticity and even originality in this sort of attempt, but it is still a far cry from what many philosophers in Europe and the United States routinely do, or at least attempt to do.

Some critics of Latino philosophy go even farther than this, claiming that there are in fact no philosophers in Latin America, and there is little of philosophical value in the history of Latin American philosophy. After all, as we saw in the last chapter, they ask: Where is the evidence of the impact of Latino philosophy outside of Latin America? Indeed, most Latinos think so poorly of their own philosophers that they seldom refer to their views as

---

[2] Augusto Salazar Bondy, *¿Existe una filosofía de nuestra América?* (Mexico City: Siglo XXI, 1968) and *The Meaning and Problem of Hispanic American Thought*, ed. John P. Augelli (Lawrence, KN: Center for Latin American Studies of the University of Kansas, 1969). Part of the English text is reprinted in Jorge J. E. Gracia and Elizabeth Millán-Zaibert (eds.), *Latin American Philosophy for the 21st Century: The Human Condition, Values, and the Search for Identity* (Buffalo, NY: Prometheus Books, 2004).

[3] Enrique Dussel, *Philosophy of Liberation*, trans. Aquilina Martínez and Christine Morkovsky (New York: Orbis Books, 1985), ch. 1.

[4] An early attempt in this direction is Carlos Mariátegui's adaptation of Marxism to the Peruvian situation in his *Seven Interpretative Essays on Peruvian Reality*, trans. Marjory Urquidi (Austin, TX: University of Texas Press, 1971), as we saw in ch. 8.

anything deserving attention. Yes, they often talk of them as important figures in the development of ideas in their countries, or even in Latin America as a whole.[5] But do Latinos take seriously the ideas of their philosophical ancestors and of many of their contemporaries who presumably engage in philosophizing when they are addressing philosophical issues and problems? Not often. When Latinos look for philosophical views to adopt, or even to criticize, most of them turn away from other Latinos and pay attention rather to those of European and North American philosophers. In short, Latino philosophy is generally regarded as lacking originality and is not taken seriously even by the Latino philosophical community.

II.   Reasons for the Disparaging View of Latino Philosophers among Latinos

One reason for this situation is that Latinos themselves generally use the history of philosophy in their philosophizing and in their teaching in a non-philosophical way, suppressing rather than developing genuine philosophical activity and originality as a consequence. The disparagement that Latino philosophy suffers, both within and without Latin America, is not so much that it does not quite measure up to the philosophy carried out in Europe and North America for, in spite of its faults and shortcomings, there is much merit in what many Latino philosophers have done. The reason for the neglect goes beyond a question of quality; it is that the history of Latino philosophy is, like all the history of philosophy in Latin America, generally done non-philosophically. Latino philosophy has had very little success in, we might say, selling itself to philosophers because its historians have treated it non-philosophically and therefore as philosophically uninteresting.

But what does it mean to say that Latino philosophy is studied and taught non-philosophically? This should become clear as we go along, particularly when I reveal the shortcomings of different historiographical methodologies commonly used by Latinos, but also when I present the way I believe it should be studied and taught. Nonetheless, let me anticipate what I say later by adding three points here. The first is that the aim of philosophy is to develop a view of the world, or any of its parts, which seeks to be accurate, consistent, comprehensive, and supported by sound evidence. As such, philosophy can be distinguished from other disciplines of learning in two ways: (1) it is more

---

[5]   This is the attitude revealed in the historical works of authors such as Abelardo Villegas. See, for example, his *Panorama de la filosofía ibero-americana actual* (Buenos Aires: EUDEBA, 1963).

general insofar as all other disciplines are concerned with restricted areas of knowledge involving specific methodologies, particular objects or kinds of objects, or both; and (2) it involves areas of investigation that are uniquely philosophical such as ethics, logic, and metaphysics. The second point is that philosophy involves the solution of philosophical problems, that is, of problems that surface precisely when one tries to achieve the aim just stated, either because of conceptual inconsistencies, empirical evidence, or inadequacies of other sorts. Finally, philosophy is not merely a descriptive enterprise; it also involves interpretation and evaluation. To proceed philosophically, then, is to proceed so as to achieve the aims of the discipline; and to proceed non-philosophically is precisely to proceed in ways that divert oneself from achieving those aims.

If the culprit of both the state of Latino philosophy and the lack of reputation it enjoys is in part the way the history of philosophy is studied, one way to try to remedy the situation is to eliminate the culprit. Let us do away completely with the study of the history of philosophy and concentrate on doing philosophy. And, indeed, there have been Latino voices who have suggested just that. Some, echoing Rudolph Carnap, have gone so far as to say that the knowledge of certain dead languages, such as Latin, is an obstacle to philosophy.

This solution seems to be an easy way out, but in fact it is not a realistic alternative for at least four reasons. First, although it is in principle possible to do philosophy without engaging in any kind of study of the history of philosophy, in fact this is almost impossible, and even those philosophers who pride themselves in doing philosophy non-historically, often present their views in reaction to the views of others. That these others may be contemporaries of theirs does not change the fact that their views, having been presented in texts, are part of history, even if only recent history. Second, philosophy is taught with texts from historical figures, however recent they may be, and to teach it otherwise would be both difficult and undesirable. It is important to recognize that most philosophers everywhere rely heavily on historical texts of philosophy for teaching the discipline and to expect a change in this would be unrealistic. Third, the probability that Latino philosophers will abandon the interest in their own intellectual history, and even in their own philosophical history, is remote at a time when most parts of the world are seeing a revival of nationalism, particularism, ethnicity, and in general a desire to search for roots and cultural identity.[6] Finally, the history of philosophy is an incredibly rich reservoir of philosophical opinion which, if treated correctly, can and does serve to help the contemporary philosopher.

[6] Indeed, among Latinos/Hispanics/Latin Americans, this is very strong. See Jorge J. E. Gracia, *Hispanic/Latino Identity: A Philosophical Perspective* (Oxford: Blackwell,

In principle, there is no reason why the study of the history of philosophy should be an obstacle to philosophy. Rather than completely discarding the history of philosophy, both the history of philosophy in general and the history of Latino philosophy in particular, the solution to the problematic situation of Latino philosophy today is to teach and do both histories in a way that can help the philosophical task and underscore the philosophical worth of Latino philosophy.

A.   Wrong approaches to the history of philosophy

How do Latino philosophers use the history of philosophy? It would be easy to answer this question if the ways the history of philosophy is used by Latinos were uniform. Unfortunately, there is not a single way in which it is used in philosophical contexts, and indeed there is such variety in that use that an accurate description of it would require more space and time than I can give it here.[7] We must content ourselves with the brief examination of some of the ways in which Latino philosophers use the history of philosophy, so that we may later compare them with a more philosophically fruitful approach. These examples, although limited, represent some of the most popular approaches to the history of philosophy and thus should be sufficient to make my point, even if they do not prove in any conclusive way the view I wish to propose. I shall refer to three historiographical approaches: the culturalist, the ideological, and the doxographical.[8]

1.   Culturalism

The culturalist approach tries to understand the philosophical ideas from the past as expressions of the complex cultural matrix from which they germinated. The emphasis in this approach is not to understand philosophical ideas

---

2000), and Jorge J. E. Gracia and Iván Jaksić (eds.), *Filosofía e identidad cultural en América Latina* (Caracas: Monte Avila, 1988). Keep in mind, however, that this interest is of the sort I mentioned earlier, often ideological or purely historical.

[7]   I discuss these historiographical approaches in more detail, but in a general context, in Jorge J. E. Gracia, *Philosophy and Its History: Issues in Philosophical Historiography* (Albany, NY: State University of New York Press, 1992), ch. 5.

[8]   The history of Latin American philosophical historiography is still to be written. A first step in this direction was Diego Pró's study of this topic in the Argentinean context, *Historia del pensamiento filosófico argentino* (Mendoza: Universidad Nacional de Cuyo, 1973). Another is Horacio Cerutti-Guldberg's *Hacia una metodología de la historia de las ideas (filosóficas) en América Latina* (Guadalajara: Universidad de Guadalajara, 1986).

considered as ideas that are supposed to address specific philosophical issues and solve specific philosophical problems formulated by particular persons. This approach conceives philosophical ideas as part and parcel of a culture, as representative phenomena from a period or epoch. Historians who employ this strategy concentrate on the description, and to a certain extent, on the interpretation of the past, but they are opposed to its evaluation. The culturalist understands past philosophies as part of a general cultural development, but is not interested in the philosophical value of those philosophies. The preoccupation with tying philosophical ideas with other aspects of culture, such as art, literature, science, religion, social customs, and the like, results in general rather than particular analyses of these ideas.

Culturalists, moreover, are concerned with the whole picture and because of that they often neglect details. This leads frequently to the neglect of arguments and particular philosophical views. The historical accounts of culturalists have little use for even the cursory analysis of past arguments and philosophical views of individual philosophers. They seek general conclusions that they can then relate to other cultural phenomena.

Proponents of this approach seek to explain why this or that idea arose, but they do so in terms of forces external to philosophy and to what the great majority of philosophers consider their task. The analysis of arguments or particular opinions, then, is regarded as unimportant unless it can be used to tell us something about the spirit or mind of the times. Philosophical ideas are treated as symptoms of other factors which are more important for the historian to understand.

The aim of historians of philosophy is not to evaluate past ideas or to see them as products of individual minds. Rather, their aim is to reveal the connections between those ideas and the cultural mentality and background from which they sprung and which they represent. Ideas, so the argument goes, are not disembodied abstractions and do not result from formal arguments; ideas are acts which take place in particular circumstances. Histories of ideas that discuss ideas abstractly, treating them as entities isolated from the cultural matrix that gave them birth, are neither history nor philosophy. The task of the history of philosophy, in brief, is to make clear the relations among ideas, considered as cultural human responses and reactions, to the circumstances that give rise to them, thus revealing the conceptual foundations of the culture in which they originate.

In Latin America, the culturalist approach has been extensively used in part as a result of the great influence of José Ortega y Gasset's perspectival and culturalist conception of philosophy, beginning in the second decade of this century. Among the most important exponents of this kind of historiography are Samuel Ramos and Félix Schwartzmann, for whom the study of Latino thought is closely related to Latino culture.[9] For both, Latino philosophy, and indeed any philosophy, must be approached as an expression of the culture in which it is found and, therefore, as a product that makes no sense unless it is placed in the cultural context in which it originated.

Ramos's *El perfil del hombre y la cultura en México* is not a good example of the culturalist approach in the history of philosophy insofar as it is not a book about the history of philosophy. Yet, it was this book that created the framework which was eventually adopted for the culturalist study of philosophical ideas. For this reason, it is a classic locus.

The book begins with a chapter entitled, "The Imitation of Europe in the XIXth Century," which in turn begins with a discussion of method. It is here that we find the parameters for the study of philosophy as the cultural study of the history of philosophy. The discussion of method ends with the following significant paragraph:

> Let us leave aside for a moment the question of whether "Mexican culture" has a reality or not, and let us devote ourselves to think *how* that culture *would be* in case it existed. This does not mean that we locate abstract deduction in a different plane than effective realities. We know that a culture is determined by a certain mental structure of man and the accidents of his history. Let us find out these facts, and then the question may be formulated as follows: given a specific human mentality and certain accidents of its history, what type of culture can it have?

To this must be added that Ramos and his followers had inherited Ortega's view that philosophy is a cultural expression. Obviously, if this is the nature of philosophy, the history of philosophy is the history of a cultural expression and must be studied in the same way other cultural expressions are studied. Philosophical interpretation and evaluation independently of cultural considerations are superfluous, if not impossible; what counts is the discovery of the relation of philosophy to the culture at large. The job of the philosopher in general, and the historian of philosophy in particular, is to uncover these

---

[9]   The classic text which initiated this approach in Latin America is Samuel Ramos's *El perfil del hombre y la cultura en México* (Mexico City: Universidad Nacional Autónoma de México, 1934 and 1963). This was followed by *Hacia un nuevo humanismo* (Mexico City: La Casa de España en México, 1940). The most representative work of Félix Schwartzmann is *El sentimiento de lo humano en América*, 2 vols. (Santiago: Universidad de Chile, 1950 and 1953). Many historians and philosophers have followed in the footsteps of Ramos and Schwartzmann. Among the most influential are Zea, Villegas, Nicol, Salazar Bondy, and Ricaurte Soler.

relations. Abstract questions of metaphysics and logic must be translated into concrete questions about the attitudes, values, and customs of particular cultures. It is significant that Ramos's book goes on to discuss such topics as cultural context, indigenism, the Mexican bourgeoisie, the influence of Spanish and French cultures on Mexico, and so on.

It is not my intention to criticize this approach insofar as it reveals the relations between philosophical ideas on one hand and the profound and frequently unconscious cultural currents which lead us to develop and adopt those ideas on the other. Culturalists often provide us with interesting and useful insights, in many cases their conclusions and explanations are not only correct but also enlightening. For example, it may be true that the main reason Latin American philosophers ultimately rejected nineteenth-century positivism is that this philosophy was contrary to cultural values deeply ingrained in Latino culture and society. But that has only limited interest for the philosopher. It does no doubt illustrate how non-philosophical factors play a role in philosophy, but it tells us nothing concerning the philosophical reasons Latin American philosophers gave for rejecting it. From the philosophical perspective, it is not important that Latin American philosophers rejected the position because they were culturally Latinos, but rather that they proposed philosophical reasons in support of their rejection.

The kind of cultural particularism involved in the culturalist approach has never been, nor is it in the present, something attractive to philosophers in general, including those who study the history of Latino philosophy. Philosophers are attracted by philosophical reasons. The cultural analysis helps us to understand what the thinkers of a particular culture have in mind, or had in mind if they belong to the past, and the cultural reasons why they do, or did, so. But this kind of analysis does not make clear the philosophical reasons they consider to be the foundations of those ideas and, therefore, it does not help, and in fact it may be an obstacle to the philosophical evaluation of such ideas. The kind of causal explanation favored by culturalists separates them from those who take a philosophical approach to the history of philosophy.[10]

But this is not all; philosophers from the present cannot expect to understand philosophers from the past unless they themselves play the role of philosophers. This is the only way in which one can truly understand what one's philosophical ancestors had in mind. The similarity in the enterprises between the two is what makes success possible.

[10] I have discussed the contribution of this and other so-called sociological approaches to the history of philosophy in Jorge J. E. Gracia, "Sociological Accounts and the History of Philosophy," in Martin Kusch (ed.), *The Sociology of Philosophical Knowledge* (Dordrecht, Netherlands. Kluwer, 2000), pp. 193–211.

In short, the fundamentally non-philosophical character of the culturalist approach, so popular among Latinos, both in the teaching of the history of philosophy and in the writing of the history of Latin American philosophy, stands in the way of the development of a truly philosophical spirit and of the appreciation of the contributions of Latino philosophers to philosophy.

2.   Ideology

The principal characteristic of this approach is that it involves a commitment to something alien to the history of philosophy. Those who use this approach study the history of philosophy because they think that study helps them reach a goal to which they are committed but which is neither philosophical nor historical. In some cases the goal is disinterested and worthy of admiration, but in other cases it is not. In the majority of cases it is mixed, and results from a lack of clear awareness in those who adopt it concerning what they believe and the aims they pursue. Ideologues, in contrast with philosophers and historians, do not seek the truth; they believe they have already found it, or they think it is impossible to find. They therefore use the history of philosophy only for rhetorical reasons, that is, to convince an audience of what they themselves have already accepted. As a consequence, this approach often displays an apologetic tone, and uses well-known formulas and clichés that it takes from the ideological current within which it functions. Also characteristic of it is an excessive sensitivity to criticism, as well as a marked belligerence against any comment that might be construed even as remotely critical.

The non-philosophical goal of the ideological approach allows for the use of non-philosophical means to spread philosophical ideas. Proselytizing and even force are not to be ruled out. And there is also the possibility of a cynical aim in ideology and that there is no real and true belief in the ideas promoted by the ideologue. For the ideologue, what is important is the object of commitment, which is neither philosophy nor history.

A very interesting case of the use of the ideological approach in Latin America occurred in the nineteenth century. At the time, Latin America was going through one of its many periods of social, political, and economic instability, and Latin American intellectuals, concerned about the situation, imported from Europe the set of ideas we now know as positivism. In Mexico, as Zea tells us, positivism became the official philosophy of Porfirio Díaz's dictatorship.[11] Some of those who adopted the new ideology and studied the ideas of Comte, Spencer, and other favorite positivists, did so because they were convinced that the positivist program was the best way to put an end to the instability of Latin America. This was clearly a worthy motive that we find

[11]   Leopoldo Zea, *Positivism in Mexico* (Austin, TX: University of Texas Press, 1974).

in some Latin American positivists such as, for example, the Argentinean José Ingenieros.[12] Others, however, were interested in personal gain, the continuity of the status quo that allowed them to have and preserve a privileged position in society. This latter motive, obviously, was not disinterested. Regardless of the motive Latin American positivists had, their commitment was something alien to the ideas they adopted to reach it. The ideas they studied, defended, and discussed were nothing more than instruments and means to get something else. The interest of many Latin American positivists in the philosophical thought that preceded them was ideological.

The reasons for the popularity of the ideological approach are quite obvious. No one can fail to understand the temptation to use and endorse ideas to bring about benefits to ourselves and those we care for. Indeed, I doubt anyone would object to the use of ideas to bring about beneficial changes to society. But the benefits this approach produces are unrelated to the history of philosophy, for they involve social and practical gains, not the understanding of the philosophical past. In fact, it is difficult to see that ideas from the past can be truly understood, when the overall aim of the one who seeks to understand them is something other than understanding. In short, there does not seem to be any advantage in adopting the ideological approach to study the history of philosophy, but its adoption has plenty of disadvantages.

Among the most serious of these disadvantages is the loss of objectivity. The emphasis on useful results, whether intended for the social group or the individual, interferes with the objective grasp of ideas themselves, leading to interpretations polluted by mercenary considerations derived from the value they have for something else. This attitude is a step backwards to the time preceding the discovery of science by the pre-Socratics, for it is characterized by a non-liberal understanding of knowledge and the history of thought, where knowledge and history have value only insofar as they can be used for some practical purpose. This devaluation of objectivity may not just result in an unintended distortion of the past, but sometimes leads to intended revisions of it in order to bring it in line with the positions necessary to reach desired goals.

A second important disadvantage of the ideological approach is that it is impossible to carry on a dialogue with those who adopt it. The practical aim the ideologue pursues is an obstacle to dialogue. True dialogue requires the exchange of ideas with a view toward mutual and deeper understanding because in all dialogue there is the implication of the possibility of change in

---

[12] José Ingenieros wrote two important historiographical works: *Direcciones filosóficas de la cultura argentina* (Buenos Aires: EUDEBA, 1963; first published in 1915), and *Evolución de las ideas argentinas*, 5 vols. (Buenos Aires 1918–20).

perspective in those engaged in dialogue. But ideologues leave no room for such possibility. They are interested in pushing their point of view so they can achieve the practical aim they have in mind. If they engage in what appears to be a dialogue, they do so only as a means of achieving their predetermined goal and only insofar as it does not interfere with that goal. There is no exchange of ideas, and there is no possibility of change of opinion on the part of the ideologue.

This closed attitude and the duplicity with which ideologues engage in what appears to be dialogue, has earned them both a bad name and the contempt of serious historians of philosophy and philosophers. For the conscious and willing use of the history of philosophy for aims alien to that history is repugnant to the historical spirit. It reveals either a cynical and sophistical attitude toward historical knowledge or a naive, quasi-religious commitment to a cause, and both are insurmountable obstacles to the history of philosophy. The history of philosophy requires description in addition to interpretation and evaluation, but ideologues are concerned only with the last two. And the interpretative and evaluative judgments they reach are based on non-philosophical considerations. As a result, their historical accounts of the history of philosophy are non-philosophical and of little interest to philosophers.

Perhaps an analogy with E. D. Hirsch, Jr's argument against the non-authorial interpretation of texts might be useful. His argument is that to interpret a text independently from what its author intended is morally reprehensible. As he puts it:

> To treat an author's words merely as grist for one's own mill is ethically analogous to using another man merely for one's own purposes. I do not say such ruthlessness of interpretation is never justifiable in principle, but I cannot imagine a situation where it would be justifiable in the professional practice of interpretation. The peculiarly modern anarchy of every man for himself in matters of interpretation may sound like the ultimate victory of the Protestant spirit. Actually, such anarchy is the direct consequence of transgressing the fundamental ethical norms of speech and its interpretation.[13]

Hirsch's point is that there is something immoral in the interpretation of a text that disregards an author's intention. I do not favor this kind of intentionalist interpretation in all cases, but I do think we can apply this point to our situation. We can do it by saying that there is something radically wrong with a non-philosophical, ideological interpretation of a philosophical text that is passed as philosophical but has little to do with the text.

---

[13]   E. D. Hirsch, Jr, "Three Dimensions of Hermeneutics," *New Literary History* 3, 2 (1972), 260.

Moreover, what prestige can a historiography have which is guided by interests that are not intrinsically tied with the ideas that are supposed to be studied? Who will take seriously a history of philosophy that does not itself take seriously the history of philosophy, but subordinates it to interests alien to it? In fact, not only historical narratives and analyses of the philosophy favored by Latin American positivists, but also the ideas themselves that they proposed lost credibility owing to their association with an ideological program.[14] And, finally, how can a student of philosophy bred in ideology learn to philosophize? The ideological teaching of the history of philosophy not only destroys any possibility of learning how to do philosophy but gives Latino philosophy a bad name. The reason is that it promotes methods that are not conducive to the achievement of the philosophical goal of developing a view of the world that is accurate, consistent, comprehensive, and supported by sound evidence. If what is important is the defense of a point of view already accepted and unquestionable, there can be very little hope of achieving the goals of philosophy, for the road to ideology and apology is very different to those necessary for the development of philosophy.

3. Doxography

The main feature of doxography is the emphasis on uncritical description. The doxographer aims to present views and ideas in a descriptive fashion without critical evaluation, and even discourages interpretation. Elsewhere I have distinguished three different kinds of doxography found in histories of philosophy: life-and-thought, univocal-question, and history-of-ideas doxographies.[15] Because of restrictions of space and the fact that in Latin America it is the first that has been most frequently used, I only discuss life-and-thought doxography here.

The most important feature of the life-and-thought doxographical approach is its concentration on the facts of the life and what are considered to be the fundamental ideas of various authors who are discussed serially. No attempt is made to discuss the reasons on the basis of which the figures in question reach their conclusions, nor is there much in the way of subtle interpretation or evaluation of their views. Although the aim of life-and-thought doxography is historical, to the degree that it seeks to provide accurate information about the past, those who practice this method treat philosophers and their ideas to a great extent as atomic units unconnected with each other. They usually pay

---

[14] The consequence is the well-known vitalist and spiritualist reaction against positivism in general. See Jorge J. E. Gracia, "Introduction: Latin American Philosophy Today," *Philosophical Forum* 20 (1988–9), 4–8.

[15] Gracia, *Philosophy and Its History*, ch. 5, pp. 246–53.

no attention to the historical circumstances that may have had a bearing on the philosophers' thinking, and their ideas are treated, for the most part, as single occurrences, and listed as parts of a kind of creed to which the philosophers in question adhered.

It is true that doxographers sometimes gather philosophers into schools, but this is done rather mechanically and serves more to keep them separate than to show the historical connections among them. Thus, for example, Locke, Berkeley, and Hume are gathered and treated together in the group of British empiricists because they all had similar views concerning human understanding. And Descartes, Malebranche, and Leibniz are put together into the group of Continental rationalists because they also held similar views of human knowledge, which differed substantially from the view of empiricists. But in both cases doxographers tend to ignore the connections among members of the groups. In contrast, they pay particular attention to chronology. A very important aspect of doxographies of the kind we are examining is temporal succession. Authors are arranged chronologically rather than in an order that expresses the historical interrelations among them.

This kind of history of philosophy does not reveal the historical connections among past philosophers and their views. Moreover, it distorts our perception of the way in which philosophical ideas are generated and develop because it does not present them as solutions to the problems that philosophers intended to solve through them. An accurate historical account of philosophical ideas must present ideas in their proper context as solutions to problems if that is in fact how they were meant. To this extent, then, the life-and-thought doxographical approach may be considered not only unhistorical but also historically distorting. In addition, this approach is philosophically superficial, because it does not consider ideas and arguments in depth and evades the kind of interpretation and evaluation that are essential to a good philosophical account of the past.

Still, we should not judge this approach too harshly. First, it should be noted that some of those who have adopted it have had a limited aim in mind. They are not trying to reconstruct the history of philosophy or to give a detailed account of it. They are trying rather to present us with some basic information about past philosophers and their views. They write information manuals, the sort of thing we find in encyclopedias and the like. Clearly, this information is useful, and the task of gathering it is not only legitimate but also historically relevant and necessary. We need to have works of reference where we can look up dates, titles of books, summaries of thought, and biographical information. This is, in fact, what we find in some classic doxographical works.

The main problem with life-and-thought doxography when used in the history of philosophy is not what it achieves, but the fact that it may be taken for more than it is, and some historians will consider themselves satisfied with it. The history of philosophy entails much more than the doxographer of this sort gives us: it requires critical analyses of ideas and the arguments used to support them, and also historically accurate accounts of the relations among authors and their views. Doxographies have a place in the history of philosophy, but it is a very limited place. Moreover, if the history of philosophy is treated doxographically in the classroom, it gives a distorted view of the discipline, discouraging such fundamental elements of its practice as argumentation and evaluation.

Among Latinos, the doxographical approach is frequently used in the classroom and in the writing of histories of philosophy. Examples of its use in studies of Latin American philosophy are common.[16] Among these, perhaps one that stands out is the *History of Philosophical Doctrines in Latin America* by Francisco Larroyo and Edmundo Escobar.[17] This book is little more than a compilation of data on the history of Latin American philosophy and yet it has been used widely to teach philosophy in Latin America.

The book is divided into three sections. The first two are devoted to methodological issues concerning philosophy and philosophical historiography. They take up about a fifth of the book. In the remaining 200 pages, the authors go through the complete history of Latin American philosophical ideas, from pre-Columbian thought to the present. These are divided into seven chapters arranged chronologically and *seriatim* as follows: (1) Pre-Columbian Thought; (2) Transplantation, Propagation, and Doctrinal Controversies; (3) Introduction to Modern Philosophy; (4) Americanist Doctrine, Enlightenment and Idealism; (5) Eclecticism, Utopian Socialism, and Positivism; (6) Overcoming Positivism and Philosophy of Freedom; and (7) Catholic Philosophy, Historical Materialism, Critical Idealism, Phenomenology, Existentialism, Material Theory of Values, Analytical Philosophy, History of Ideas. In these chapters, facts about the life and doctrines of the main representatives of the schools listed are packed together mercilessly. Consider, for example, the discussions of Phenomenology, Existentialism, and the Material Theory of Values, which takes up 11 pages of the 65 devoted to chapter 7. More than 30 authors are

---

[16] Examples of doxography are: José Luis Abellán, *Filosofía española en América (1936–1966)* (Madrid: Ediciones Guadarrama, 1967); Manfredo Kempff Mercado, *Historia de la Filosofía en Latinoamérica* (Santiago: Zig Zag, 1958); Harold Eugene Davis, *Latin American Thought: A Historical Introduction* (New York: The Free Press, 1974), and Guillermo Francovich, *La filosofía en Bolivia* (Buenos Aires: Losada, 1945).

[17] Francisco Larroyo and Edmundo Escobar, *Historia de las doctrinas filosóficas en Latinoamérica* (Mexico City: Editorial Porrúa, 1968).

discussed. Most of them receive no more than a brief mention or a short paragraph with a few important facts about their lives and doctrines. Their philosophical views are summarized in brief, descriptive statements which make no attempt at interpreting these views or explaining their significance. In general these "descriptions," devoid of interpretation and evaluation, lack both historical and philosophical interest. Consider the following comments:

> In Bolivia, Augusto Pescador, a Spanish emigree, was professor of the Universidad of La Paz from 1939 to 1955. His thought was articulated based on Hartmann. Since 1955, he is professor at the Universidad Austral of Chile. (Works: *Lógica, Sobre lo que no sirve*, etc.)

> In the Dominican Republic, Andrés Avelino has been concerned with logical problems.

> Risieri Frondizi (b. 1910), professor in Buenos Aires since 1935 and founder of the Department of Philosophy of the University of Tucumán (1938–40), has been in charge of chairs of logic, aesthetics, and history of ideas, in Argentina, Venezuela, and the USA. For Frondizi, philosophy is a theory of the totality of human experience. Underlining the importance of the self as a dynamic structure constituted by living, interacting acts with other subjects and things, he criticizes substantialist anthropology and psychology. In axiology, he takes a position contrary to subjectivism and objectivism, maintaining that value has to be understood in a relation of dependence to a complex of social and individual elements and circumstances (Works: *El punto de partida del filosofar*, 1945; *Substancia y función en el problema del yo*, 1952; *¿Qué son los valores?* 1958).

In short, because of its non-philosophical character, the doxographical approach interferes with the development of philosophy in Latin America and also is an obstacle to the proper appreciation of the contribution of Latinos to philosophy. Doxography lacks the dimensions of interpretation and evaluation essential to the philosophical task of developing a comprehensive and adequate view of the world.

4. Other approaches

In spite of the great differences between the three historiographical approaches I have described – the culturalist, the ideological, and the doxographical – there is a common factor to them that functions as an obstacle for the philosophical appreciation of the ideas about which they try to give a historical account: they lack the appreciation of philosophical ideas in themselves, of their relations, and of the value of those ideas. Philosophers are interested in truth and in what the history of philosophy has contributed to that truth. They want to advance their knowledge not only of the facts from the past, but more importantly of truth itself; they want their study of the history of philosophy to help them deepen their philosophical understanding. But none of the three approaches presented makes possible this kind of advancement, or furthers the appreciation of the contribution of historical ideas to philosophy. This is the reason why histories that use the approaches we have described do not help create interest in Latino thought or promote the practice of philosophy among Latinos.

Historians and teachers of Latino philosophy have not restricted themselves to the approaches I have described. For example, many use what I have called elsewhere, the scholarly approach, which seeks to establish facts from the past in an objective form, isolating them as far as possible from interpretation and evaluation.[18] There are also socio-political approaches, which search for the connection between the development of philosophical ideas and social and political events from the past.[19] Eschatologists present us with historical teleologies that move toward predetermined ends.[20] More recently, liberationist and postmodernist histories have become fashionable.[21] According to these, the function of the historian is to construct (perhaps I should say "make up") the history of Latino philosophical thought in accordance with the underlying political program favored by members of this movement. And there are many others. But I need not say more, for the common denominator to all these approaches is the same one shared by those I have given as examples before: the lack of philosophical aim.

What should we do then? Is there no solution to this problem? Is there a historiographical approach that could overcome the mentioned obstacle and is available to Latino philosophers? The answer to this question is affirmative. The approach I propose for the study of Latino philosophy, and for the study

---

[18] Some good examples are works of Mauricio Beuchot and Fernando Salmerón. For Beuchot, see *The History of Philosophy in Colonial Mexico* (Washington, DC: The Catholic University of America Press, 1999), and *Estudios de historia y de filosofía en el México colonial* (Mexico City: Universidad Nacional Autónoma de México, 1991), and for Salmerón, see *Cuestiones educativas y páginas sobre México* (Xalapa: Universidad Veracruzana, 1980).

[19] The work of Zea, to which I referred in note 11, fits this approach.

[20] Most of the work of José Vasconcelos falls within this category. See in particular, *La raza cósmica* (Barcelona: Agencia Mundial de Librería, 1925), *Indología* (Paris: Agencia Mundial de Librería, 1926), and *Historia del pensamiento filosófico* (Mexico City: Universidad Nacional Autónoma de México, 1937).

[21] Horacio Cerutti-Guldberg defends this historiographical approach in *Hacia una metodología de la historia de las ideas (filosóficas) en América Latina* (Guadalajara: Universidad de Guadalajara, 1986).

of the history of philosophy among Latinos, is what I have called elsewhere, *the framework approach.*

B. The framework approach

The framework approach holds that in order to do history of philosophy it is necessary to begin by laying down a conceptual map of the issues in the history of philosophy that the historian proposes to investigate. This conceptual map is composed of five basic elements: first, the analysis and definitions of the main concepts involved in the issues under investigation; second, the precise formulation of those issues, together with a discussion of their interrelationships; third, the exposition of solutions that may be given to those issues; fourth, the presentation of basic arguments for and objections against those solutions; and, finally, the articulation of criteria to be used in the evaluation of the solutions to the problems under investigation and the arguments and objections brought to bear on them. In short, the framework is a set of carefully defined concepts, formulated problems, stated solutions, articulated arguments and objections, and adopted principles of evaluation, all of which are related to the issues the historian proposes to explore in the history of philosophy.

In the case, for example, of an investigation into the notion of individuality in Francisco Romero's *Theory of Man*, the conceptual map would consist in at least the following: (1) the definition and analysis of terms such as 'individual,' 'individuality,' 'individuation,' 'person,' 'subject,' 'universal,' and so on, that is, terms that are commonly used, or that the historian thinks should be used, in the analysis of individuality; (2) the formulation of problems related to individuality (e.g., ontological status, identification); (3) the presentation of various types of theories of individuality (e.g., as difference, non-predicability, non-instantiability); (4) the investigation of arguments both for and against these theories (the need for parsimony prevents me from giving examples); and (5) a set of criteria that will be used in the evaluation of theories of individuality and of the arguments that are used to support or undermine such theories.[22] In (5) could be included general rules that have to do, for example, with coherence, although the most useful rules are specific ones, that is, rules the historian thinks have to do particularly with the topic in question.

---

[22] I have discussed some of these in Jorge J. E. Gracia, "Prolegomena," in *Individuality: An Essay on the Foundations of Metaphysics* (Albany, NY: State University of New York Press, 1988), and I have written a brief article on Romero on this topic: see Jorge J. E. Gracia, "Romero y la individualidad," in Ernesto Mayz Vallenilla (ed.), *Francisco Romero: Maestro de la filosofía latinoamericana* (Caracas: SIF, 1983), pp. 85–102.

The function of the framework is to serve as a conceptual map for determining the location and relation of ideas and figures in the history of philosophy relative to each other and to us. It does not seek to eliminate the complexity of the issues, positions, or figures by arbitrarily simplifying them. Nor is the framework guided by the teleological aim of the eschatologist's historical goal, where philosophical developments are described, interpreted, and evaluated only to the extent they fit a developmental schema leading to a pre-recognized aim. Finally, the framework should not ignore or try to eliminate real differences among views, authors, and cultures as a doxography does. The function of the conceptual framework in the approach I am proposing here is rather to help establish the differences and similarities among ideas that otherwise would be very difficult to compare. It is not to confirm a predetermined historical direction or to blur existing distinctions. The conceptual framework makes possible the translation of diverse nomenclatures and traditions to a common denominator that will allow the development of an overall understanding. It reduces the cacophony of ideas to certain parameters according to which positions may be more easily understood, and it lays down the basis for possible evaluations and the determination of their development throughout history. In this sense, the approach satisfies the need for objectivity required by the accurate description of history and also provides the foundations for interpretation and evaluation that are essential to a philosophical approach to the history of philosophy.

An explicit framework makes clear, moreover, the way in which ideas and authors are being interpreted by the historian and the criteria according to which they are being judged. Most historians of philosophy consciously or unconsciously engage in surreptitious judgments that are passed on as part of historical description. Because a conceptual framework is always operational in any discourse, it is inevitable that its categories affect any account being proposed in that discourse. Anachronism cannot be completely eradicated from historical accounts, for historians are not *tabulae rasae*, nor should they be. Moreover, the aim of a historical account is more than just the re-creation of the acts of understanding of philosophers from the past. Historians of philosophy go beyond those in order to make explicit the relations that could not have been made explicit in the past and to make judgments on the basis of evidence unavailable to the players in the historical drama. On the other hand, historical objectivity requires that interpretation and evaluation be clearly identified as such and distinguished as much as possible from description. We need practical ways of recognizing what is or may be anachronistic, and a sure way to make headway in the preservation of objectivity is by making the conceptual map at work in the historian's mind as explicit and clear as possible. This obviously makes it easier to disagree with the resulting account. Clarity invites disagreement, whereas obscurity helps consensus. This is the reason why ambiguity is so useful in political and legal documents. Rhetoricians know this fact very well and put it to good practical use. But philosophy and history are by nature opposed to such gimmicks. If the aims pursued are truth and understanding, either in philosophy or in history, then clarity is essential and any hidden assumptions and presuppositions must be exposed. Obviously, it is not possible to lay bare every assumption one holds. But the attempt must be made to do so as far as possible. This is the reason why the attempt at uncovering the interpretative and evaluative conceptual map at work in historical accounts must be made at the outset.

Finally, another advantage of the framework approach should not be overlooked: it considers essential to the historical account the description, interpretation, and evaluation not only of positions, but also of problems and arguments. Some of the approaches described earlier were predisposed to concentrate on certain aspects of the past. The doxographical approach, for example, seemed to be concerned almost exclusively with positions to the neglect of arguments and problems. In the framework approach, the very procedure requires paying attention to, and taking into account, problems, positions, and arguments. The preparation of the conceptual framework used for the understanding of the past involves systematically distinguishing the various problems and issues that are pertinent, formulating different alternative solutions, examining the fundamental ideas involved in them, and analyzing the sorts of arguments used for and against the solutions in question. And all of this is accompanied by a statement of the criteria used for historical selection, interpretation, and evaluation as well as a clear indication of the historian's own views on the issues under discussion.

The features that have been pointed out allow the framework approach to capture and integrate the most beneficial aspects of other historiographical approaches. There is, however, a limiting aspect of the framework approach that should not be ignored. The framework approach works best when it deals with an idea or problem or a closely knit set of ideas or problems, rather than with the large-scale description of all philosophical dimensions of a historical period.

The reason for this is that the development and exposition of a conceptual framework of the sort that this historiographical approach requires would not be feasible if such a framework were to cover all aspects of the thought of a period. The framework approach, therefore, faces limitations when it comes to the production of comprehensive histories of philosophy. Such general works need to rely on more specialized studies that themselves use the framework approach, although they cannot themselves use it to the fullest. Considering the breadth that comprehensive histories must have, they must of necessity be doxographical. This is an important corollary, for it suggests that comprehensive histories of philosophy cannot be carried out with the method I am arguing best suits the history of philosophy. Therefore, either they must be done using less philosophically appropriate methods, or they must not be done at all. Some historiographers have argued that they must not be done at all.[23] I believe there is some merit in them, however, provided they are themselves based on more probing analyses which use the framework approach, and their aim is informational rather than philosophical. In this way, they are supported by conclusions reached through a sound methodology, and at the same time make modest claims about the data they present.

The advantages of the framework approach are not a consequence of the eclectic aggregation of the methodologies of other historiographical methods. It would be fruitless to try to put together the techniques used by an ideologue and a doxographer, for example, for such a combination would be undesirable to the extent that its components have little to recommend for themselves. Finally, even if such a combination were desirable, the eclectic result would not necessarily constitute an effective procedure. To be so, it would have to come up with a concrete proposal for guidelines that the historian of philosophy should follow. And that can be accomplished only through the sensitivity developed in the awareness of the need to balance the descriptive, interpretative, and evaluative elements that enter into the historical account, not just by the eclectic aggregation of various procedures that by themselves have been found wanting.

There are at least two serious criticisms that can be brought to bear against the framework approach. The first is that it assumes too much.[24] It can be argued that this approach assumes that it is possible to develop a general and neutral conceptual framework that can serve as the grounds for comparison among widely differing views. But this assumption is contradicted by our experience of the wide conceptual chasm that separates the present from the past and one culture from another. There is, therefore, no general framework that could be used to compare views from different periods of history. Moreover, the conceptual framework could not be neutral, because it would be the product of a historical figure in a particular culture. The notion of a general

---

[23] Richard Rorty, "The Historiography of Philosophy: Four Genres," in Rorty, J. B. Schneewind, and Quentin Skinner (eds.), *Philosophy in History: Essays on the Historiography of Philosophy* (Cambridge: Cambridge University Press, 1984), p. 75.

[24] Paul Eisenberg raises this objection in a discussion of *Philosophy and Its History* that appeared as "*La filosofía y su historia*, de Jorge Gracia," in *Revista Latinoamericana de Filosofía* 22, 1 (1996), 119–21.

and neutral conceptual framework, therefore, is nothing but a projection of a historian's desire for objectivity, and can never be realized.

In response, I would like to say that the endorsement of the framework approach and its implementation do not require the actual existence of a perfectly general and neutral conceptual framework. Indeed, part of the rationale for the framework approach is the awareness of the biased and culturally oriented perspective of every historian of philosophy. No historian is free from conceptual assumptions or looks at history from a completely neutral stance. This is why it is necessary to develop procedures that will promote, if not ensure, as much objectivity as possible. The function of the conceptual framework in the framework approach is to make explicit, as far as possible, both the historians' understanding of the issues, arguments, and views with which they are dealing and their own views about how those issues are to be understood, as well as the relative value of contending arguments and views with respect to them. The generality and neutrality of the conceptual framework are not conceived as something given and required at the beginning of the historical inquiry, but rather as a methodological goal that regulates the process whereby historians try to understand and recover the philosophical past.

The other serious criticism I would like to bring up is that the framework approach may become a kind of Procrustean bed in which ideas that do not fit are cut off and discarded, and others are stretched beyond what their proper elasticity allows. In short, the accusation is of having a pre-established schema that historians set out to see substantiated in history, as did eschatologists such as Hegel and Augustine.[25]

This is certainly a danger for the framework approach. But those who practice the approach need not fall into it. First of all, the framework must be broad and general enough to include as many alternatives as possible, and it should also be open to alteration. The framework is not a system, a complete and circular set of ideas, but rather an open-ended set of guidelines. There has to be a reciprocal relationship between the conceptual framework and the textual study. Developments in the textual study should prompt modification in the conceptual framework and developments in the conceptual framework should heighten the awareness about possible interpretations of the texts. Moreover, if the historical context is kept ever-present, the danger of extravagant interpretations and wild evaluations will be substantially reduced. Finally, the explicitness of the conceptual framework should help guard against the implicit

---

[25] This criticism is usually made by those who favor a scholarly approach. Kenneth Schmitz brings it up against my view in "La naturaleza actual de la filosofía se revela en su historia," *Revista Latinoamericana de Filosofía* 22, 1 (1996), 97ff.

and disguised interrelations and evaluations that are woven into most historical accounts.

III.   Role of, and Approach to, the History of Philosophy

In conclusion, I see the framework approach as the best way to study the history of philosophy, including the history of Latino philosophy. The synchronic and diachronic integration of ideas that it makes possible cannot be found in any other approach and its eminently philosophical character serves to train students of philosophy in the discipline and to present Latino philosophy in the philosophical light necessary for it to be regarded with respect and interest by philosophers everywhere. The benefits of the framework approach are twofold: first, it serves as a proper tool to teach the history of philosophy insofar as, in this way, the study of the history of philosophy ceases to be an obstacle to philosophy and becomes a tool of it; second, its use in the study of the history of Latino philosophy in particular should make possible the appreciation of the value of this history by making clear its philosophical contribution to the history of philosophy in general. This in turn should help draw the attention of philosophers, both Latinos and non-Latinos, toward this substantial body of work.

Latinos in America

I began this book by pointing out that the growing population of Latinos in the United States has attracted attention and generated fear both in the Latino and the non-Latino communities. Latinos are perceived as posing various threats to the non-Latino population, and Latinos themselves feel threatened by both how we are perceived and the consequences of our Latino identity. These perceptions are revealed in the interaction of Latinos in American society, particularly the marketplace, affirmative action, and linguistic rights.

My response to this situation has been to argue that an important, and often neglected, contributing factor to the generation of these perceptions is a misconception of Latino identity. It is common to think of Latinos as having something in common with each other and as being essentially different from non-Latinos. This is a source of the fear that the growing numbers of Latinos will result in the elimination of values that are distinctive of the American way of life. Yet, the reality is very different, for there is nothing common to all Latinos. We are not homogeneous, but diverse, even though we are united by historical relations and contingent and contextual properties draw us together. We are a kind of family, and it is familial historical connections that tie us and allow us to use the term 'Latino' effectively in context. But the bases for the use of this term have nothing to do with homogeneity, although it has been easy for many, including some Latinos, to think they do.

I presented and defended this view of Latino identity in chapter 1, where I also showed how two conceptual formulations, the Globalism vs Particularism and the Essentialism vs Eliminativism dilemmas, were at the heart of the misconceptions concerning Latino identity. Next, I defended the view against two objections based on circularity and demarcation, and finally I finished the first part of the book by showing how the use of ethnic names has political implications that need to be taken into account. I also claimed that 'Latino' and similar ethnic labels function as proper names, and as such their primary use is to refer and they are established through a kind of baptism. Still, we learn to employ these terms through contingent descriptions which reflect the historical and familial nature of Latino identities.

The second part of the book turned to the situation of Latinos in the marketplace, affirmative action, and linguistic rights, three areas where Latinos are at the center of controversy and which affect their place in American society. Using the philosophy marketplace as an illustration, I argued that Latinos become marginalized because of the structures of power along which the philosophy profession is organized. Unless Latinos become de-Latinized in the sense that they are alienated from their Latino communities and intellectual roots, they have difficulty finding jobs and becoming public voices in America. The existence of these difficulties justifies the establishment of affirmative procedures that ensure the full participation of Latinos in the life of our democratic nation. I also claimed that the English-first argument in the context of the linguistic education of Latino children is unsound and may be inspired by mistaken conceptions of American nationality as an ethnos, and of ethnicity as necessarily involving a set of properties. These views go contrary to the position on identity I have proposed.

The third part of the book moves to the way Latinos think of themselves and of their intellectual heritage. I begin with the question of how to conceive Latino philosophy in view of the controversies that have surrounded the notion of Latin American philosophy. I conceived this philosophy as ethnic and distinct from what is often thought of as "scientific" philosophy. Understanding Latino philosophy in this way creates a framework in which problems of historiographical inclusion and exclusion can be more easily understood and resolved. It also facilitates a better understanding of the relations between Latino philosophy on one side and American philosophy on the other.

This led to the consideration of the canon of philosophy and the exploration of the exclusion of Latino philosophy from it. Although many historical and philosophical reasons have been proposed for this phenomenon, and most of them have some validity, one that is commonly neglected is the important role that tradition plays in the development of a canon, and particularly in that used in the United States. Tradition, conceived as a web of practices adopted by a community that designates some of its members as authorities, partly accounts for the absence of Latino philosophy both in the American and world canons of philosophy.

Finally, the last chapter argued that a contributing factor to the neglect of Latino philosophy in the United States and the world is the negative attitude that Latinos themselves have concerning Latino philosophy. This negative attitude is the result of many factors. In part it has to do with a well-known colonial mentality in which what comes from outside, from a dominator, is regarded as good, and what comes from inside, what is native, is regarded as bad. But an important element frequently neglected is that the history of Latino philosophy is generally studied and taught using the wrong approaches. In order for our philosophy to be regarded as valuable, it must be taught philosophically. This entails that Latino philosophy should be taken seriously as philosophy and that it should be subjected to the same conceptual standards of interpretation and evaluation to which other philosophies are subjected.

The view I have proposed is intended to make it easier for both Latinos and non-Latinos to grasp that we are not inexorably estranged from each other in America. Neither of us is "an other," necessarily opposed, different, and alien. Latinos and non-Latinos belong to different social groups, but these groups are not homogeneous and should not be regarded as foreign to each other. There is a you and an I, but there is also a we. There is no need to fear, and there is no real threat with which we need to be concerned. Latinos and non-Latinos are not like nations, political units separated by legal and territorial boundaries. They are rather like families, and as families, they may be related in some important respects and unrelated in others. Some Latinos and some non-Latinos share important things in common, just as some do not. But nothing is written on stone. Nothing is inexorably dividing. Nothing stands in the way of joining forces. There is no reason at all, indeed, why we cannot engage in constructive negotiation and productive dialogue.

Bibliography

Abellán, José Luis (1967) *Filosofía española en América (1936–1966)*. Madrid: Ediciones Guadarrama.

Acosta-Belén, Edna (1988) "From Settlers to Newcomers: The Hispanic Legacy in the United States." In Acosta-Belén, Edna, and Sjostrom, Barbara (eds.) *The Hispanic Experience in the United States: Contemporary Issues and Perspectives*. New York: Praeger, pp. 81–106.

—— (ed.) (1986) *The Puerto Rican Woman: Perspectives on Culture, History, and Society*. 2nd ed. New York: Praeger.

Acosta-Belén, Edna, and Sjostrom, Barbara (eds.) (1988) *The Hispanic Experience in the United States: Contemporary Issues and Perspectives*. New York: Praeger.

Acuña, Rodolfo (1971) *A Mexican American Chronicle*. New York: American Book Co.

Albó, Xavier (1995) "Our Identity Starting from Pluralism in the Base." In Beverly, J., Aronna, M., and Oviedo, J. (eds.) *The Postmodernism Debate in Latin America*. Durham, NC: Duke University Press, pp. 18–33.

Alcoff, Linda Martín (2006) *Visible Identities: Race, Gender, and the Self*. New York: Oxford University Press.

—— (2005) "Latino vs. Hispanic: The Politics of Ethnic Names." *Philosophy and Social Criticism* 31, 4: 395–408.

—— (2001) "Toward a Phenomenology of Racial Embodiment." In Bernasconi, Robert (ed.) *Race*. Oxford: Blackwell, pp. 267–83.

—— (2000) "Is Latina/o Identity a Racial Identity?" In Gracia, Jorge J. E. and De Greiff, Pablo (eds.) *Hispanics/Latinos in the United States: Ethnicity, Race, and Rights*. New York: Routledge, pp. 23–44.

—— (2000) "On Judging Epistemic Credibility: Is Social Identity Relevant?" In Zack, Naomi (ed.) *Women of Color and Philosophy: A Critical Reader*. Oxford: Blackwell, pp. 255–61.

—— (2000) "Who's Afraid of Identity Politics?" In Moya, Paula M. L. and Hames-García, Michael R. (eds.) *Reclaiming Identity: Realist Theory and the Predicament of Postmodernism*. Berkeley, CA: University of California Press, pp. 312–44.

—— (1999) "Philosophy and Racial Identity." In Bulmer, Martin, and Solomos, John (eds.) *Ethnic and Racial Studies Today*. London: Routledge, pp. 29–44.

—— (1995) "*Mestizo* Identity." In Zack, Naomi (ed.) *American Mixed Race: The Culture of Microdiversity*. Lanham, MD: Rowan and Littlefield Publishers, pp. 257–78.

Allen, Anita L. (2000) "Interracial Marriage: Folk Ethics in Contemporary Philosophy." In Zack, Naomi (ed.) *Women of Color and Philosophy: A Critical Reader*. Oxford: Blackwell, pp. 182–205.

American Philosophical Association Committee on Hispanics (2000) "Report on the Status of Hispanics in Philosophy." Posted on the APA webpage (http://www.apaonline.org/apa/).

Anderson, Benedict (1983) *Imagined Communities: Reflections on the Origin and Spread of Nationalism*. London: Verso Editions/NLB; rev. ed. 1990.

Andreasen, Robin O. (2005) "The Meaning of 'Race': Folk Conceptions and the New Biology of Race." *Journal of Philosophy* 102: 94–106.

—— (1998) "A New Perspective on the Race Debate." *British Journal for the Philosophy of Science* 49: 199–225.

Anzaldúa, Gloria (1987) *Borderlands/La Frontera: The New Mestiza*. San Francisco, CA: Spinsters/Aunt Lute.

Appiah, Kwame Anthony (2007) "Does Truth Matter to Identity?" In Gracia, Jorge J. E. (ed.) *Race or Ethnicity? On Black and Latino Identity*. Ithaca, NY: Cornell University Press, pp. 19–44.

—— (1996) "Race, Culture, Identity: Misunderstood Connections." In Appiah, Kwame Anthony, and Gutmann, Amy, with an Introduction by David B. Wilkins, *Color Conscious: The Political Morality of Race*. Princeton, NJ: Princeton University Press, pp. 30–105.

—— (1992) *In My Father's House: Africa in the Philosophy of Culture*. New York: Oxford University Press.

—— (1990) "'But Would That Still Be Me?' Notes on Gender, 'Race,' Ethnicity, as Sources of 'Identity.'" *Journal of Philosophy* 87: 493–9.

—— (1990) "Racisms." In Goldberg, D. T. (ed.) *Analysing Racism*. Minneapolis, MN: University of Minnesota Press, pp. 3–17.

—— (1985) "The Uncompleted Argument: Du Bois and the Illusion of Race." *Critical Inquiry* 12, 1: 21–37; rep. in Gates, Jr, Henry Louis (ed.) (1986) *Race, Writing and Difference*. Chicago, IL: University of Chicago Press; and in Bernasconi, Robert, and Lott, Tommy L. (eds.) (2000) *The Idea of Race*. Indianapolis, IN: Hackett, pp. 118–35.

Appiah, K. Anthony, and Gutmann, Amy, with an Introduction by Wilkins, David B. (1996) *Color Conscious: The Political Morality of Race*. Princeton, NJ: Princeton University Press.

Aristotle (1984) *The Complete Works of Aristotle*, 2 vols. Barnes, Jonathan (ed.) Princeton, NJ: Princeton University Press.

Babbitt, S. E., and Campbell, S. (eds.) (1999) *Racism and Philosophy*. Ithaca, NY: Cornell University Press.

Barron, Ana et al. (eds.) (1995) *¿Porqué se fueron? Testimonios de argentinos en el exterior*. Buenos Aires: EMECE.

Barth, Fredrick (ed.) (1969) *Ethnic Groups and Boundaries: The Social Organization of Culture Difference*. Oslo: Universitetsforlaget.

Baumeister, R. (1986) *Identity: Cultural Change and the Struggle for Self*. Oxford: Oxford University Press.

Bell, B. E. R., Grosholz, E., and Stewart, J. B. (1996) *W. E. B. Du Bois on Race and Culture*. New York: Routledge.

Belliotti, Raymond A. (1995) *Seeking Identity: Individualism versus Community in an Ethnic Context*. Lawrence, KN: University Press of Kansas.

Bernal, Martha E., and Knight, George Pitt (eds.) (1993) *Ethnic Identity: Formation and Transmission among Hispanics and Other Minorities*. Albany, NY: State University of New York Press.

Bernasconi, Robert (ed.) (2001) *Race*. Oxford: Blackwell.

Bernasconi, Robert, and Lott, Tommy L. (eds.) (2000) *The Idea of Race*. Indianapolis, IN: Hackett.

Bernstein, Richard (2001) "Comment on *Hispanic/Latino Identity* by J. J. E. Gracia." *Philosophy and Social Criticism* 27, 2: 44–50.

—— (1987) "Philosophical Rift: A Tale of Two Approaches." *New York Times*, Dec. 29.

Berreman, G. (1972) "Race, Caste and Other Invidious Distinctions in Social Stratifications." *Race* 13: 385–414.

Beuchot, Mauricio (1999) *The History of Philosophy in Colonial Mexico*. Washington, DC: The Catholic University of America Press.

—— (1991) *Estudios de historia y de filosofía en el México colonial*. Mexico City: Universidad Nacional Autónoma de México.

Black, Max (1963) *Philosophical Analysis: A Collection of Essays*. Englewood Cliffs, NJ: Prentice-Hall.

Block, Ned (2001) "How Heritability Misleads about Race." In Boxill, Bernard (ed.) *Race and Racism*. Oxford: Oxford University Press, pp. 114–45.

Block, N. D., and Dworkin, G. (1976) *The IQ Controversy*. New York: Pantheon.

Blum, L. (1999) "Ethnicity, Identity, and Community." In Blum, L. *Justice and Caring: The Search for Common Ground*. New York: Teachers College, pp. 127–45.

Boethius (1968) *The Theological Tractates*. Stewart, H. F., and Rand, E. R. (ed. and trans.) Cambridge, MA: Harvard University Press.

Boxill, Bernard (2001) "Introduction." In Boxill, Bernard (ed.) *Race and Racism*. Oxford: Oxford University Press, pp. 1–42.

—— (ed.) (2001) *Race and Racism*. Oxford: Oxford University Press.

Brennan, Andrew (1988) *Conditions of Identity: A Study of Identity and Survival*. Oxford: Clarendon Press.

Brewer, Robert E., and Brewer, Marilyn (1971) "Expressed Evaluation toward a Social Object as a Function of Label." *Journal of Social Psychology* 84: 257–60.

Brown, Michael E. (1997) "Causes and Implications of Ethnic Conflict." In Guibernau, M., and Rex, J. (eds.) *The Ethnicity Reader: Nationalism, Multiculturalism and Migration.* Cambridge: Polity Press, pp. 80–99.

Buchanan, Allen (1991) *Secession: The Morality of Political Divorce from Fort Summers to Lithuania and Quebec.* Boulder, CO: Westview.

Bulmer, Martin, and Solomos, John (eds.) (1999) *Ethnic and Racial Studies Today.* London: Routledge.

Bunge, Mario (1995) "Testimonio de Mario Bunge." In Barron, Ana et al. (eds.) *¿Porqué se fueron? Testimonios de argentinos en el exterior.* Buenos Aires: EMECE.

Butler, R. E. (1986) *On Creating a Hispanic America: A Nation within a Nation?* Special Report. Washington, DC: Council for Inter-American Security.

Cafferty, Pastora San Juan, and McCready, William C. (eds.) (1985) *Hispanics in the United States: A New Social Agenda.* New Brunswick, NJ: Transaction Books.

Calderón, F. (1995) "Latin American Identity and Mixed Temporalities; or, How to Be Postmodern and Indian at the Same Time." In Beverly, J., Oviedo, J., and Aronna, M. (eds.) *The Postmodernism Debate in Latin America.* Durham, NC: Duke University Press, pp. 55–64.

—— (1979) *Las democracias latinas de América.* Caracas: Biblioteca Ayacucho; first published in French in 1912.

Card, C. (1995) "On Race, Racism, and Ethnicity." In Bell, L. A., and Blumenfeld, D. (eds.) *Overcoming Racism and Sexism.* Lanham, MD: Rowan and Littlefield, pp. 141–52.

Carens, Joseph H. (1995) "Aliens and Citizens: The Case for Open Borders." In Kymlicka, Will (ed.) *The Rights of Minority Cultures.* Oxford: Oxford University Press, pp. 331–49.

Carter, Bob (2000) *Realism and Racism: Concepts of Race in Sociological Research.* London: Routledge.

Cashmore, E. (1988) *Dictionary of Race and Ethnic Relations.* London: Routledge

Castañeda, Héctor-Neri (1975) "Individuation and Non-Identity." *American Philosophical Quarterly* 12: 131–40.

Cavalli-Sforza, L. L. et al. (1994) *The History and Geography of Human Genes.* Princeton, NJ: Princeton University Press.

Cerutti-Guldberg, Horacio (ed.) (1992) *América Latina. Historia y destino. Homenaje a Leopoldo Zea.* Mexico City: Universidad Nacional Autónoma de México.

—— (1986) *Hacia una metodología de la historia de las ideas (filosóficas) en América Latina.* Guadalajara: Universidad de Guadalajara.

Chew, Matthew (2000) "Politics and Patterns of Developing Indigenous Knowledge under Western Disciplinary Compartmentalization: The Case of Philosophical Schools in Modern China and Japan." In Kusch, Martin (ed.) *The Sociology of Philosophical Knowledge,* Dordrecht, Netherlands: Kluwer, pp. 125–54.

Churrión, Pedro Lange, and Mendieta, Eduardo (1996) "Philosophy and Literature: The Latin American Case." *Dissens: Revista Internacional de Pensamiento Latinoamericano,* 2: 31–44.

Cohen, Avner, and Dascal, Marcelo (eds.) (1989) *The Institution of Philosophy: A Discipline in Crisis?* La Salle, IL: Open Court.

Cohen, Roger (2001) "How Open to Immigrants Should Germany Be? An Uneasy Country's Debate Deepens." *New York Times International,* Sunday, May 13.

Cohen, P. (ed.) (1999) *New Ethnicities, Old Racism?* London: Zed Books.

Collins, F. (1997) *Social Reality.* New York: Routledge.

Connolly, William (1991) *Identity/Difference: Democratic Negotiations of Political Paradox.* Ithaca, NY: Cornell University Press.

Copp, David (1997) "Democracy and Communal Self-Determination." In McKim, Robert, and McMahan, Jeff (eds.) *The Morality of Nationalism.* Oxford: Oxford University Press, pp. 277–300.

Corlett, J. Angelo (2002) *Race, Racism and Reparations.* Ithaca, NY: Cornell University Press.

—— (2001) "Latino/a Identity." *APA Newsletter on Hispanic/Latino Issues in Philosophy* (Fall): 97–104.

—— (2000) "Latino Identity and Affirmative Action." In Gracia, Jorge J. E. and De Greiff, Pablo (eds.) *Hispanics/Latinos in the United States: Ethnicity, Race, and Rights.* New York: Routledge, pp. 201–22.

—— (1999) "Latino Identity." *Public Affairs Quarterly* 13, 3: 273–95.

—— (1998) "Analysing Racism." *Public Affairs Quarterly* 12, 1: 23–50.

—— (1997) "Parallels of Ethnicity and Gender." In Zack, Naomi (ed.) *Race/Sex: Their Sameness, Difference and Interplay.* New York: Routledge, pp. 83–93.

Crawford, William Rex (1966) *A Century of Latin American Thought,* 3rd ed. New York: Praeger.

Cross, W. (1991) *Shades of Black: Diversity in African American Identity.* Philadelphia, PA: Temple University Press.

Dane, Leila, F. (1997) "Ethnic Identity and Conflict Transformation." *Peace Review* 9, 4: 503–7.

Davis, C. et al. (1988) "U.S. Hispanics: Changing the Face of America." In Acosta-Belén, E. and Sojstrom, B. R. (eds.) *The Hispanic Experience in the United States: Contemporary Issues and Perspectives.* New York: Praeger, pp. 3–78.

Davis, Harold Eugene (1974) *Latin American Thought: A Historical Introduction.* New York: The Free Press.

—— (1972) *Latin American Thought: A Historical Introduction.* Baton Rouge, LA: Louisiana State University Press.

—— (1961) *Latin American Social Thought: The History of Its Development since Independence, with Selected Readings.* Washington, DC: University Press of Washington.

Davis, David Brion (1997) "Constructing Race: A Reflection." *William and Mary Quarterly* 54, 1: 7–18.

De Greiff, Pablo (2000) "Deliberation and Hispanic Representation." In Gracia, Jorge J. E., and De Greiff, Pablo (eds.) *Hispanics/Latinos in the United States: Ethnicity, Race, and Rights.* New York: Routledge, pp. 235–52.

Delfino, Robert (ed.) (2006) *What Are We To Understand Gracia To Mean? Realist Challenges to Metaphysical Neutralism.* New York: Rodopi.

Dickie, George (1974) *Art and the Aesthetic: An Institutional Analysis.* Ithaca, NY: Cornell University Press.

Dinnerstein, Leonard, and Reimers, David M. (1975) *Ethnic Americans: A History of Immigration and Assimilation.* New York: Dodd, Mead & Co.

Donnellan, K. (1977) "Reference and Definite Descriptions." In Schwartz, S. P. (ed.) *Naming, Necessity and Natural Kinds.* Ithaca, NY: Cornell University Press, pp. 42–65.

—— (1977) "Speaking of Nothing." In Schwartz, S. P. (ed.) *Naming, Necessity and Natural Kinds.* Ithaca, NY: Cornell University Press, pp. 216–44.

—— (1970) "Proper Names and Identifying Descriptions." *Synthese* 21: 335–58.

Donoso, Antón (1976) "The Society for Iberian and Latin American Thought (SILAT): An Interdisciplinary Project." *Los ensayistas: Boletín Informativo* 1–2: 38–42.

Du Bois, W. E. B. (1976) *The World and Africa.* Millwood, NY: Kraus-Thomas Organization.

—— (1968) *The Health and Physique of the Negro American. Report of a Social Study Made Under the Direction of Atlanta University; Together with the Proceedings of the Eleventh Conference for the Study of the Negro Problems, Held at Atlanta University, on May the 29th, 1906.* Rep. in *Atlanta University Publications (Numbers 7–11–1902– 1906),* vol. II. New York: Octagon Books.

—— (1940) *Dusk of Dawn: An Essay Toward an Autobiography of a Race Concept.* New York: Harcourt, Brace and Co.

—— (1897) *The Conservation of Races.* The American Negro Academy Occasional Papers, No. 2. Washington, DC: The American Negro Academy, pp. 5–15. Rep. in Bernasconi, Robert (ed.) *Race.* Oxford: Blackwell, pp. 84–92.

Dussel, Enrique (1985) *Philosophy of Liberation.* Martínez, Aquilina, and Morkovsky, Christine (trans.) New York: Orbis Books.

—— (1973) *América Latina: dependencia y liberación.* Buenos Aires: Fernando García Cambeiro.

Educational Testing Service (1990) *Black, Hispanic, and White Doctoral Students: Before, During, and After Enrolling in Graduate School.* Princeton, NJ: Educational Testing Service.

Eisenberg, Paul (1996). "*La filosofía y sus historia,* de Jorge Gracia." *Revista Latino-americana de Filosofía* 22, 1: 109–21.

Elshtein, Jean Bethke (1995) *Democracy on Trial.* New York: Basic Books.

Epstein, Steven (1987) "Gay Politics, Ethnic Identity: The Limits of Social Construc-tionism." *Socialists Review* 17: 9–54.

Eriksen, Thomas Hylland (1997) "Ethnicity, Race, and Nation." In Guibernau, M., and Rex, J. (eds.) *The Ethnicity Reader: Nationalism, Multiculturalism and Migration.* Cambridge: Polity Press, pp. 33–42.

—— (1993) *Ethnicity and Nationalism: Anthropological Perspectives.* London: Pluto Press.

Fairchild, H. H., and Cozens, J. A. (1981) "Chicano, Hispanic or Mexican American: What's in a Name?" *Hispanic Journal of Behavioral Sciences* 3: 191–8.

Fernández, Carlos A. (1992) "*La Raza* and the Melting Pot: A Comparative Look at Multiethnicity." In Root, Maria P. P. (ed.) *Racially Mixed People in America.* Newbury Park, CA: Sage Publications, pp. 126–43.

Fernández Retamar, Roberto (1980) *Calibán and Other Essays*. Baker, Edward (trans.). Minneapolis, MN: University of Minnesota Press.

Flower, Elizabeth, and Murphy, Murray G. (1977) *A History of Philosophy in America*. New York: Capricorn Books.

Fox, Geoffrey (1996) *Hispanic Culture, Politics, and the Constructing of Identity*. New York: Carol Publishing Group.

Francis, E. K. (1976) *Interethnic Relations*. New York: Elsevier.

Francovich, Guillermo (1968) "Pachamama." In Zea, Leopoldo (ed.) *Antología de la filosofía americana contemporánea*. Mexico City: B. Costa Amic, pp. 79–87.

—— (1945) *La filosofía en Bolivia*. Buenos Aires: Losada.

Freyre, Gilberto (1963) *The Mansions and the Shanties (Sobrados e mucambos): The Making of Modern Brazil*. Onís, Harriet de (trans.) New York: Knopf.

Frondizi, Risieri (1971) *The Nature of the Self*. Carbondale, IL: Southern Illinois University Press.

—— (1951) "On the Unity of the Philosophies of the Two Americas." *Review of Metaphysics* 4: 617–22.

—— (1948–9) "Is There an Ibero-American Philosophy?" *Philosophy and Phenomenological Research* 9: 345–55.

—— (1948) "¿Hay una filosofía latinoamericana?" *Realidad* 3: 158–70.

Frondizi, Risieri, and Gracia, Jorge J. E. (eds.) (1975) *El hombre y los valores en la filosofía latinoamericana del siglo XX*. Mexico City: Fondo de Cultura Económica; rep. 1981.

Furlong, Guillermo (1944) *Bibliotecas argentinas durante la dominación hispánica*. Buenos Aires: Editorial Huarpes.

Gaos, José (1980) *En torno a la filosofía mexicana*. Introduction by Leopoldo Zea. Mexico City: Alianza.

—— (ed.) (1945) *Antología del pensamiento de lengua española en la edad contemporánea*. Mexico City: Séneca.

García Calderón, Francisco (1979) *Las democracias latinas de América: La creación de un continente*. Caracas: Biblioteca Ayacucho; first published in French in 1912.

García, Jorge L. A. (2007) "Racial and Ethnic Identity?" In Gracia, Jorge J. E. (ed.) *Race or Ethnicity? On Black and Latino Identity*. Ithaca, NY: Cornell University Press, pp. 45–77.

—— (2001) "Is Being Hispanic an Identity? Reflections on J. J. E. Gracia's Account." *Philosophy and Social Criticism* 27, 2: 29–43.

Garn, Stanley M. (1993) "Modern Human Populations." In *The New Encyclopedia Britannica*. Chicago, IL: Encyclopedia Britannica, Inc., vol. 18, pp. 844–54.

—— (1971) *Human Races*. Springfield, IL: Charles C. Thomas.

Gates, Jr, Henry Louis (ed.) (1986) *Race, Writing and Difference*. Chicago, IL: University of Chicago Press.

Geertz, Clifford (1973) *The Interpretation of Cultures: Selected Essays*. New York: Basic Books.

218 Bibliography

—— (1963) "The Integrative Revolution." In Geertz, Clifford (ed.) *Old Societies and New States: The Quest for Modernity in Asia and Africa.* New York: Free Press, pp. 105–57.

—— (ed.) (1963) *Old Societies and New States: The Quest for Modernity in Asia and Africa.* New York: Free Press.

George, David (1996) "National Identity and Self-Determination." In Caney, Simon, George, David, and Jones, Peter (eds.) *National Rights, International Obligations.* Boulder, CO: Westview, pp. 13–33.

Gilroy, Paul (1993) *The Black Atlantic: Modernity and Double Consciousness.* Cambridge, MA: Harvard University Press.

Gil-White, Francisco J. (2001) "Are Ethnic Groups Biological 'Species' to the Human Brain? Essentialism in Our Cognition of Some Social Categories." *Current Anthropology* 42, 4: 515–54.

—— (2001) "Sorting Is Not Categorization: A Critique of the Claim that Brazilians Have Fuzzy Racial Categories." *Cognition and Culture* 1, 3: 1–23.

—— (1999) "How Thick Is Blood? The Plot Thickens . . . : If Ethnic Actors Are Primordialists, What Remains of the Circumstantialist/Primordialist Controversy?" *Ethnic and Racial Studies* 22, 5: 789–820.

Giménez, Martha (1989) "'Latino?/Hispanic' – Who Needs a Name? The Case Against a Standardized Terminology." *International Journal of Health Services* 19, 3: 557–71.

Glasgow, Joshua M. (2003) "On the New Biology of Race." *Journal of Philosophy* 100: 456–74.

Glazer, Nathan (1995) "Individual Rights Against Group Rights." In Kymlicka, Will (ed.) *The Rights of Minority Cultures.* Oxford: Oxford University Press, pp. 123–38.

—— (1982) "Government and the American Ethnic Pattern." In Van Horne, Winston (ed.) *Ethnicity and Public Policy.* Milwaukee, WI: University of Wisconsin, pp. 24–41.

Glazer, Nathan, and Moynihan, Daniel P. (1963) *Beyond the Melting Pot: The Negroes, Puerto Ricans, Jews, Italians, and Irish of New York City.* Cambridge, MA: MIT Press.

Glazer, Nathan, and Moynihan, Daniel P. (eds.) (1975) *Ethnicity: Theory and Experience.* Cambridge, MA: Harvard University Press.

Gleason, P. (1992) "Identifying Identity: A Semantic History." In Gleason, P. *Speaking of Diversity: Language and Ethnicity in Twentieth-Century America.* Baltimore, MD: Johns Hopkins University Press, p. 123–49.

Goldberg, David T. (1993) *Racist Culture: Philosophy and the Politics of Meaning.* Oxford: Blackwell.

Goldberg, David T., and Solomos, John (eds.) (2002). *A Companion to Racial and Ethnic Studies.* Oxford: Blackwell.

Gómez Martínez, José Luis (ed.) (1997–2005) *Proyecto Ensayo Hispánico.* Available from (www.ensayistas.org).

—— (1996) "Posmodernidad, discurso antrópico y ensayística latinoamericana." *Dissens, Revista Internacional de Pensamiento Latinoamericano* 2.

—— (1995) *Pensamiento de la liberación: Proyección de Ortega en América*. Mexico City: Ediciones EGE.

Gómez Robledo, Antonio (1946) *La filosofía en el Brasil*. Mexico City: Imprenta Universitaria.

González, Justo L. (1992) "Hispanics in the United States." *Listening: Journal of Religion and Culture* 27, 1: 7–16.

Gooding-Williams, Robert (2001) "Comment on J. J. E. Gracia's *Hispanic/Latino Identity*." *Philosophy and Social Criticism* 27, 2: 3–10.

—— (2001) "Race, Multiculturalism and Democracy." In Bernasconi, Robert (ed.) *Race*. Oxford: Blackwell, pp. 237–59.

Gordon, L. (1995) *Bad Faith and Antiblack Racism*. Atlantic Highlands, NJ: Humanities Press.

Gordon, Milton (1964) *Assimilation in American Life*. New York: Oxford University Press.

Gracia, Jorge J. E. (forthcoming) "Identity and Latin American Philosophy." In Nuccetelli, Susana (ed.) *Blackwell Companion to Latin American Philosophy*. Oxford: Blackwell.

—— (2007) "Individuation of Racial and Ethnic Groups: The Problems of Circularity and Demarcation." In Gracia, Jorge J. E. (ed.) *Race or Ethnicity? On Black and Latino Identity*. Ithaca, NY: Cornell University Press, pp. 78–99.

—— (2007) "What Is Latin American Philosophy?" In Yancy, George (ed.), *Philosophy in Multiple Voices*. Lanham, MD: Rowman & Littlefield, pp. 175–96.

—— (ed.) (2007) *Race or Ethnicity? On Black and Latino Identity*. Ithaca, NY: Cornell University Press.

—— (2005) "The History of Philosophy and Latin American Philosophy." In Salles, Arleen and Millán-Zaibert, Elizabeth (eds.) *The Role of History in Latin American Philosophy: Contemporary Perspectives*. Albany, NY: State University of New York Press, pp. 21–42.

—— (2005) "A Political Argument in Favor of Ethnic Names." *Philosophy and Social Criticism* 31, 4: 409–17.

—— (2005) *Surviving Race, Ethnicity, and Nationality: A Challenge for the Twenty-First Century*. New York: Rowman & Littlefield Publishers, Inc.

—— (2004) "Language Priority in the Education of Children: Pogge's Argument in Favor of English-First for Hispanics." *Journal of Social Philosophy* 35, 3: 420–32.

—— (2003) "Ethnic Labels and Philosophy." In Mendieta, Eduardo (ed.) *Latin American Philosophy: Currents, Issues, Debates*. Bloomington, IN, Indiana University Press, pp. 57–67.

—— (2003) *Old Wine in New Skins: The Role of Tradition in Communication, Knowledge, and Group Identity*. The 67th Aquinas Lecture. Milwaukee, WI: Marquette University Press.

—— (2002) "Globalization, Philosophy, and Latin America." In Sáenz, Mario (ed.) *Latin American Perspectives on Globalization: Ethics, Politics, and Alternative Visions*. Lanham, MD: Rowan & Littlefield, pp. 123–31.

—— (2002) "Minorities in the Philosophical Marketplace." *Metaphilosophy* 33, 2: 535–51.

—— (2001) "Response to the Critics of *Hispanic/Latino Identity: Tahafut Al-Tahafut.*" *Philosophy and Social Criticism* 27, 2: 51–75.

—— (2000) "Affirmative Action for Latinos? Yes and No." In Gracia, Jorge J. E., and De Greiff, Pablo (eds.) *Latinos in the United States: Ethnicity, Race, and Rights.* New York: Routledge, pp. 201–21.

—— (2000) *Hispanic/Latino Identity: A Philosophical Perspective.* Oxford: Blackwell.

—— (2000) "Hispanic/Latino Identity: Homogeneity and Stereotypes," *Ventana Abierta* 2, 8: 17–25.

—— (2000) "Sociological Accounts and the History of Philosophy." In Kusch, Martin (ed.) *The Sociology of Philosophical Knowledge.* Dordrecht, Netherlands: Kluwer, pp. 193–211.

—— (1999) "Hispanics, Philosophy, and the Curriculum." *Teaching Philosophy* 22, 3: 241–8.

—— (1999) *Metaphysics and Its Task: The Search for the Categorial Foundation of Knowledge.* Albany, NY: State University of New York Press.

—— (1999) "The Nature of Ethnicity with Special Reference to Hispanic/Latino Identity." *Public Affairs Quarterly* 13, 1: 25–42.

—— (1998) "El escolasticismo ibérico: Puente entre la antigüedad clásica y el pensamiento colonial iberoamericano." In Gracia, Jorge J. E. *Filosofía hispánica: Concepto, origen y foco historiográfico.* Pamplona: Universiad de Navarra, pp. 45–81.

—— (1998) *Filosofía hispánica: Concepto, origen y foco historiográfico.* Pamplona: Universidad de Navarra.

—— (1993) "Hispanic Philosophy: Its Beginning and Golden Age." *Review of Metaphysics* 46, 3: 475–502; reprinted in White, K. (ed.) (1997) *Hispanic Philosophy in the Age of Discovery.* Washington, DC: The Catholic University of America Press, pp. 3–27.

—— (1992) "La liberación como foco utópico del pensamiento latinoamericano." In *La utopía en América: Simposio internacional sobre el quinto centenario.* Santo Domingo: Universidad Autónoma de Santo Domingo, pp. 28–44.

—— (1992) *Philosophy and Its History: Issues in Philosophical Historiography.* Albany, NY: State University of New York Press. Sánchez, Juan José (trans. into Spanish) (1998) *La filosofía y su historia: Cuestiones de historiografía filosófica.* Mexico City: Universidad Nacional Autónoma de México.

—— (1992) "Zea y la liberación latinoamericana." *América Latina: historia y destino. Homenaje a Leopoldo Zea.* Mexico City: UNAM, pp. 95–105.

—— (1988–9) "Introduction: Latin American Philosophy Today." *Philosophical Forum* 20: 4–32.

—— (ed.) (1988–9) *Latin American Philosophy Today.* Double issue of *Philosophical Forum* 20, 1–2.

—— (1988) *Individuality: An Essay on the Foundations of Metaphysics.* Albany, NY: State University of New York Press.

—— (1988) *Introduction to the Problem of Individuation in the Early Middle Ages.* 2nd rev. ed. Munich: Philosophia Verlag.

—— (ed.) (1988) *Directory of Latin American Philosophers.* Buffalo, NY: Council on International Studies and Programs.

—— (ed.) (1986) *Latin American Philosophy in the Twentieth Century: Man, Values, and the Search for Philosophical Identity.* Buffalo, NY: Prometheus Books.

—— (1983) "Romero y la individualidad." In Mayz Vallenilla, Ernesto (ed.) *Francisco Romero: Maestro de la Filosofía latinoamericana.* Caracas: SIF, pp. 85–102.

—— (1975) "Importance of the History of Ideas in Latin America: Zea's *Positivism in Mexico.*" *Journal of the History of Ideas* 36: 177–84.

Gracia, Jorge J. E., Bosch, Lynette, and Alvarez-Borland, Isabel (eds.) (2007) *Identity, Memory, and Diaspora: Voices of Cuban-American Artists, Writers, and Philosophers.* Albany, NY: State University of New York Press.

Gracia, Jorge J. E., and Camurati, Mireya (eds.) (1989) *Philosophy and Literature in Latin America: A Critical Assessment of the Current Situation.* Albany, NY: State University of New York Press.

Gracia, Jorge J. E., and De Greiff, Pablo (eds.) (2000) *Hispanics/Latinos in the United States: Ethnicity, Race, and Rights.* New York: Routledge.

Gracia, Jorge J. E., and Jaksić, Iván (eds.) (1988) *Filosofía e identidad cultural en América Latina.* Caracas: Monte Avila.

Gracia, Jorge J. E., and Jaksić, Iván (1984) "The Problem of Philosophical Identity in Latin America: History and Approaches." *Inter-American Review of Bibliography* 34: 53–71.

Gracia, Jorge J. E., Korsmeyer, Carolyn, and Gasché, Rodolphe (eds.) (2002). *Literary Philosophers: Borges, Calvino, Eco.* New York: Routledge.

Gracia, Jorge J. E., and Millán-Zaibert, Elizabeth (eds.) (2004) *Latin American Philosophy for the 21st Century: The Human Condition, Values, and the Search for Identity.* Buffalo, NY: Prometheus Books.

Gracia, Jorge J. E. et al. (eds.) (1984) *Philosophical Analysis in Latin America.* Dordrecht, Netherlands: D. Reidel; more extensive Spanish ed.: *El análisis filosófico en América Latina* (1985) Mexico City: Fondo de Cultura Económica.

Greeley, Andrew M. (1974) *Ethnicity in the United States: A Preliminary Reconnaissance.* New York: John Witley.

Grosfoguel, Ramón, and Georas, Chloé S. (1996) "The Racialization of Latino Caribbean Migrants in the New York Metropolitan Area." *CENTRO Journal of the Center for Puerto Rican Studies* 8, 1–2: 191–201.

Guibernau, M. (1997) "Nations Without States: Catalonia, a Case Study." In Guibernau, M. and Rex, J. (eds.) *The Ethnicity Reader: Nationalism, Multiculturalism and Migration.* Cambridge: Polity Press, pp. 133–53.

—— (1996) *Nationalisms: The Nation-State and Nationalism in the Twentieth Century.* Cambridge: Polity Press.

Guibernau, M., and Rex, John (1997) "Introduction." In Guibernau, M. and Rex, J. (eds.) *The Ethnicity Reader: Nationalism, Multiculturalism and Migration.* Cambridge: Polity Press, pp. 1–12.

Guibernau, M., and Rex, John (eds.) (1997) *The Ethnicity Reader: Nationalism, Multiculturalism and Migration.* Cambridge: Polity Press.

Gurr, Ted Robert (2000) "Ethnic Warfare on the Wane." *Foreign Affairs* 79, 3: 52–64.
—— (1993) *Minorities at Risk: A Global View of Ethnopolitical Conflict.* Washington, DC: Institute of Peace Press.
Gurr, Ted Robert, and Harff, Barbara (1994) *Ethnic Conflicts in World Politics.* Boulder, CO: Westview Press.
Gurr, Ted Robert, Marshall, Monty, and Khosla, Deepa (2000) *Peace and Conflict 2000: A Global Survey of Armed Conflicts, Self-Determination Movements, and Democracy.* College Park, MD: Center for International Development and Conflict Management, University of Maryland.
Habermas, J. (1992–3) "Citizenship and National Identity: Some Reflections on the Future of Europe." *Praxis International* 12: 1–19.
Hacker, Andrew (1992) *Two Nations: Black and White, Separate, Hostile, Unequal.* New York: Scribner's.
Hacking, Ian (2002) *Historical Ontology.* Cambridge, MA: Harvard University Press.
—— (1999) *The Social Construction of What?* Cambridge, MA: Harvard University Press.
—— (1986) "Making Up People." In Thomas C. Heller et al. (eds.) *Reconstructing Individualism: Autonomy, Individuality and the Self in Western Thought.* Stanford, CA: Stanford University Press, pp. 222–36.
Haddox, John H. (1970) "Latin America: One and/or Many: A Philosophical Exploration." In Jones, E. and Dean, F. (eds.) *The Americas and Self-Identification.* College Station, TX: Texas A & M University Press, pp. 62–75.
Hall, Stuart (1994) "Ethnicity." W. E. B. Du Bois Lecture. Cambridge, MA: Harvard University.
Hames-García, Michael R. (2000) "'Who Are Our Own People?': Challenges for a Theory of Social Identity." In Moya, Paula M. L., and Hames-García, Michael R. (eds.) *Reclaiming Identity: Realist Theory and the Predicament of Postmodernism.* Berkeley, CA: University of California Press, pp. 102–32.
Hanchard, Michael G. (2000) "Racism, Eroticism, and the Paradodoxes of a U.S. Black Researcher in Brazil." In Twine, France Winddance, and Earren, Jonathan W. (eds.) *Racing Research, Researching Race: Methodological Dilemmas in Critical Race Studies.* New York: New York University Press, pp. 165–86.
Hanke, Lewis (1974) *All Mankind is One: A Study of the Disputation Between Bartolomé de Las Casas and Juan Ginés de Sepúlveda in 1550 on the Intellectual and Religious Capacity of the American Indians.* DeKalb, IL: Northern Illinois University Press.
—— (1959) *Aristotle and the American Indians: A Study in Race Prejudice in the Modern World.* Bloomington, IN, Indiana University Press.
Hardimon, Michael O. (2003) "The Ordinary Concept of Race." *Journal of Philosophy* 100: 437–55.
Hargreaves, A. G., and Leaman, J. (eds.) (1995). *Racism, Ethnicity, and Politics in Contemporary Europe.* Aldershot, UK: Elgar.
Harris, Leonard (2002) "Prolegomenon to a Tradition: What is American Philosophy?" In Harris, Leonard, Pratt, Scott L., and Waters, Anne S. (eds.) *American Philosophies: An Anthology.* Oxford: Blackwell, pp. 5–6.

—— (ed.) (1999) *Racism*. Amherst, NY: Humanities Press.

Harris, Leonard, Pratt, Scott L., and Waters, Anne S. (eds.) (2002) *American Philosophies: An Anthology*. Oxford: Blackwell.

Hayes-Bautista, David E. (1983) "On Comparing Studies of Different *Raza* Populations." *American Journal of Public Health* 73: 274–6.

—— (1980) "Identifying 'Hispanic' Populations: The Influence of Research Methodology upon Public Policy." *American Journal of Public Health* 70: 353–6.

Hayes-Bautista, David E., and Chapa, Jorge (1987) "Latino Terminology: Conceptual Bases for Standardized Terminology." *American Journal of Public Health* 77: 61–8.

Henry, D. P. (1984) *That Most Subtle Question (Quaestio Subtilissima): The Metaphysical Bearing of Mediaeval and Contemporary Linguistic Disciplines*. Manchester: Manchester University Press.

Hintzen, Percy C. (2002) "The Caribbean: Race and Creole Ethnicity." In Goldberg, D. T., and Solomos, J. (eds.) *A Companion to Race and Ethnicity*. Oxford: Blackwell, pp. 475–94.

Hirsch, Jr, F. D. (1972) "Three Dimensions of Hermeneutics." *New Literary History* 3, 2: 245–61.

Hobsbawm, Eric (1997) "An Anti-Nationalist Account of Nationalism Since 1989." In Guibernau, M. and Rex, J. (eds.) *The Ethnicity Reader: Nationalism, Multiculturalism and Migration*. Cambridge: Polity Press, pp. 69–79.

—— (1992) "Ethnicity and Nationalism in Europe Today." *Anthropology Today* 8, 1: 3–8.

Hobsbawm, Eric, and Ranger, Terence (eds.) (1983) *The Invention of Tradition*. Cambridge: Cambridge University Press.

Hofstede, G. (1980) *Culture's Consequences: International Differences in Work-Related Values*. Beverly Hills, CA: SAGE Publishers.

Hollinger, David A. (2006) "From Identity to Solidarity." *Daedalus* (Fall): 23–31.

—— (2006) *Postethnic America: Beyond Multiculturalism*. Revised and updated. New York: Basic Books.

hooks, bell (1990) *Yearning: Race, Gender, and Cultural Politics*. Boston, MA: South End Press.

Horowitz, Donald L. (1985) *Ethnic Groups in Conflict*. Berkeley, CA: University of California Press.

—— (1975) "Ethnic Identity." In Glazer, N., and Moynihan, D. P. (eds.) *Ethnicity: Theory and Experience*. Cambridge, MA: Harvard University Press, pp. 111–40.

Huntington, Samuel P. (2004) "The Hispanic Challenge." *Foreign Affairs* (March–April). 30–45.

—— (2004) *Who Are We? The Challenges to America's National Identity*. New York: Simon and Schuster.

Hutchinson, J., and Smith, A. D. (eds.) (1996) *Ethnicity*. Oxford: Oxford University Press.

Ignatiev, Noel (1935) *How the Irish Became White*. New York: Routledge.

Ingenieros, José (1918–20) *Evolución de las ideas argentinas*, 5 vols. Buenos Aires.

—— (1963) *Direcciones filosóficas de la cultura argentina*. Buenos Aires: EUDEBA; first published in 1915.

Ingle, Dwight J. (1978) "Fallacies in Arguments on Human Differences." In Travis Osborne, T. (ed.) *Human Variation: The Biopsychology of Age, Race, and Sex*. New York: Academic Press, pp. 5–27.

Isaacs, Harold R. (1975) "Basic Group Identity." In Glazer, N., and Moynihan, D. P. (eds.) *Ethnicity: Theory and Experience*. Cambridge, MA: Harvard University Press, pp. 29–52.

Jaffe, A. J. et al. (1980) *The Changing Demography of Spanish Americans*. New York: Academic Press.

Jaksić, Iván. (2007) *Ven conmigo a la España lejana: los intelectuales norteamericanos ante el mundo hispano, 1820–1880*. Mexico City: Fondo de Cultura Económica.

—— (1989) *Academic Rebels in Chile: The Role of Philosophy in Higher Education and Politics*. Albany, NY: State University of New York Press.

Jenkins, Richard (1999) "Ethnicity Etcetera: Social Anthropological Points of View." In Bulmer, Martin and Solomos, John (eds.) *Ethnic and Racial Studies Today*. London: Routledge, pp. 85–97.

—— (1997) *Rethinking Ethnicity: Arguments and Explorations*. London: Sage.

—— (1996) *Social Identity*. London: Routledge.

—— (1994) "Rethinking Ethnicity: Identity, Categorization and Power." *Ethnic and Racial Studies* 17: 196–223.

Jones, Siân (1999) "Peopling the Past: Approaches to 'Race' and Ethnicity in Archeology." In Bulmer and Solomos, John (eds.) *Ethnic and Racial Studies Today*. London: Routledge, pp. 152–66.

Kellas, James (1991) *The Politics of Ethnicity and Nationalism*. New York: St Martin's Press.

Kennedy, Kenneth K. R. (1973) "Race and Culture." In Naroll, Raoul and Naroll, Frada (eds.) *Main Currents in Cultural Anthropology*. New York: Appleton-Century-Crofts, pp. 123–55.

Keyes, Charles F. (1981) *Ethnic Change*. Seattle, WA: University of Washington Press.

Kitcher, Philip (1999) "Race, Ethnicity, Biology, Culture." In Harris, Leonard (ed.) *Racism*. Amherst, NY: Humanities Press, pp. 87–120.

Knight, Alan (1990) "Racism, Revolution, and *Indigenismo*: Mexico, 1910–1940." In Graham, Richard (ed.) *The Idea of Race in Latin America, 1870–1940*. Austin, TX: University of Texas Press, pp. 71–113.

Kripke, Saul (1981) *Naming and Necessity*. Oxford: Blackwell.

Kusch, Martin (ed.) (2000) *The Sociology of Philosophical Knowledge*. Dordrecht, Netherlands: Kluwer.

—— (1995) *Psychologism: A Case Study in the Sociology of Philosophical Knowledge*. London: Routledge.

Kymlicka, Will (1997) "Do We Need a Liberal Theory of Minority Rights?" *Constellations* 4, 1: 72–87.

—— (1997) "Ethnicity in the USA." In Guibernau, M., and Rex, J. (eds.) *The Ethnicity Reader: Nationalism, Multiculturalism and Migration*. Cambridge: Polity Press, pp. 229–47.

—— (1995) "Introduction." In Kymlicka, Will (ed.) *The Rights of Minority Cultures.* Oxford: Oxford University Press, pp. 1–27.

—— (1995) *Multicultural Citizenship: A Liberal Theory of Minority Rights.* Oxford: Oxford University Press.

—— (ed.) (1995) *The Rights of Minority Cultures.* Oxford: Oxford University Press.

Larroyo, Francisco, and Escobar, Edmundo (1968) *Historia de las doctrinas filosóficas en Latinoamérica.* Mexico City: Editorial Porrúa.

Las Casas, Bartolomé de (1992) *In Defense of the Indians: The Defense of the Most Reverend Lord, Don Fray Bartolomé de las Casas, of the Order of Preachers, Late Bishop of Chiapa, Against the Persecutors and Slanderers of the Peoples of the New World Discovered Across the Seas.* Poole, Stafford (trans. and ed.) DeKalb, IL: Northern Illinois University Press.

Lauret, Maria (1999) "'The Approval of Headquarters': Race and Ethnicity in English Studies." In Bulmer, Martin, and Solomos, John (eds.) *Ethnic and Racial Studies Today.* London: Routledge, pp. 124–35.

Lentz, C. (1995) "'Tribalism' and 'Ethnicity' in Africa: A Review of Four Decades of Anglophone Research." *Cahiers des Sciences Humanes* 31: 303–28.

León-Portilla, Miguel (1988) *Time and Reality in the Thought of the Maya.* 2nd ed. Norman, OK: University of Oklahoma Press.

Levinson, Daniel J. (1950) "The Study of Ethnocentric Ideology." In Adorno, Theodor et al. *The Authoritarian Personality.* New York: Norton, pp. 102–15.

Lewontin, R. C. (1998) "Race." In *Encyclopedia Americana.* Danbury, CN: Grolier, vol. 23, pp. 116–22.

—— (1972) "The Apportionment of Human Diversity." *Evolutionary Biology* 6: 381–98.

Liss, S. B. (1984) *Marxist Thought in Latin America.* Berkeley, CA: University of California Press.

Lissak, Rivka Shpak (1989) *Pluralism and Progressives: Hull-House and the New Immigrants, 1890–1919.* Chicago, IL: University of Chicago Press.

Litt, E. (1970) *Ethnic Politics in America: Beyond Pluralism.* Glenview, IL: Scott, Foresman.

Llobera, J. (1994) *The God of Modernity: The Development of Nationalism in Western Europe* Oxford: Berg.

Lowry, I. S. (1982) "The Science and Politics of Ethnic Enumeration." In Van Horne, W. A. (ed.) *Ethnicity and Public Policy.* Milwaukee, WI: University of Wisconsin System, American Ethnic Studies Coordinating Committee/Urban Corridor Consortium, pp. 42–61.

Löwy, M. (ed.) (1990) *Marxism in Latin America from 1909 to the Present: An Anthology.* Pearlman, M. (trans.) Atlantic Highlands, NJ: Humanities Press.

Lynn, Richard (1978) "Ethnic and Racial Differences in Intelligence: International Comparisons." In Travis Osborne, R. et al. (eds.) *Human Variation: The Biopsychology of Age, Race, and Sex.* New York: Academic Press, pp. 261–86.

Mandt, A. J. (1989) "The Inevitability of Pluralism: Philosophical Practice and Philosophical Excellence." In Cohen, Avner, and Dascal, Marcelo (eds.) *The Institution of Philosophy: A Discipline in Crisis?* La Salle, IL: Open Court, pp. 77–101.

Mariátegui, Carlos (1971) *Seven Interpretative Essays on Peruvian Reality.* Urquidi, Marjory (trans.) Austin, TX: University of Texas Press.

Martiniello, Marco (2002) "Citizenship." In Goldberg, D. T., and Solomos, J. (eds.) *A Companion to Race and Ethnicity.* Oxford: Blackwell, pp. 114–23.

Marín, G. (1984) "Stereotyping Hispanics: The Differential Effect of Research Method, Label and Degree of Contact." *International Journal of International Relations* 8: 17–27.

Marín, G., and Triandis, H. C., (1985) "Allocentrism as an Important Characteristic of the Behavior of Latin Americans and Hispanics." In Díaz-Guerrero, R. (ed.) *Cross-Cultural and National Studies in Social Psychology: Proceedings of the XXIII International Congress of Psychology of the International Union of Psychological Science (IUPsyS), Acapulco, Mexico, September 2–7, 1984: Selected/Revised Papers.* Amsterdam; Elsevier Science Publishers, vol. 2, pp. 85–104.

Marín, G., and VanOss Marín, B. (1991) *Research with Hispanic Populations.* Newbury Park, CA: SAGE Publications.

Martí, José (1946) "La verdad sobre los Estados Unidos." In Martí, José *Obras completas.* Havana: Editorial Lex, vol. 1, pp. 2035–8.

Martí, Oscar R. (1983) "Is There a Latin American Philosophy?" *Metaphilosophy* 1: 46–52.

Martínez, Elizabeth (2001) "Seeing More Than Black and White: Latinos, Racism, and the Cultural Divides." In Andersen, Margaret, and Collins, Patricia Hill (eds.) *Race, Class, and Gender: An Anthology.* Belmont, CA: Wadsworth, pp. 108–14.

Martínez-Echazábal, Lourdes (1998) "*Mestizaje* and the Discourse of National/Cultural Identity in Latin America, 1845–1959." *Latin American Perspectives* 25: 21–42.

Mason, David (1999) "The Continuing Significance of Race? Teaching Ethnic and Racial Studies in Sociology." In Bulmer, Martin, and Solomos, John (eds.) *Ethnic and Racial Studies Today.* London: Routledge, pp. 13–28.

Mayz Vallenilla, Ernesto (1992) *El problema de América.* Caracas, Venezuela: Ediciones de la Universidad Simón Bolívar; formerly published in 1969.

—— (1983) *Francisco Romero: Maestro de la Filosofía latinoamericana.* Caracas: SIF.

McGarry, J. and B. O'Leary (eds.) (1993) *The Politics of Ethnic Conflict Regulation.* London: Routledge.

McGary, Howard (2007) "Racial Assimilation and the Dilemma of Racially Defined Institutions." In Gracia, Jorge J. E. (ed.) *Race or Ethnicity? On Black and Latino Identity.* Ithaca, NY: Cornell University Press, pp. 155–69.

McKee, Jesse O. (ed.) (2000) *Ethnicity in Contemporary America: A Geographical Appraisal.* 2nd ed. Lanham, MD: Rowman & Littlefield.

McKim, Robert, and McMahan, Jeff (eds.) (1997) *The Morality of Nationalism.* Oxford: Oxford University Press.

McLemore, S. D. (1994) *Race and Ethnicity in America.* 4th ed. Boston, MA: Allyn and Bacon.

McWilliams, Carey (1990) *North from Mexico: The Spanish-Speaking People of the United States.* New York: Greenwood Press.

Medina, José (forthcoming) "*Latinidad,* Hispanicity, and Ethnic-Group Terms." In Susana Nuccetelli (ed.) *Blackwell Companion to Latin American Philosophy.* Oxford: Blackwell.

—— (2004) "Pragmatism and Ethnicity: Critique, Reconstruction, and the New Hispanic." *Metaphilosophy* 35: 115–46; reprinted in Shusterman, R. (ed.) (2004) *The Range of Pragmatism and the Limits of Philosophy.* Oxford: Blackwell, pp. 112–43.

—— (2003) "Identity Trouble: Disidentification and the *Problem* of Difference." *Philosophy and Social Criticism* 29, 6: 655–80. See also the discussion of this article in *Symposia on Gender, Race, and Philosophy* (http://web.mit.edu/sgrp).

Medina, Vicente (1992) "The Possibility of an Indigenous Philosophy: A Latin American Perspective." *American Philosophical Quarterly* 29, 4: 373–80.

Mendieta, Eduardo (ed.) (2003) *Latin American Philosophy: Currents, Issues, Debates.* Bloomington, IN, Indiana University Press.

—— (2002) "Review of Leonard Harris's *Racism.*" *Continental Philosophy Review* 35, 1: 108–15.

—— (2001) "The 'Second *Reconquista,*' or Why Should a 'Hispanic' Become a Philosopher." *Philosophy and Social Criticism* 27, 2: 11–19.

—— (2000) "The Making of New Peoples: Hispanizing Race." In Gracia, Jorge J. E., and De Greiff, Pablo (eds.) *Hispanics/Latinos in the United States: Ethnicity, Race, and Rights.* New York: Routledge, pp. 45–59.

—— (1999) "Is There Latin American Philosophy?" *Philosophy Today* 43 (Supp., 50–2): 50–61.

Mercado, Manfredo Kempff (1958) *Historia de la Filosofía en Latinoamérica.* Santiago de Chile: Zig Zag.

Michaels, Walter Benn (1997) "Identity and Liberation." *Peace Review* 9, 4: 494–502.

—— (1994) "The No-Drop Rule," *Critical Inquiry* 20, 4: 758–69.

—— (1992) "Race and Culture: A Critical Genealogy of Cultural Identity." *Critical Inquiry* 18, 4: 655–85.

Michel, Luo (1998) "Group Claims Some Police Officers Posed as Hispanics in Order to Gain Employment." *Buffalo News,* January 20: B1 and B10.

Midgley, Mary (1999) "Towards an Ethic of Global Responsibility." In Dunne, Tim, and Wheeler, N. G. (eds.) *Human Rights in Global Politics.* Cambridge: Cambridge University Press, pp. 195–213.

Mignolo, Walter (2005) *The Idea of Latin America,* Blackwell Manifestos. Malden, MA: Blackwell.

—— (2000) "Latinos (and Latino Studies) in the Colonial Horizon of Modernity." In Gracia, Jorge J. E., and De Greiff, Pablo (eds.) *Latinos in the United States: Ethnicity, Race, and Rights.* New York: Routledge, pp. 99–124.

—— (2000) *Local Histories/Global Designs: Coloniality, Subaltern Knowledges, and Border Thinking.* Princeton, NJ: Princeton University Press.

—— (1999) "Philosophy and the Colonial Difference." *Philosophy Today* 43 (Supp. 1): 36–41.

Mill, John Stuart (1872) *A System of Logic*. London: Longman.

Miller, Mara (1993) "Canons and the Challenge of Gender." *Monist* 76, 4: 477–93.

Miller, Robin, L. (1992) "The Human Ecology of Multiracial Identity." In Root, Maria P. P. (ed.) *Racially Mixed People in America*. Newbury Park, CA: SAGE Publications, pp. 24–36.

Mills, Charles W. (1998) "'But What Are You Really?' The Metaphysics of Race." In Mills, Charles M. *Blackness Visible: Essays on Philosophy and Race*. Ithaca, NY: Cornell University Press, pp. 41–66.

—— (ed.) (1998) *Blackness Visible: Essays on Philosophy and Race*. Ithaca, NY: Cornell University Press.

—— (1997) *The Racial Contract*. Ithaca, NY: Cornell University Press.

Mindel, Charles H. et al. (eds.) (1988). *Ethnic Families in America: Patterns and Variations*. Englewood Cliffs, NJ: Prentice-Hall.

Minow, Martha (1990) *Making All the Difference: Inclusion, Exclusion and American Law*. Ithaca, NY: Cornell University Press.

Miró Quesada, Francisco (1976) *El problema de la filosofía latinoamericana*. Mexico City: Fondo de Cultura Económica.

Modood, Tariq (2001) "'Difference,' Cultural Racism and Anti-Racism." In Boxill, Bernard (ed.) *Race and Racism*. Oxford: Oxford University Press, pp. 238–56.

Mohanty, Satya P. (2000) "The Epistemic Status of Cultural Identity: On *Beloved* and the Postcolonial Condition." In Moya, Paula L. M., and Hames-García, Michael R. (eds.) *Reclaiming Identity: Realist Theory and the Predicament of Postmodernism*. Berkeley, CA: University of California Press, pp. 29–66.

Montville, Joseph (ed.) (1990) *Conflict and Peacemaking in Multiethnic Societies*. Washington, DC: Lexington Books.

Moore, Joan, and Pachón, Harry (1985) *Hispanics in the United States*. Englewood Cliffs, NJ: Prentice-Hall.

—— (1976) *Mexican-Americans*. 2nd ed. Englewood Cliffs, NJ: Prentice-Hall.

Morales Padrón, F. (1955) *Fisonomía de la conquista indiana*. Sevilla: Escuela de Estudios Hispanoamericanos de Sevilla.

Mörner, Magnus (1967) *Race Mixture in the History of Latin America*. Boston, MA: Little, Brown.

Morse, Richard (1964) "The Heritage of Latin America." In Hartz, L. (ed.) *The Founding of New Societies: Studies in the History of the United States, Latin America, South Africa, Canada, and Australia*. New York: Harcourt, Brace and World, pp. 123–77.

Moya, Paula M. L. (2002) *Learning from Experience: Minority Identities, Multicultural Struggles*. Berkeley, CA: University of California Press.

—— (2001) "Why I Am Not Hispanic: An Argument with Jorge Gracia." *The American Philosophical Association Newsletter on Hispanic/Latino Issues in Philosophy* 2 (Spring): 100–5.

—— (2000) "Introduction: Reclaiming Identity." In Moya, Paula L. M., and Hames-García, Michael R. (eds.) *Reclaiming Identity: Realist Theory and the Predicament of Postmodernism*. Berkeley, CA: University of California Press, pp. 1–26.

—— (2000) "Potmodernism, 'Realism,' and the Politics of Identity: Cherríe Moraga and Chicana Feminism." In Moya, Paula L. M., and Hames-García, Michael R. (eds.) *Reclaiming Identity: Realist Theory and the Predicament of Postmodernism*. Berkeley, CA: University of California Press, pp. 67–101.

Moya, Paula M. L., and Hames-García, Michael R. (eds.) (2000) *Reclaiming Identity: Realist Theory and the Predicament of Postmodernism*. Berkeley, CA: University of California Press.

Murguia, Edward (1991) "On Latino/Hispanic Ethnic Identity." *Latino Studies Journal* 2: 8–18.

Nascimento, Amós (1997) "Identities in Conflict? Latin (African) American." *Peace Review* 9, 4: 489–95.

National Research Council (1987) *Summary Report: Doctorate Recipients from the United States Universities*, Appendix C. Washington, DC: National Academy Press, pp. 66–71.

Nelson, C., and Tienda, Marta (1985) "The Structuring of Hispanic Identity: Historical and Contemporary Perspectives." *Ethnic and Racial Studies* 8, 1: 49–74.

Nicol, Eduardo (1961) *El problema de la filosofía hispánica*. Madrid: Tecnos.

Nuccetelli, Susana (ed.) (forthcoming) *Blackwell Companion to Latin American Philosophy*. Oxford: Blackwell.

—— (2004) "Reference and Ethnic-Group Terms." *Inquiry* 6: 528–44.

—— (2002) *Latin American Thought: Philosophical Problems and Arguments*. Boulder, CO: Westview Press.

—— (2001) "'Latinos,' 'Hispanics,' and 'Iberoamericans': Naming or Describing?" *Philosophical Forum* 32, 2: 175–88.

Nuccetelli, Susana, and Seay, Gary (eds.) (2004) *Latin American Philosophy: An Introduction with Readings*. Upper Saddle River, NJ: Prentice-Hall.

Oboler, Suzanne (2000) "It Must Be a Fake! Racial Ideologies, Identities, and the Question of Rights." In Gracia, Jorge J. E., and De Greiff, Pablo (eds.) *Hispanics/Latinos in the United States: Ethnicity, Race, and Rights*. New York: Routledge.

—— (1995) *Ethnic Labels/ Latino Lives: Identity and the Politics of (Re)presentation in the United States*. Minneapolis, MN: University of Minnesota Press.

O'Leary, Brendan, and McGarry, John (1995) "Regulating Nations and Ethnic Communities." In Breton, Albert et al. (eds.) *Nationalism and Rationality*. Cambridge: Cambridge University Press, pp. 245–89.

Omi, Michael, and Winant, Howard. (1994) *Racial Formation in the United States: From the 1960s to the 1990s*. 2nd ed. New York: Routledge.

Outlaw, Jr, Lucius T. (2001) "Toward a Critical Theory of 'Race.'" In Boxill, Bernard (ed.) *Race and Racism*. Oxford: Oxford University Press, pp. 58–82.

—— (1996) *On Race and Philosophy*. New York: Routledge.

Padilla, Félix (1985) *Latino Ethnic Consciousness: The Case of Mexican Americans and Puerto Ricans in Chicago*. Notre Dame, IN, University of Notre Dame Press.

Pappas, Gregory (2001) "Jorge Gracia's Philosophical Perspective on Hispanic Identity." *Philosophy and Social Criticism* 27, 2: 20–8.

—— (1998) "The Latino Character of American Pragmatism." *Transactions of the Charles S. Peirce Society* 34: 93–112.

Parsons, Talcott (1975) "Some Theoretical Considerations on the Nature and Trends of Change of Ethnicity." In Glazer, N., and Moynihan, D. P. (eds.) *Ethnicity: Theory and Experience*. Cambridge, MA: Harvard University Press, pp. 53–83.

París Pombo, M. D. (1990) *Crisis e identidades colectivas en América Latina*. Mexico City: Plaza y Valdés.

Peterson, William (1982) "Concepts of Ethnicity." In Peterson, William, Novak, Michael, and Gleason, Philip (eds.) *Concepts and Ethnicity*. Cambridge, MA: Harvard University Press, pp. 1–26.

Peterson, William, Novak, Michael, and Gleason, Philip (eds.) (1982). *Concepts and Ethnicity*. Cambridge, MA: Harvard University Press.

"Philosophy in America in 1994." (1996) *Proceedings and Addresses of the American Philosophical Association*. Newark, DE: American Philosophical Association, 70, 2: 131–53.

Pogge, Thomas W. (2000) "Accommodation Rights for Hispanics in the United States." In Gracia, Jorge J. E., and De Greiff, Pablo (eds.) *Latinos in the United States: Ethnicity, Race, and Rights*. New York: Routledge, pp. 181–200.

—— (1997) "Group Rights and Ethnicity." *NOMOS* 39: 187–221.

Portes, Alejandro, and Rumbaud, Rubén C. (1997) *Immigrant America: A Portrait*. 2nd rev. ed. Berkeley, CA: University of California Press.

Pratt, Scott L. (2002) *Native Pragmatism: Rethinking the Roots of American Philosophy*. Bloomington, IN: Indiana University Press.

Pró, Diego (1973) *Historia del pensamiento filosófico argentino*. Mendoza: Universidad Nacional de Cuyo.

Quesada, Vincent G. (1910) *La vida intelectual de la América española durante los siglos XVI, XVII y XVIII*. Buenos Aires: Arnoldo Moen y Hermano.

Quijano, Aníbal (1995) "Modernity, Identity, and Utopia in Latin America." In Beverly, J., Aronna, M., and Oviedo, J. (eds.) *The Postmodernist Debate in Latin America*. Durham, NC: Duke University Press, pp. 201–16.

Quiles, Ismael (1940) "La libertad de investigación en la época colonial." *Estudios*: 511–24.

Rabossi, Eduardo (2005) "History and Philosophy in the Latin American Setting: Some Disturbing Comments." In Salles, Arlene, and Millán-Zaibert, Elizabeth (eds.) *The Role of History in Latin American Philosophy: Contemporary Perspectives*. Albany, NY: State University of New York Press, pp. 57–73.

Ramos, Samuel (1940) *Hacia un nuevo humanismo*. Mexico City: La Casa de España en México.

—— (1934 and 1963) *El perfil del hombre y la cultura en México*. Mexico City: Universidad Nacional Autónoma de México.

Redmond, W. (1972) *Bibliography of the Philosophy in the Iberian Colonies of America*. The Hague: Nijhoff.

Rex, J. (1986) *Race and Ethnicity*. Milton Keynes: Open University Press.

—— (1967) *Race, Community and Conflict*. Oxford: Oxford University Press.

Rex, J., and Mason, D. (ed.) (1986) *Theories of Race and Ethnic Relations*. Cambridge: Cambridge University Press.

Ringer, Benjamin B., and Lawless, Elinor R. (1989) *Race-Ethnicity and Society*. London: Routledge.

Rivano, Juan (1965) *Punto de partida de la miseria*. Santiago: Universidad de Chile.

Robles, Laureano (ed.) (1992). *Filosofía iberoamericana en la época del Encuentro*. Madrid: Editorial Trotta: Consejo Superior de Investigaciones Científicas.

Roig, Arturo Andrés (1992) "Nuestra América frente al panamericanismo y el hispanismo: la lectura de Leopoldo Zea." In Cerutti-Guldberg, Horacio (ed.) *América Latina. Historia y destino. Homenaje a Leopodo Zea*. Mexico City: UNAM, pp. 279–84.

—— (1981) *Teoría y crítica del pensamiento latinoamericano*. Mexico City: Fondo de Cultura Económica.

Romero, Francisco (1964) *Theory of Man*. Cooper, William (trans.) Berkeley, CA: University of California Press.

—— (1952) *Sobre la filosofía en America*. Buenos Aires: Raigal.

Root, Maria P. P. (ed.) (1992). *Racially Mixed People in America*. Newbury Park, CA: SAGE Publications.

Rorty, Richard. (1989) *Contingency, Identity, Solidarity*. Cambridge: Cambridge University Press.

—— (1984) "The Historiography of Philosophy: Four Genres." In Rorty, Richard, Schneewind, J. B., and Skinner, Quentin (eds.) *Philosophy in History: Essays on the Historiography of Philosophy*. Cambridge: Cambridge University Press, pp. 44–75.

Rorty, Richard, Schneewind, J. B., and Skinner, Quentin (eds.) (1984) *Philosophy in History: Essays on the Historiography of Philosophy*. Cambridge: Cambridge University Press.

Rosenblat, Angel (1954) *La población indígena y el mestizaje en América*. 2 vols. Buenos Aires: Editorial Nova.

Rothschild, Joseph (1981). *Ethnopolitics*. New York: Columbia University Press.

Roychoudhury, A. K. (1976) "Genetic Distance and Gene Diversity among Linguistically Different Tribes of Mexican Indians." *American Journal of Physical Anthropology* 42: 449–54.

Ruch, E. A. (1981) "African Philosophy: The Origins of the Problem." In Ruch, E. A., and Anyanwu, K. C. (eds.) *African Philosophy: An Introduction to the Main Philosophical Trends in Contemporary Africa*. Rome: Catholic Book Agency, pp. 180–98.

Russell, Bertrand (1956) *Logic and Knowledge, Essays 1901–1950*. Marsh, Robert C. (ed.) London: Allen and Unwin.

—— (1905) "On Denoting." *Mind*, new series, 14: 479–93.

Sáenz, Mario (ed.) (2002) *Latin American Perspectives on Globalization: Ethics, Politics, and Alternative Visions*. Lanham, MD: Rowman & Littlefield.

Salles, Arlene, and Millán-Zaibert, Elizabeth (eds.) (2005) *The Role of History in Latin American Philosophy: Contemporary Perspectives*. Albany, NY: State University of New York Press.

Salmon, Nathan (1989) "Names and Descriptions." In Gabbay, D., and Guenthner, F. (eds.) *Handbook of Philosophical Logic*. Vol. IV: *Topics in the Philosophy of Language*. Dordrecht, Netherlands: D. Reidel, pp. 409–61.

Salazar Bondy, Augusto (1969) *The Meaning and Problem of Hispanic American Thought*. Augelli, John P. (ed.) Lawrence, KN: Center for Latin American Studies of the University of Kansas.

—— (1969) *Sentido y problema del pensamiento hispano-americano*, with English trans. by Donald L. Schmidt. Kansas City, KN: University of Kansas Center for Latin American Studies.

—— (1968) *¿Existe una filosofía de nuestra América?* Mexico City: Siglo XXI.

Salmerón, Fernando (1980) *Cuestiones educativas y páginas sobre México*. Xalapa: Universidad Veracruzana.

Sánchez Reulet, A. (ed.) (1954) *Contemporary Latin American Philosophy: A Selection with an Introduction and Notes*. Trask, W. R. (trans.) Albuquerque, NM: University of New Mexico Press.

Sasso, Javier (1998) *La filosofía latinoamericana y las construcciones de su historia*. Caracas, Venezuela: Monte Ávila.

Schacht, Richard (1993) "On Philosophy's Canon." *Monist* 76, 4: 421–35.

Schaefer, Richard (1990) *Racial and Ethnic Groups*. 4th ed. Glenview, IL: Scott, Foresman.

Schermerhorn, R. A. (1970) *Comparative Ethnic Relations: A Framework for Theory and Research*. New York: Random House.

Schlesinger, Jr, Arthur M. (1998) *The Disuniting of America: Reflections on a Multicultural Society*. New York: W. W. Norton.

Schmitz, Kenneth (1996) "La naturaleza actual de la filosofia se revela en su historia." *Revista Latinoamericana de Filosofía* 22, 1: 97–109.

Schutte, Ofelia (2000) "Negotiating Latina Identities." In Gracia, Jorge J. E., and De Greiff, Pablo (eds.) *Hispanics/Latinos in the United States: Ethnicity, Race, and Rights*. New York: Routledge, pp. 61–75.

—— (1993) *Cultural Identity and Social Liberation in Latin American Thought*. Albany, NY: State University of New York Press.

—— (1987) "Toward an Understanding of Latin American Philosophy: Reflections on the Foundations of Cultural Identity." *Philosophy Today* 31: 21–34.

Schwartzmann, Félix (1950) *El sentimiento de lo humano en América*. 2 vols. Santiago: Universidad de Chile.

Searle, John (1995) *The Construction of Social Reality*. New York: Free Press.

—— (1984) *Intentionality: An Essay in the Philosophy of Mind*. Cambridge: Cambridge University Press.

—— (1969) *Speech Acts: An Essay in the Philosophy of Language*. Cambridge: Cambridge University Press.

—— (1967) "Proper Names and Descriptions." In *The Encyclopedia of Philosophy*. 8 vols. London: Macmillan, vol. 6, pp. 487–91.

—— (1958) "Proper Names." *Mind* 67: 166–73.

Sedillo López, Antoinette (1995) *Historical Themes and Identity: Mestizaje and Labels.* Latinos in the United States: History, Law and Perspective Series, 1. New York: Garland Publishing.

Seigfried, Charlene Haddock (1998) "Advancing American Philosophy." *Transactions of the Charles S. Peirce Society* 34, 4: 807–39.

Sen, A. (2002) "Civilizational Imprisonments." *New Republic* (June 10): 28–33.

—— (2001) "Being and Being of Mixed Race." *Social Theory and Practice* 27: 285–307.

—— (1999) *Reason before Identity.* Oxford: Oxford University Press.

Sharpley-Whiting, T. Denean (2001) "Paulette Nardal, Race Consciousness and Antillean Letters." In Bernasconi, Robert (ed.) *Race.* Oxford: Blackwell, pp. 95–106.

Shibutani, R., and Kwan, K. M. (1965) *Ethnic Stratification.* New York: Macmillan.

Skrentny, John David (1996) *The Ironies of Affirmative Action: Politics, Culture, and Justice in America.* Chicago: University of Chicago Press.

Smedley, Audrey (1993) *Race in North America: Origin and Evolution of a Worldview.* Boulder, CO: Westview Press.

Smith, Anthony D. (1997) "Structure and Persistence of Ethnie." In Guibernau, M., and Rex, J. (eds.) *The Ethnicity Reader: Nationalism, Multiculturalism and Migration.* Cambridge: Polity Press, pp. 27–33.

—— (1994) "The Problem of National Identity: Ancient, Medieval and Modern?" *Ethnic and Racial Studies* 17: 375–99.

—— (1992) "Ethnicity and Nationalism." In Smith, Anthony D. (ed.) *Ethnicity and Nationalism.* Leiden: E. J. Brill, pp. 1–4.

—— (ed.) (1992) *Ethnicity and Nationalism.* Leiden: E. J. Brill.

—— (1991) *National Identity.* Reno, NV: University of Nevada Press.

—— (1986) *The Ethnic Origins of Nations.* Oxford: Blackwell.

—— (1981) *The Ethnic Revival.* Cambridge: Cambridge University Press.

Smith, Dan (2000) "Ethical Uncertainties of Nationalism." *Journal of Peace Research* 37, 4: 489–502.

Smith, Dan, and Østerud, Øyvind (1995) *Nation-State, Nationalism and Political Identity.* Oslo: Advance Research on the Europeanisation of the Nation-State, University of Oslo.

Smith, M. G. (1986) "Pluralism, Race and Ethnicity in Selected African Countries." In Rex, J., and Mason, D. (eds.) *Theories of Race and Ethnic Relations.* Cambridge: Cambridge University Press, pp. 177–208.

Smith, J., and Kornberg, A. (1969) "Some Considerations Bearing Upon Comparative Research in Canada and the United States." *Sociology* 3: 341–57.

Sollors, Werner (2002) "Ethnicity and Race." In Goldberg, D. T., and Solomos, J. (eds.) *A Companion to Race and Ethnicity.* Oxford: Blackwell, pp. 97–104.

—— (ed.) (1997) *Theories of Ethnicity: A Classical Reader.* Basingstoke, UK: Macmillan.

Sowell, Thomas (1994) *Race and Culture: A World View.* New York: Basic Books.

Spinner, J. (1994) *The Boundaries of Citizenship: Race, Ethnicity, and Nationality in the Liberal State*. Baltimore, MD: The Johns Hopkins University Press.

Spoonley, P. (1993) *Racism and Ethnicity*. Oxford: Oxford University Press.

Stabb, Martin S. (1995) *The Dissenting Voice: The New Essay of Spanish America, 1960–1985*. Austin, TX: University of Texas Press.

—— (1967) *In Quest of Identity: Patterns in the Spanish American Essay of Ideas, 1890–1960*. Chapel Hill, NC: University of North Carolina Press.

Stephan, Cookie White (1992) "Mixed-Heritage Individuals: Ethnic Identity and Trait Characteristics." In Root, Maria P. P. (ed.) *Racially Mixed People in America*. Newbury Park, CA: SAGE Publishers, pp. 50–63.

Strawson, Peter F. (1950) "On Referring." *Mind* 59: 320–44.

Stubblefield, Anna (2005) *Ethics along the Color Line*. Ithaca, NY: Cornell University Press.

Stuhr, John J. (1998) "Sidetracking American Philosophy." *Transactions of the Charles S. Peirce Society* 34, 4: 841–60.

Sweet, James (1997) "The Iberian Roots of American Racist Thought." *William and Mary Quarterly* 54, 1: 143–66.

Szalay, Lorand B., and Díaz-Guerrero, Rogelio (1985) "Similarities and Differences between Subjective Cultures: A Comparison of Latin, Hispanic, and Anglo Americans." In Díaz-Guerrero, Rogelio (ed.) *Cross-Cultural and National Studies in Social Psychology: Proceedings of the XXIII International Congress of Psychology of the International Union of Psychological Science (IUPsyS), Acapulco, Mexico, September 2–7, 1984: Selected/Revised Papers*. Amsterdam: Elsevier Science Pub., vol. 2, pp. 105–32.

Takaki, Ronald (2002) "The Twenty-First Century: We Will All Be Minorities." In Takaki, Ronald (ed.) *Debating Diversity: Clashing Perspectives on Race and Ethnicity in America*. New York: Oxford University Press, pp. 1–4.

—— (1993) *A Different Mirror: A History of Multicultural America*. Boston, MA: Little Brown.

Taylor, Charles (1993) "The Politics of Recognition." In Gutmann, Amy (ed.) *Multiculturalism and the 'Politics of Recognition.'* Princeton, NJ: Princeton University Press, pp. 25–74.

Taylor, Paul (2000) "Appiah's Uncompleted Argument: W. E. B. Du Bois and the Reality of Race." *Social Theory and Practice* 26: 103–28.

Taylor, Rupert (1999) "Political Science Encounters 'Race' and 'Ethnicity.'" In Bulmer, Martin, and Solomos, John (eds.) *Ethnic and Racial Studies Today*. London: Routledge, pp. 115–23.

El Tercer Congreso Interamericano de Filosofía (1950) La Habana: Publicaciones de la Sociedad Cubana de Filosofía.

Thernstrom, Stephan (1982) "Ethnic Groups in American History." In Liebman, Lance (ed.) *Ethnic Relations in America*. Englewood Cliffs, NJ: Prentice-Hall, pp. 3–27.

Thomas, Laurence (2001) "Group Autonomy and Narrative Identity: Blacks and Jews." In Boxill, Bernard (ed.) *Race and Racism*. Oxford: Oxford University Press, pp. 357–70.

—— (2001) "Sexism and Racism: Some Conceptual Differences." In Boxill, Bernard (ed.) *Race and Racism*. Oxford: Oxford University Press, pp. 344–56.

Thompson, E. P. (1963) *The Making of the English Working Class*. New York: Pantheon Books.

Tienda, M., and Ortíz, V. (1986) "'Hispanicity' and the 1980 Census." *Social Sciences Quarterly* 67: 3–20.

Todorov, Tzvetan (1984) *The Conquest of America: The Quest of the Other*. Howard, Richard (trans.) New York: Harper and Row.

Treviño, Fernando (1987) "Standardized Terminology for Hispanic Populations." *American Journal of Public Health* 77: 69–72.

Triandis, Harry. C. et al. (1984) "*Simpatía* as a Cultural Script of Hispanics." *Journal of Personality and Social Psychology* 47: 1363–75.

Twine, France Winddance, and Warren, J. (eds.) (2000) *Racing Research, Researching Race: Methodological Dilemmas in Critical Race Studies*. New York: New York University Press.

Unamuno, Miguel de (1968) "Hispanidad." In Unamuno, Miguel de, *Obras completas*. Vol. 4. Madrid: Exelsior (first published in 1927), pp. 1,081–4.

US Bureau of the Census (1988). *Development of the Race and Ethnic Items for the 1990 Census*. Washington, DC: US Bureau of the Census.

—— (1966) *Statistical Abstract of the United States, 1966*. 116th ed. Washington DC: US Government Printing Office.

Vallenilla, Ernesto Mayz (1969 and 1992) *El problema de América*. Caracas, Venezuela: Ediciones de la Universidad Simón Bolívar.

van den Berghe, Pierre L. (2001) "Does Race Matter?" In Boxill, Bernard (ed.) *Race and Racism*. Oxford: Oxford University Press, pp. 101–13.

—— (1981) *The Ethnic Phenomenon*. New York: Elsevier.

—— (1967) *Race and Racism: A Comparative Perspective*. New York: Wiley.

Van Dyke, Vernon (1995) "The Individual, the State, and Ethnic Communities in Political Theory." In Kymlicka, Will (ed.) *The Rights of Minority Cultures*. Oxford: Oxford University Press, pp. 31–56.

Van Horne, Winston A. (ed.) (1982). *Ethnicity and Public Policy*. Vol. 1. Milwaukee, WI: University of Wisconsin.

Vasconcelos, José (1957) *Obras completas*. 4 vols. Mexico City: Libreros Mexicanos.

—— (1937) *Historia del pensamiento filosófico*. Mexico City: Universidad Nacional Autónoma de México.

—— (1926) *Indología: una interpretación de la cultura iberoamericana*. Paris: Agencia Mundial de Librería.

—— (1925) *La raza cósmica*. Barcelona: Agencia Mundial de Librería.

Villegas, Abelardo (1963) *Panorama de la filosofía ibero-americana*. Buenos Aires: Editorial Universitaria de Buenos Aires.

Vincent, Joan (1974) "The Structuring of Ethnicity." *Human Organization* 33, 4: 375–9.

Vobejda, Barbara (1998) "Hispanic Children Are Leading Edge of the U.S. Demographic Wave." *Washington Post*; rep. *Buffalo News* (July 15): A-6.

Wagley, C., and Harris, M. (1958) *Minorities in the New World*. New York: Columbia University Press.

Waldron, Jeremy (1995) "Minority Cultures and the Cosmopolitan Perspective." In Kymlicka, Will (ed.) *The Rights of Minority Cultures*. Oxford: Oxford University Press, pp. 93–119.

Wallman, S. (1986) "Ethnicity and the Boundary Process in Context." In Rex, J., and Mason, D. (eds.) *Theories of Race and Ethnic Relations*. Cambridge: Cambridge University Press, pp. 296–313.

—— (1978) "The Boundaries of Race: Processes of Ethnicity in England." *Man* 13: 200–17.

Walzer, Michael (1997) "The Politics of Difference: Statehood and Toleration in a Multicultural World." In McKim, Robert, and McMahan, Jeff (eds.) *The Morality of Nationalism*. Oxford: Oxford University Press, pp. 245–57.

—— (1995) "Pluralism: A Political Perspective." In Kymlicka, Will (ed.) *The Rights of Minority Cultures*. Oxford: Oxford University Press, pp. 139–54.

—— (1993) "Comment." In Gutman, Amy (ed.) *Multiculturalism and the 'Politics of Recognition.'* Princeton, NJ: Princeton University Press, pp. 100–1.

—— (1992) *What It Means to be an American*. New York: Marsilio.

—— (1970) "The Obligations of Oppressed Minorities." In Walzer, Michael. *Obligations: Essays on Disobedience, War, and Citizenship*. Cambridge, MA: Harvard University Press, pp. 46–73.

Warren, Jonathan W., and Twine, F. Winddance (2002) "Critical Race Studies in Latin America: Recent Advances, Recurrent Weaknesses." In Goldberg, D. T., and Solomos, J. (eds.) *A Companion to Race and Ethnicity*. Oxford: Blackwell, pp. 538–60.

Waters, Mary C. (1990) *Ethnic Options: Choosing Identities in America*. Berkeley, CA: University of California Press.

Weber, Max (1997) "What Is an Ethnic Group?" In Guibernau, M, and Rex, J. (eds.) *The Ethnicity Reader: Nationalism, Multiculturalism and Migration*. Cambridge: Polity Press, pp. 15–26.

Webster's Third New International Dictionary (1966) Chicago: Encyclopaedia Britannica.

Weinberg, Julius (1964) *A Short History of Medieval Philosophy*. Princeton, NJ: Princeton University Press.

West, Cornel (1993) *Race Matters*. Boston, MA: Beacon Press.

Westphal, Merold (1993) "The Canon as Flexible, Normative Fact." *Monist* 76, 4: 436–49.

Weyr, Thomas (1988) *Hispanic U.S.A.: Breaking the Melting Pot*. New York: Harper and Row.

Whitehead, Alfred North, and Russell, Bertrand (1962) *Principia mathematica to *56*. Cambridge: University Press; abridged edition of "Principia mathematica." 2nd ed. Cambridge, 1927.

Wieseltier, L. (1996) *Against Identity*. New York: William Drenttel.

Wieviorka, Michel (2002) "The Development of Racism in Europe." In Goldberg, D. T., and Solomos, J. (eds.) *A Companion to Race and Ethnicity*. Oxford: Blackwell, pp. 460–74.

Wilterlink, N. (1993) "An Examination of European and National Identity." *Archives Eurepéenes de Sociologie* 34: 119–36.

Wittgenstein, Ludwig (1965) *Philosophical Investigations*. Anscombe, G. E. M. (trans.). New York: Macmillan.

—— (1961) *Tractatus logico-philosophicus*. Pears, D. F., and McGuiness, B. F. (trans.). London: Routledge and Kegan Paul.

Woodward, R. L. (ed.) (1971) *Positivism in Latin America: 1850–1900: Are Order and Progress Reconcilable?* Lexington, MA: Heath.

Young, C. (1983) "The Temple of Ethnicity." *World Politics* 35, 4: 652–62.

Young, Iris Marion (2001) "Social Movements and the Politics of Difference." In Boxill, Bernard (ed.) *Race and Racism*. Oxford: Oxford University Press, pp. 383–421.

—— (2000) "Structure, Difference, and Hispanic/Latino Claims of Justice." In Gracia, Jorge J. E., and De Greiff, Pablo (eds.) *Hispanics/Latinos in the United States: Ethnicity, Race, and Rights*. New York: Routledge, pp. 147–66.

—— (1997) "Asymmetrical Reciprocity: On Moral Respect, Wonder, and Enlarged Thought." In Young, Iris Marion, *Intersecting Voices: Dilemmas of Gender, Political Philosophy, and Policy*. Princeton, NJ: Princeton University Press.

—— (1995) "Together in Difference: Transforming the Logic of Group Political Conflict." In Kymlicka, Will (ed.) *The Rights of Minority Cultures*. Oxford: Oxford University Press, pp. 155–76.

—— (1990) *Justice and the Politics of Difference*. Princeton, NJ: Princeton University Press.

Zack, Naomi (2001) "Race and Philosophic Meaning." In Boxill, Bernard (ed.) *Race and Racism*. Oxford: Oxford University Press, pp. 43–57.

—— (ed.) (2000) *Women of Color and Philosophy: A Critical Reader*. Oxford: Blackwell.

—— (ed.) (1997) *Race/Sex: Their Sameness, Difference, and Interplay*. New York: Routledge.

—— (ed.) (1995) *American Mixed Race: The Culture of Microdiversity*. Lanham, MD: Rowman & Littlefield.

—— (1993) *Race and Mixed Race*. Philadelphia, PA: Temple University Press.

Zaibert, Leonardo, and Millán-Zaibert, Elizabeth (2000) "Universalism, Particularism, and Group Rights: The Case of Hispanics." In Gracia, Jorge J. E. and De Greiff, Pablo (eds.) *Hispanics/Latinos in the United States: Ethnicity, Race, and Rights*. New York: Routledge, pp. 167–80.

Zea, Leopoldo (2004) "The Actual Function of Philosophy in Latin America." In Gracia, Jorge J. E., and Millán-Zaibert, Elizabeth (eds.) *Latin American Philosophy for the 21st Century: The Human Condition, Values, and the Search for Identity*. Buffalo, NY: Prometheus Books, pp. 357–68.

—— (2004) "Identity: A Latin American Philosophical Problem." In Gracia, Jorge J. E., and Millán-Zaibert, Elizabeth (eds.) *Latin American Philosophy for the 21st Century: The Human Condition, Values, and the Search for Identity*. Buffalo, NY: Prometheus Books, pp. 369–78.

—— (1992) *The Role of the Americas in History*. Savage, MD: Rowman & Littlefield.

—— (1988–9) "Identity: A Latin American Philosophical Problem." *The Philosophical Forum* 20, 1–2: 33–42.

—— (1976) *El pensamiento latinoamericano.* Barcelona: Ariel.

—— (1974) *Positivism in Mexico.* Austin, TX: University of Texas Press.

—— (1963) *The Latin American Mind.* Abbott, James H., and Dunham, Lowell (trans.) Norman, OK: University of Oklahoma Press.

—— (1948) "En torno a una filosofía americana." *Ensayos sobre filosofía en la historia.* Mexico City: Stylo, pp. 165–77.

Index